Inside Intuit

Inside Intuit

**How the Makers of Quicken Beat Microsoft
and Revolutionized an Entire Industry**

Suzanne Taylor
Kathy Schroeder

Harvard Business School Press

Boston, Massachusetts

07 06 05 04 03   5 4 3 2 1

Library of Congress Cataloging-in-Publication Data

Schroeder, Kathrine K.
    Inside Intuit : how the makers of Quicken beat Microsoft and revolutionized
an entire industry / Kathrine K. Schroeder and Suzanne E. Taylor.
      p. cm.
    ISBN 1-59139-136-9 (alk. paper)
    1. Intuit (Firm)—History. 2. Microsoft Corporation. 3. Quicken (Computer
file) 4. Computer software industry—United States. 5. Competition—United
States. I. Taylor, Suzanne E. II. Title.
    HD9696.63.U64I587 2003
    338.7'61332024—dc21

                        2003009333

This book is dedicated to our husbands, Scott and Brad, who unstintingly supported our efforts by watching the kids, fixing dinners, carpooling the kids, folding laundry, washing the kids, cleaning up, caring for the kids, and—despite it all—endlessly believing in us. We're both so incredibly fortunate to be married to you guys.

It's also dedicated to the kids who required the watching, feeding, and washing: Jacob, Valerie, Amanda, Jessie, and Andy. You are the best kids in the whole world, bar none, and you continually inspire us.

And we dedicate this (finally) finished work to each other, because, despite a constant string of unexpected obstacles, our spirit of friendship prevailed.

And finally, to Peet's coffee, without which at least one of us would not function at all.

CONTENTS

MISSIONARIES VERSUS MERCENARIES

Inside Intuit is a tale of missionaries, not mercenaries. It's about a founding team that prevails through tenacity, frugality, and an obsession with the customer experience. It's about great people who put the organization ahead of themselves and who embrace the mission and values articulated clearly and consistently by Intuit's leaders. Through meticulous research, including scores of interviews with managers, executives, competitors, and ex-employees, the authors take you behind the scenes, from the trenches to the boardroom, immersing you in the struggles inside Intuit.

Kleiner Perkins first learned about Intuit in 1985 after backing and working with software start-ups such as Lotus, Symantec, and Electronic Arts. Those firms' products seemed like "must haves" to us. But when it came to large numbers of households using their home computers to manage their checkbooks, we just couldn't see it.

Scott Cook was a former Crisco marketing manager for Procter & Gamble; Tom Proulx was a Stanford engineering student. Neither of them had created a new product nor started a company from scratch, let alone single-handedly faced nearly forty competitors. So when Intuit's flagship product, Quicken, began to take off in the marketplace, my partners and I at Kleiner Perkins—along with the entire burgeoning shrink-wrapped software industry—took notice.

When Intuit's founders approached Kleiner Perkins about investing, and we began to dig into the business in detail, we discovered just how far off-base our initial skepticism had been. These founders were building something different—something we wanted to be a part of.

What Scott Cook had achieved so far at Intuit already separated him from hundreds of other entrepreneurial pretenders. But the "bake-off" he staged to help him choose from an array of eager potential investors really distinguished him from the crowd. More than a dozen venture capitalists vied to get a piece of Intuit. Cook and his team tested each finalist with a new, pressing, real problem: What should Intuit do if Microsoft entered the personal finance market to compete with Quicken?

At Kleiner Perkins, we soon saw that Intuit differed in more ways than merely its approach to venture fund-raising. At the first Intuit board meeting I attended, I was surprised: more than half the meeting took place at Intuit's tech support center, listening to tech reps answer customers' product questions and fix their problems. Cook's uniquely intense focus on happy customers and firsthand customer feedback impresses me to this day.

The more we learned about Intuit, the more we understood that listening to customers is key to Intuit's culture. Customers don't just use Intuit's products and services; they love them. Part of the reason is that Intuit has made a science of listening to, understanding, and responding to their needs. With each product release, Intuit sends engineers out to interview customers using the product. The company focuses on customer-driven innovation, not technology-driven innovation like many other high-tech firms. Innovations in Intuit's Quicken, TurboTax, and Quick-Books have simplified the financial lives of more than a fourth of U.S. households and more than six million small businesses.

As part of Intuit's board of directors since 1990, I've seen Cook and his team learn from the successes of other high-tech institutions. For example, from Apple and Software Publishing, they learned how to design software for ease of use. From Intel

Intuit modeled its first strategic planning, seeking to "insulate itself from the whims of competitors." From Microsoft they saw the importance of developers.

MICROSOFT, AND THE INTERNET

Another insight embraced by Intuit came from software legend and Sun Microsystems cofounder Bill Joy, who once observed, "No matter how much talent your company has, most of the smart people don't work for you." As Intuit grew, Joy's dictum became the basis for an aggressive effort to attract and leverage as much outside talent as possible. Cook and his team built relationships through external partnerships, resellers, developers, and acquisitions. Indeed, it even agreed to be taken over by Microsoft, its main rival, in 1994. Microsoft wanted more than Intuit's products. Although in the past Microsoft had typically absorbed its acquisitions fully, in this case Bill Gates assured Intuit that Microsoft would allow the company to run independently to maintain Intuit's unique strengths and culture.

But the Microsoft merger was not to be; the Department of Justice sued to stop it from happening. Almost immediately thereafter, the company faced another disruptive change: the Internet. We at Kleiner Perkins were early investors in Netscape and watched Marc Andreessen's world-changing browser go from zero to twenty million users in a few months in late 1994—a spurt of growth unprecedented in the history of the software business.

Characteristically, Intuit realized that the Internet was not only a profound challenge but also an enormous opportunity. The Internet would transform the financial services industry, and Intuit scrambled to keep up. Intuit's franchise was solid enough to withstand the changes wrought by the Internet frenzy as the company's products and services extended well into the online world. Despite the growing pains and missteps described frankly in this book, Intuit is one of the few software-and-service providers that surfed the Internet wave without crashing. In fact, after the Internet bubble burst in 2000, Intuit emerged stronger than before the Web became commonplace.

Many people have asked how Intuit beat Microsoft, winning against the software world's fiercest competitor in several product categories. I believe the answer lies in two factors: the quality of its people and the quality of its culture—one grounded in a complete, disciplined focus on continual improvement and customer satisfaction.

The company's culture is deeply rooted in values (see appendix). Intuit has paradoxically achieved excellence without arrogance. The team is ruthlessly, intellectually honest—supersmart and supertalented. Intuit encourages risk taking, acknowledges and learns from mistakes, and moves on. Cook has long studied Japanese business practices such as teamwork and continuous process improvement for quality. His inquiring mind ensures that Intuit's innovations are encouraged vigorously—and evaluated rigorously.

At the root of both these factors is the company's exceptional leadership over the years. Scott Cook personifies customer-driven innovation, and his brilliance shepherded Intuit through its initial stellar growth. Cook has an unusual ability to ask the right questions (which my partner Vinod Khosla insists is more important than getting the right answers; in business, there are often several right answers). But underneath Cook's keen intellect is a warm, wonderful human being who really cares about family, customers, people, and doing the right thing.

"COACH" BILL CAMPBELL

In 1993, Cook realized before any of the rest of us that Intuit needed a new CEO to help the company reach the next level. How unusual, I thought at the time, for a company founder to know and admit that he might be holding his company back.

Cook acted on his self-knowledge and willingly passed the reins to someone with different skills and expertise.

Bill Campbell had been general manager of Consumer Products–Europe at Kodak, executive VP of sales and marketing at Apple, the CEO of Claris—and, once upon a time, the football coach at Columbia University. I knew Bill as the CEO of GO, a failed venture on which we worked together, and gently recommended him to Cook and the Intuit board. Once Campbell was hired—after exhaustive interviews and diligence—he perfectly complemented Cook, in much the same way that Andy Grove complemented Gordon Moore, or that Steve Ballmer complements Bill Gates. Bill "the Coach" Campbell connects with your heart; Scott "the Visionary" Cook connects with your intellect. This one-two punch, the Campbell-Cook dynamic, carried Intuit to the next level of entrepreneurial success—from a growing, mid-sized public company to a large, established, billion-dollar enterprise.

Campbell is the single best mentor and coach of CEOs, teams, and talent I've ever met. Period. His experience, decisiveness, integrity, and bedrock "sense of reasonableness" inspires enormous loyalty. Campbell relies on experience but doesn't manage by rote. He sizes up each business challenge and individual contributor as a special situation. Bill's great gift to you, after a hearty hug and earthy oath, is prescribing a personal, customized development plan that allows you and your team to grow to be the best you can be. That's tough love—a rare and invaluable quality in a CEO.

Campbell groomed as his successor Bill Harris, who joined Intuit through the acquisition of TurboTax, and rose to chief operating officer. Harris was a prime mover in Intuit's embrace of the Internet, a savvy, aggressive deal maker, and major contributor. The board named Harris CEO and Campbell chairman in 1998. But orchestrating a billion-dollar enterprise wasn't Harris's forte. His entrepreneurial passions led him to a financial services start-up, X.com, where he led the immensely successful acquisition of PayPal, now part of eBay.

STEVE BENNETT

So the board turned outside with a CEO search led by Norbert Gottenberg and quarterbacked by Campbell and Cook. One candidate stood out—Steve Bennett, a twenty-three-year GE veteran, then running many of GE's financial services.

Bennett embodies the key values of Intuit regarding people and commitment to customers, while bringing yet another set of talents to the table. Bennett embraced the things working well at Intuit and eliminated those that did not fit. He changed just one word in Intuit's values statement ("think fast, move fast" to "think *smart,* move fast"). He put the right people in the right places, attracting new leaders to new opportunities while retaining top leaders by growing their skills and responsibilities. Bennett sets high expectations and helps the team achieve them.

Bennett's found new ways to extend Intuit values throughout the organization. Great CEOs are great teachers. Exiting the dot-com boom, Bennett taught everyone how to focus on good strategy and good profitability, making each and every Intuit business better. He teaches classes on management, leadership, and rigor. Bennett leads by example, showing that you learn by teaching and that leaders are learners. Bennett's commitment to a learning, leading organization inspires in employees a deep loyalty, delight, and energy—you know, and feel, that Intuit's getting better, you are getting better, and Bennett deeply cares.

While gifted with operational prowess, Bennett possesses a fertile, strategic mind. He has formulated a new strategic direction that shows great promise. Bennett has energized employees, and Intuit's bottom line results prove his (and his team's) effectiveness. Watch Steve Bennett—you'll find he's one of the best CEOs in Silicon Valley and the country.

In Cook, Campbell, and Bennett, Intuit has enjoyed three generations of exceptional leaders. Each of them displays the "Level 5" leadership qualities described in Jim Collins's terrific book *Good to Great*. Specifically, they combine personal humility with great ambition—for the company and its customers, not for themselves.

What is unusual about Intuit is that these three leaders are all still actively engaged in building the company. As CEO, Bennett has "the last call," setting the tempo, directing the team. As chairman of the board, Campbell holds sway from an off-campus office, advising the team, turning up on campus, and walking the halls. And Cook, as founder and chairman of the executive committee, provokes and celebrates strategy rethinking, inspires innovations, and continues, as ever, to obsess on the customers. As a leadership trio, they are unique in Silicon Valley. Together they have built one of the best-managed organizations I know, and one of the best meritocracies for the development of great products and people.

THE NEXT TWO DECADES

Intuit's progress over the next two decades will be even more interesting than the last. The company, now large, must keep innovating, changing, and finding new ways to address the large, unmet needs of businesses and individuals as they simplify their financial lives. But what won't change are Intuit's core values: integrity, doing right by customers, and valuing its people. The size and loyalty of Intuit's twenty-five-million-strong customer base demonstrates how enduring these deeply rooted values are.

Not every businessperson aspires to be an institution-builder. Some simply want the freedom to be their own bosses, to achieve financial independence, to call the shots. Others want to solve problems and push the boundaries with their solutions; they work hard to "change the game" by innovating, rethinking, or breaking the rules. And yet, for all their efforts, business to them will always be just that—a game.

For still others, however, and they're a rare breed indeed, business is about striving for something more fundamental: to alter and improve their customers' lives. These people aim to create companies that will transcend their creators, that will remain strong and productive from generation to generation. They aim to build lasting institutions.

Achieving that goal is no mean feat. Every decade the technology industry produces only one or two companies that remotely qualify as true institutions. Intel is one; so are Cisco, Hewlett-Packard, and Microsoft. And so, I believe, is Intuit.

I've always been awed by entrepreneurs, by how little they have to work with when they start and by how much they sometimes accomplish. *Inside Intuit* is an honest story of entrepreneurship. The authors detail the pain and triumph of growth, the challenges of intense competition, the disruptiveness of new technologies, and the succession of transformational leadership. Intuit's journey over the last twenty years is remarkable and fascinating.

One year after the news of Wall Street accounting scandals and the shocking deceit of the scumbag CEOs and CFOs at Enron and WorldCom, it is a pleasure to introduce you to what I believe will be an enduring business institution. Companies like Intuit, and the story *Inside Intuit,* highlight the contrast between the best entrepreneurs have to offer and the rest.

John Doerr
Kleiner Perkins Caufield & Byers
April 2003

ACKNOWLEDGMENTS

This project, particularly since we had never before tackled one like it, depended on the contributions of others, of those who witnessed events firsthand and were willing to share what they remembered. From Scott Cook, who from the first enthusiastically supported our efforts, to former Microsofties and ex-Intuit employees, many people gave generously of their time for the express purpose of helping us write this book. We sincerely appreciate all the input we received and could not have written an accurate, compelling, and balanced book without these people giving us material to use in this book.

We must mention first those whose stories and remembrances we sought multiple times, and whose insights anchored this work. Our story rests on the memories of these helpful, dedicated people: Scott Cook, Bill Campbell, Eric Dunn, Tom Proulx, Bill Harris, Mari Baker, Virginia Boyd, Tom LeFevre, John Monson, and John Doerr. Thank you for so much time, for the endless fact checking, and for caring so much about Intuit. Your stories and passion for the company motivated us.

Other contributors lent us time, memories, and encouragement, including Dennis Adsit, Steven Aldrich, Tom Allanson, Ron Artigues, Roger Bass, Steve Bennett, Tapan Bhat, Jane Boutelle, Dan Caine, Craig Carlson, Mike Chipman, Andy Cohen, Matt Cone, Ted Cooper, Caroline Donahue, Ridge Evers, Brooks Fisher, Charlie Gaylord, Alan Gleicher, Mark Goines, Steve Grey,

Mike Grossman, Mike Hallman, Jim Heeger, Judee Humburg, Linda Itskovitz, Karen Jacke, Barb Karlin, Richard Katz, Steve Katz, Larry King Jr., Dave Kinser, Sam Klepper, Sanjeev Kriplani, Lisa Lang, Jacqueline Maartense, Mike Maples, Bob Meighan, Bryan Mistele, Darryl Mobley, Lorrie Norrington, Carol Novello, Jay O'Connor, Mark Ostrau, Steve Pelletier, Leo Redmond, Joanne Reed, Carl Reese, Laura Rippy, Tanya Roberts, Roy Rosin, Dan Rudolph, Jeni Sall, Eric Shenk, Pankaj Shukla, Todd Stanley, Raymond Stern, Tim Villanueva, Alison Berkley Wagonfeld, Sal Webber, Peter Wendell, Larry Wolfe, and Lun Yuen.

Others helped us significantly along the way with finding photos, setting up interviews, and helping with publicity: Karen Cleeve, Diane Kohl, Noelani Luke, Heather McLellan, Lorraine Rossini, I. Brian Taylor, Angela Valles, Jeanette Voss, and Toni Werner.

And thanks to our editors and others at Harvard Business School Press, who provided much needed guidance for our fledgling work: Kirsten Sandberg, Constance Hale, Hollis Heimbouch, Julia Ely, and Erin Korey.

We appreciate these other business book writers who generously gave us insight and encouragement: Andrea Butter, Emanuel Rosen, Phil Carpenter, and Jim Collins.

When we first met with Scott Cook to pitch the idea of our writing this story, he listened carefully to our proposal and then gave us the highest of compliments: "Tom and I," he told us, "were untried and inexperienced, but we were the right pair to create Quicken. You two are just like we were back in 1983. I think you're the right pair to write this book."

Thank you, Scott. We hope you still think so, and we can certainly return the compliment. You were exactly the right person at the right time for Intuit—and stayed that way by evolving tirelessly as the needs of the company changed. Few others could have succeeded as you have. As we finish this journey, you have earned our highest respect.

CHAPTER 1

CALIFORNIA DREAMIN'

E ven in California, fall brings chilly air and earlier nights. As dusk deepened into twilight on one of those crisp fall nights in 1982, Signe Ostby sat at her refinished kitchen table in a small house in Burlingame, near the San Francisco airport. In one of the straight-back chairs around the old oak table, Ostby frowned as she paid bills and balanced the checkbook. Absorbed in a business journal, her husband, Scott Cook, sat nearby to keep her company.

Silence reigned in the kitchen, where the smell of dinner lingered. Cook, an avid businessman with entrepreneurial leanings, devoured stories of new software businesses as his wife worked. Abstracted, he barely noticed when she rose abruptly to refill her teacup, her chair scraping against the wooden floor.

"I hate paying bills," she grumbled. "Really, Scott, this has got to be one of the most tedious, repetitive tasks around."

Jerked from his concentration, Cook looked up as his wife's words penetrated, then turned back to his magazine. But he didn't read much further that evening. Instead, he began to mull over his wife's complaint.

For years, Cook had yearned to strike out on his own and test his entrepreneurial ideas. In 1981, IBM Corporation introduced its personal computer (PC) after thirty years of producing mainframes. Even though Commodore Business Machines and

Apple Computer had already released the Commodore 64 and Apple II computers, IBM's entry transformed the PC market, setting off a swirl of opportunity and opportunism, of frenetic advancement and the marking of technical territory.[1]

The nascent software industry, which had supplied Apple with thousands of titles, exploded around the new IBM PC. With the news in 1982 of Compaq Computer Corporation's founding to make IBM-compatible PC clones, the industry inflated, fueled by technical advances and human ingenuity.[2] In January 1983, *Time* magazine named the Personal Computer as its 1982 "Man of the Year" and estimated that eighty million PCs would be in use by 2000.[3]

Those PCs would need software. Cook, a thirty-year-old graduate of Harvard Business School, had honed consumer marketing skills at Goliath Procter & Gamble and had sharpened analytical decision making at Bain & Company. The high-tech industry fascinated him, and years of watching his father's entrepreneurial efforts stoked Cook's own interest in creating a business. Chafing at his high-paying consulting job, Cook hungered to jump into the ever-evolving world of high technology.

After his wife groused, Cook realized that bill payment might be an excellent chore for a computer. A software program could easily handle the repetitive, numerical, and standardized tasks involved in paying bills and maintaining check registers. Cook had a hunch that such a program might become very popular. And a popular software program, as Cook had seen in companies such as Microsoft, Lotus, and Software Publishing Corporation, could be the genesis of a successful company and a vehicle for his transition from businessman to entrepreneur—a transition he'd been working toward his whole life.

Born in 1952, Cook grew up in La Cañada, California, a middle-class suburb of Los Angeles. His father, Chester, a child of the Great Depression, insisted on frugality, and so Scott and his younger sister, Sharon, made do or did without. The elder Cook, a former Navy lieutenant, valued obedience and education; constant home-improvement projects developed his children's manual dexterity and problem-solving skills. "My family," said Cook, "always worked hard."[4]

A construction equipment sales manager, Chester Cook traveled so much for business that the Cook family vacationed at home. While Scott was growing up, Chester moonlighted by creating two tiny businesses: He designed, and eight-year-old Scott helped build, tanks for safely storing fire-retardant chemicals; he also recorded audio-training tapes for heavy equipment salesmen. Though these entrepreneurial efforts earned little money, his relentless hard work and high standards eventually made Chester the president of the Crook Company heavy equipment dealership.

Scott Cook worked hard to please his stoic father. As soon as he started school, he earned consistently high marks. In third grade, he read all forty-one volumes of the encyclopedia in his spare time, and by fifth grade, he had absorbed enough trade magazines and technical journals to build a simple computer for a science project. Teaching himself programming from a book, Cook wrote his first program at age fifteen in 1967; he ran it on an IBM 1620 in the basement of the school district two towns away. In high school, Cook's entrepreneurial fantasies ranged from fashion to science fiction: he designed wooden cuff links to sell at men's clothing stores and dreamed of creating an electronic tablet that could read handwriting and answer math problems.

Throughout his adolescence, Cook struggled to meet his somewhat remote father's high standards. At seventeen, he applied to Stanford University, his first choice, and to the University of Southern California (USC). His father was between jobs when Cook learned that both schools had admitted him and awarded him academic scholarships. But the Stanford need-based scholarship would disappear when Chester Cook returned to work. Cook polled a few locals—all of whom happened to be USC grads who naturally favored their alma mater—and decided that Stanford was too financially risky. He stayed close to home and matriculated at USC.

Cook majored in math and economics, enjoying the problem solving and quantitative aspects of both. He and his friend Jay Helms applied for a grant to do a project on reducing air pollution in southern California by devising a tax scheme to penalize heavy polluters. They received the grant, struggled to write the paper, and ended up winning an economics contest sponsored by the Western Regional Science Association.

The prize itself was nominal, but it brought Cook to the attention of the chief economist of the Air Resource Board, who hired Cook as an intern. The fieldwork in this state agency taught Cook nonacademic lessons in economics. Most important, it taught him that he didn't want to become an economist.

During his junior year, Cook became president of the USC Ski Club. Cook viewed the club as a business and determined to master its underlying economics—what people wanted, how to give it to them, and how to attract them through advertising and marketing. To succeed, Cook sought the advice of leaders of the most successful ski clubs in the state. The tactics he learned reshaped the club, and membership exploded. By Cook's senior year, the USC Ski Club, with 650 members, was the largest in the state and the largest on-campus organization at USC.

From this experience, Cook learned that he made much better decisions when he got feedback from the best experts rather than from people nearby. Cook had come to regret the choice of USC over Stanford and faulted his own process of polling only USC partisans. The best advice, Cook had learned, rarely came from the most convenient source; making the effort to seek out advice from the best informed and most experienced always paid off. Learning from the best meant that Cook would not have to "reinvent the wheel" and could instead build on others' efforts to reach a better solution.

His ski club experience also taught Cook that he enjoyed the demands of growing a business. And so, during his senior year at USC, Cook dropped the idea of becoming an economist and decided to get a master's in business administration. He applied to

Stanford and Harvard and was accepted by both. Cook chose Harvard, curious about the East Coast and eager to explore it. After graduating from USC in June 1974, Cook moved to Boston in August.

Cook took to Harvard as if he were born crimson. He made friends easily, and felt inspired by his professors to do his best work ever. However, as the course work moved away from theory toward real-world practice, the inexperienced Cook foundered. A twenty-two-year-old with little professional experience, he strained to keep up.

THE FOUNDATION: PROCTER & GAMBLE

After his first year, Cook took an internship with Swissair, developing a marketing plan for a Mediterranean resort. He returned to Harvard with a zeal for marketing and chose his second-year classes to learn more about it. At that time, the big consumer packaged goods companies provided the best on-the-job marketing and business training post graduation. Cincinnati was not a natural magnet for a young bachelor from California, but Cook could not resist an offer from the masters of marketing and headed to Procter & Gamble with his M.B.A. in hand.

At twenty-three, the neophyte Cook had already developed many of the characteristics that would drive his business success. Thin and wiry, Cook seemed taller than his average height because of his slender build and quietly forceful presence. Cook rarely raised his voice, but his drive and confidence in his own intelligence made him passionate and outspoken about business decisions. Cook's thick glasses helped underscore both his intelligence and his fundamental geekiness; he loved thoughtful problem solving and spent long hours contemplating issues that stirred his interest.

Cook's experience with the ski club had also shaped one other salient habit: He listened actively and intently. His intense listening posture—head tilted forward, blue eyes focused on the speaker, agile brain extracting every bit of meaning from what he was hearing—drew in those speaking with him, convincing them to answer his questions honestly and thoughtfully. This unusually demanding listening—a product of his restless curiosity—helped Cook learn more rapidly and deeply than many of his peers.

And Cook learned an encyclopedia's worth of business at P&G. Beginning as assistant brand manager for Crisco shortening, Cook took assignments that taught him about all aspects of business—and especially about listening to the customer. P&G drilled its new marketing recruits on customer orientation as well as how to write reports, analyze business data, manage time, produce on deadline, attend to detail, and work very, very hard.

Among the business practices P&G drummed into its product managers was the critical role of research throughout the product life cycle. In the development phase, P&G researchers profiled behaviors and needs of customers and then identified the benefits that would satisfy them. But its research extended far beyond product development to include advertising, packaging testing, usage studies, and prospect profiles. The object? To ensure that every element of the marketing mix focused on customer needs.

Cook learned that advertising should vividly call attention to product benefits; that packaging should act as a "stop sign" on the shelves; and that distribution, promotions, and pricing all worked together to maximize sales. Proactively managing how stores stocked and merchandised products helped increase sales. Jargon like "shelf space," "out-of-stocks," and "blind test winner" crept into his vocabulary as Cook came to rely on data and analysis to solve problems.

P&G's obsession with its customers resonated with Cook, a longtime subscriber to *Consumer Reports*. Cook loved that magazine because it profiled products that best met customer needs. Cook believed that listening to customers and solving their problems should be the central focus of any business enterprise hoping to transform customers' lives through its goods and services.

Despite his affinity for P&G ideals, self-doubt tormented Cook his first year there. He worried that, with his lack of experience, he was underperforming versus his peers. Colleagues from his business school class were already CEOs while he was struggling as a brand assistant. Cook compensated for his self-doubt with gargantuan efforts. After twelve months, he was the first of his P&G "entering class" to be promoted. Less than a year later, he was promoted again and then made brand manager for Crisco, one of P&G's top five brands at the time and a cash cow for the company.

"Fundamentally, Procter & Gamble has a dedication to inventing products that change people's lives," Cook said later, adding that his experience there gave him an invaluable playbook that could be applied to other industries: hiring and growing new talent, managing and reviewing people, treating people right, and most crucially, doing right by customers.[5]

During his tenure at P&G, Cook had become romantically involved with a fellow brand manager, Signe Ostby. Daughter of the Norwegian Counsel of Wisconsin and possessing long blond hair, a warm smile, and an M.B.A. from the University of Wisconsin, Ostby intrigued Cook. The two became engaged, and thrived both personally and professionally until the arrival of an intolerable new boss for Cook. On the couple's honeymoon in 1980, Cook told Ostby that he wanted to return to California and join a business school buddy at Bain & Company. Ostby reluctantly agreed, and Cook's stint at P&G ended.

THE BIG IDEA

In 1980, Cook and Ostby moved to a cozy house surrounded by fragrant eucalyptus trees in Burlingame, some twenty miles south of San Francisco. After four years at P&G, the twenty-seven-year-old Cook joined Bain as a consultant in Menlo Park, while Ostby became a brand manager at the Clorox Company in Oakland.

Ostby soon leapt to Software Publishing Corporation (SPC), one of the first companies to market its software aggressively to consumers. As Cook commuted to San Francisco, Ostby became the first marketing manager at the start-up, which was based in Mountain View twenty minutes south of their home.

Cook worked diligently at Bain, but California and the burgeoning high-tech industry stirred the entrepreneur in him. The 1977 Apple II PC had ushered in desktop computing, but most Apple programmers created software for themselves, not for ordinary consumers. In those early days, most software programs were created by engineers for engineers. But by the early 1980s, the growing computer software industry was creating products for the less geeky owners of PCs and their broader appeal awakened Cook's business instincts.

However, Cook's first entrepreneurial experiments had nothing to do with computers. While at Bain, he explored the viability of an import-car rental business, which no one had considered before, especially because domestic cars enjoyed wide popularity. He also set up a prototype trip for a windsurfing vacation adventure business. But as he devoured the computer journals that Ostby subscribed to, met SPC executives at parties, and soaked up his wife's software marketing ideas, he began musing over how computers could change people's lives.

By late 1982, when Ostby complained about the drudgery of writing checks and managing their bills, Cook had learned enough about technology and widespread consumer needs to seize on the problem as a possible software opportunity. To explore his idea further, he did what any P&G alum should: He asked the customer about the problem. To validate Ostby's complaint, he randomly called people listed in the Palo Alto, California, and Winnetka, Illinois, phone books, as they reflected communities of upscale consumers likely to buy PCs.

Cook's cold-call customer research applied P&G business principles modified for Cook's own limited time and modest budget. The bootstrap research confirmed a consistent set of customer problems: Most people disliked managing their finances, but could not escape the burden. They stuck to the kind of basic financial tasks—writing checks, maintaining the check register, reconciling, and checking monthly balances—that software could do easily and accurately. With firsthand customer data to support his intuition, Cook believed that he had uncovered a huge unmet need and that his financial software idea had real promise.

Cook might have pursued this idea only in his spare time but for a Bain decision that enraged him. Cook and a Bain partner courted Western Digital, a California-based computer component company, as a client for Bain. When they landed the account, Bain reneged on its commitment to appoint him manager of the engagement. So Cook defiantly departed Bain in spring 1983 to start a software company that would end people's financial management headaches. Cook knew he had a big leap ahead of him—from former Crisco salesman to high-tech entrepreneur—but he believed the jump would reward him. Finally, he would prove himself as an entrepreneur.

CHAPTER 2

SELECTING THE STARTING TEAM

The year 1983 was heady for new software companies; venture capitalists were funding with a vengeance. Now unemployed, Scott Cook recognized that his inexperience at running a company might make him a risky bet for a venture firm, but he believed that if he produced a prototype of his program, he could then credibly peddle his idea. After consulting with his wife's boss, Fred Gibbons, the CEO of SPC, Cook decided to hire a college student to help him create the software quickly and inexpensively in BASIC (Beginner's All-purpose Symbolic Instruction Code)—a simple computer-programming language.

In March, during "dead week" just before winter quarter finals, Cook drove to Stanford with a stack of fliers reading: "Programmer wanted for innovative PC program." Despite having been accepted there twice, Cook did not know his way around Stanford's campus, so he parked his car and set out on foot to find the engineering school. In front of the Terman engineering library, he approached a group of students, and asked, "Where is the best place to post these fliers?"

"I'll take one," a baritone voice responded. Cook handed a flier to a lanky upperclassman. "Tell me more," the young man invited, and under the California spring sunshine Cook described the project briefly. "That sounds really interesting. I might want to work with you on this," replied the clean-cut student. "My name is Tom Proulx."

Cook posted his fliers at Stanford, UC Berkeley, and San Jose State and eventually met with several applicants. But Proulx's evident thoughtfulness after several conversations convinced Cook he'd made a beeline to the perfect candidate. Within two weeks, Tom Proulx had agreed to develop Cook's financial software program. Together, Cook and Proulx gave it a working name: Kwik-Chek.

ENTREPRENEURIAL ENGINEER

Tom Proulx (whose last name rhymes with *true*) was also from southern California—all over southern California. The upheaval caused by his family's annual moves, as his father worked to advance in his career, formed Proulx's dogged personality. Like Cook's father, both of Proulx's parents had grown up in wrenching poverty. Proulx's father had lived in a North Carolina cabin with an outhouse, no heat, and a hole in the floor for sweeping dirt out. He spent his life climbing out of that hole.

Proulx learned his work ethic from his father. By age four, the younger Proulx insisted on being awakened every morning at four o'clock so that he could accompany his father on the massive paper route he maintained while attending law school at the University of California at Los Angeles (UCLA). After delivering all the newspapers, the two enjoyed warm donuts together before Proulx's father went on to a full day of classes. Proulx's mother also worked full-time as a bookkeeper. After graduation, Proulx's father applied his law knowledge to a career in business.

By telling his personal story of success, Proulx's father instilled in his son the importance of hard work, struggle, dedication, and drive. Tom Proulx became an intense, focused worker very young, disregarding the cost of achieving the goals he set for himself. His father's stories of self-improvement also instilled in Proulx a fundamental egalitarianism and a sure sense of right and wrong. No one, thought Proulx as he listened to his father, was inherently better than anyone else, and everyone should be treated fairly and well.

During the Proulx family's brief tenure in Lancaster, California, Proulx had attended Piute Intermediate School, where his math teacher required students to score 95 percent for an A instead of the standard 90 percent. "Would you want to go to a doctor who got only a 90 percent?" he asked. Many years later, Proulx adamantly adhered to that benchmark of excellence.

Like Cook, Proulx gravitated toward computers. He wrote his first code in high school, using BASIC to program on a school district mainframe timeshare, and took a class to learn more about these wondrous machines. The pure logic required for computer programming fascinated him, and he enjoyed the process of making an idea work on a machine. By that time, Atari had released its Pong game, intriguing tech-minded individuals everywhere, and the possibilities associated with computers seemed vast.

Even though Proulx received good marks in high school, his attending college was not a given. Wanting to achieve the financial success that his father had always pursued, he considered jumping into the real estate business and riding the industry's boom in the late 1970s. But an older girlfriend, a freshman at Stanford, convinced the handsome and clever Proulx that he would profit more from college. Accepted at Stanford and the California Institute of Technology (CalTech), Proulx decided the northern California school would give him a more well-rounded undergraduate experience than the science mecca of CalTech.

At Stanford, for the first time in his life, Proulx found himself surrounded by studious intellectuals. But he was hardly outmatched. Proulx had decided to major in physics, and completing only 60 percent of his first physics final exam at the end of fall term dismayed him. When he returned to pick up his test after winter break, however, he learned that he had scored an A+

on the exam, which had been graded on a bell curve. Proulx earned three A+'s and two A's in the fall of 1979, his first quarter at Stanford.

Although the intellectual challenge of physics intrigued him, by sophomore year Proulx decided that he did not like physics enough to become a physicist. Influenced by the recent birth of personal computers and the stories he began hearing about Apple Computer founder Steve Jobs, Proulx switched to a major in electrical engineering, the closest undergraduate major to computer science that Stanford offered at the time.

By the time Cook bumped into Proulx on the Stanford campus in March 1983, Proulx was about to complete his bachelor's degree but still had one year left at Stanford to earn a concurrent master's degree in computer science. Proulx had already decided that he wanted to start a software company, hoping to emulate Jobs' success at Apple. He had begun considering ideas for a company to develop mass-market software for personal computers, but had not hit upon a suitable product. In his first conversation with Cook, Proulx realized that Cook had a big idea, one that would appeal to enough people to sustain the kind of company he had imagined.

Proulx's intelligence, work ethic, and determination to succeed echoed Cook's. So did his values; when Cook glimpsed a Bible in Proulx's dorm room, he was reassured about their association. Though Cook's experience and pragmatism brought into relief Proulx's youth, idealism, and inexperience, Cook felt that Proulx's understanding of the program's potential made him the ideal candidate. He offered Proulx the programming job, and Proulx accepted.

Cook later said of Proulx: "Tom was different from everyone who might have helped me. He had a sense of mission, of product, of wanting to build something big, not just to do code. You could see him get excited about the concepts, internalize the principles, and extend the thinking beyond where an ordinary person would take it. He was head and shoulders the standout."[1] (See figure 2-1.)

FIGURE 2-1

Cofounders Proulx (left) and Cook posed for their first formal portrait, 1989.

Source: Courtesy of Virginia Boyd.

CUSTOMER-INTUITIVE DESIGN

Once Proulx and Cook finalized terms, including Proulx's pay, they began to design the features and appearance, or user interface, of the new software. Starting in May 1983, they met regularly at Cook's house or in Proulx's dorm room. Talking directly to prospective customers had helped Cook build a deep understanding of exactly what people hated about their finances. His primal curiosity and careful analysis shaped hundreds of decisions as Cook worked with Proulx to define the product to solve those customer needs.

Cook's intuition, research, and P&G experience decreed that Kwik-Chek should look and work like the forms that people used in the real world. Apple Computer's short-lived Lisa computer, whose user interface mirrored real-world functions, had inspired Cook. Proulx immediately saw the viability of Cook's real-world concept, and agreed to create a software program that looked like a checkbook.

15

The checkbook metaphor—widely used and understood—would maximize users' comfort with the new product and minimize the time needed to learn how to use it. Proulx vowed that his program would make the standard monochrome IBM monitor green text on black screen really look like a check that people would write by hand, with data entry fields in the same places that people wrote on paper checks. And he carried the concept one important step further, by making the record-keeping part of the program look like the check register from his own Wells Fargo checkbook, down to every vertical and horizontal line. Once Proulx finished the user interface design, he was ready to begin programming.

But first, he had to focus on a summer internship at Hughes Aircraft in Newport Beach, California. Throughout the summer, Proulx amused his colleagues at Hughes Aircraft by frequently falling asleep in meetings. After the forty-plus hour work weeks for his Hughes-sponsored scholarship, Proulx put in another sixty to seventy hours each week on Kwik-Chek. Development went slowly on Kwik-Chek, so Proulx spent more time programming and less time sleeping as the summer progressed. Cook and Proulx had set a tentative product launch date of Christmas 1983—about six months after Proulx had started programming—but Proulx worried that he would not make that. By midsummer, friends and colleagues at Hughes were betting on how long it would take for the exhausted but obdurate Proulx to nod off.

Meanwhile, in northern California, Cook, drawing on his lesson from the ski club, learned more about building a software company by interviewing anyone successful who might have something to teach him. He gathered information about fundraising, retail and channel marketing, competitive products, and launch practices. Beginning with a three-hour interview of his industry-experienced wife, Cook called every software contact he could find, to learn from the best so that he could make his company the best.

Cook's determination and force of will created a driving sense of momentum for the infant company. He searched relentlessly for people to give him information and corresponded every day with Proulx about his progress. Proulx's stubborn standard of excellence and his relentless work ethic matched Cook's drive. The two men worked in tandem to wrest a company out of hard work and resolve.

To delve deeper into their prospective customers' needs, Cook commissioned his wife's sister to call hundreds of people about their personal financial habits, what they liked and what they disliked. This approach was the P&G way: understand potential customers' behaviors and needs so thoroughly that the product will completely satisfy those needs and, at best, exceed them, "wowing" customers. The research quantified what Cook's initial phone interviews had suggested: more than 80 percent of people surveyed hated dealing with their personal finances. Here was an incredible market opportunity. The key was to reduce the time spent on three main activities: paying bills, maintaining a check register, and periodically totaling and reviewing expenditures.

These findings helped Cook and Proulx focus on critical product specifications; as they corresponded over the summer, both insisted their software trim time spent on these three basic tasks, refusing to load their program with extraneous bells and whistles. The feature set would be minimal, but the execution had to be excellent—the program had to run intuitively, a phrase that Cook often used when describing his concepts.

Cook and Proulx analyzed the forty-six competitive products already on the market, later joking that they had the forty-seventh mover advantage (compared to a desirable first mover advantage) in the category. Universally, the competitors poorly met fundamental customer needs. One competitor, Home Accountant, was outselling all of its difficult-to-use competitors despite its own inscrutable complexity.[2] Home Accountant's success, Cook and Proulx speculated, was a testament to how badly customers needed a simpler alternative.

SoftSel in El Segundo, California, the leading software distributor at the time, was also launching a personal finance product, Dollars and Sense. Cook set up an interview with the SoftSel

Software CEO to learn more. If SoftSel got the product right, its distribution would allow it to own the market, and Cook and Proulx might as well give up right away. But to their relief, Soft-Sel was focused on a complex, feature-laden paradigm—not on ease or speed.

One other competitor, Managing Your Money by MECA Software of Trumbull, Connecticut, was so complicated that the staff at a software convention MECA booth failed to make it work. "This program is like an adventure game, it's so hard!" a MECA employee exclaimed to Cook. Cook compared Kwik-Chek to a speedboat and Managing Your Money to an ocean liner.

Cook believed that the other entrants in the field missed the mark because software engineers focused on features, not on customers. They seemingly lacked input from marketing or customer research. Kwik-Chek's biggest potential competitor was not any of the financial software programs already crowding retail shelves. It was what most people already used to manage their checkbooks: the pen or pencil.

It didn't take long for Cook and Proulx to decide on a name for their venture. "Instincts" was an early possibility, but Cook observed that it sounded too much like "It stinks." "Intuit," on the other hand, expressed the overarching goal of making software so easy to use that it required almost no thought. "Intuitive" became the watchword for the company's product development for years to come.

Despite Proulx's gargantuan efforts over the summer, the program was far from complete in September 1983. Frustrated by the delay, Cook pushed out launch to spring 1984. Proulx faced a difficult personal decision: he could either continue his killer two-master schedule, now juggling school by day and Kwik-Chek programming by night, or he could defer his return to Stanford. The programming—and Cook's infectious determination—won. Proulx deferred school and Cook hired Tony Tyson, a bright local high school student, as Proulx's assistant.

Cook funded the tiny business himself. Proulx, who had initially taken a salary, decided to work for equity in the company rather than drawing pay, as Cook had from the beginning. Tyson was Intuit's only paid employee. Initially, Cook worked from his den, and Proulx from the Palo Alto apartment he had moved into after returning from Hughes, but in late fall 1983, Cook took out a home-equity loan and rented a one-room, ten-by-sixteen-foot windowless office on Embarcadero Road in Palo Alto. There, he continued to assemble the business side while Proulx and his high-school assistant programmed. Throughout the fall, they all worked long hours to complete Kwik-Chek.

As they got closer to launch, Cook and Proulx realized that Intuit needed some marketing and operational expertise to help the one-product company become a real business. Cook had never developed operational skills, and Proulx's sole focus had always been programming. Neither flinched in honestly appraising this weakness, and neither hesitated about hiring someone with skills they lacked. Ideally, they wanted someone who had run an entire company's operations, hired employees, set up business books, managed manufacturing and customer service, rented offices, and purchased office equipment.

The two began keeping an eye out for other talent. Earlier that year, Cook traveled to Las Vegas with his wife as part of an SPC profit-sharing trip. There he met another SPC spouse, Tom LeFevre. LeFevre held undergraduate and graduate degrees in engineering, as well as an M.B.A. from Stanford. He had worked in marketing at P&G and Clorox, leaving Clorox in 1980 to serve as vice president of marketing and planning for Velo-Bind, a Sunnyvale, California, company that manufactured binders for reports. There, LeFevre had run operations for a growing business.

Cook's conversation with LeFevre turned into a spontaneous interview, with Cook setting up a hypothetical problem involving the roulette table for LeFevre to solve. Under Cook's intent ear, LeFevre provided a systematic and plausible solution demonstrating that he could decipher problems creatively and quickly. The next week, after consulting with Proulx, Cook offered LeFevre the job of VP of marketing and operations. LeFevre accepted, to Cook and Proulx's delight. In their eyes, Intuit had just become a real company because they had hired a professional manager.

BEATING THE PEN

LeFevre joined Intuit in December 1983 and wasted no time in boosting Cook's efforts to build a software company on the P&G model. Slight and studious, LeFevre brought a deliberate manner coupled with a keen analytical intelligence to Intuit. To balance Cook's determination and Proulx's intensity, LeFevre brought a quiet maturity, professionalism, and a seasoned perspective that helped the young entrepreneurs in many areas. LeFevre shared Cook's passion for data-driven decision making. He could communicate with Cook in P&G shorthand about business issues, and his engineering background gave him a bond in common with Proulx.

LeFevre convinced Cook and Proulx to hire two additional programmers to expedite Proulx's efforts. He set up Intuit's accounting system, created the minimal human resources policies and administrative processes required by the state, and began looking for larger, more permanent office space. LeFevre signed a lease in March 1984, making Intuit the first tenant in the "garden level" (a euphemism for basement) of a new building on vibrant University Avenue, in the heart of downtown Palo Alto just blocks from Stanford University. By April Intuit operations shifted to a new milieu of restaurants, coffee shops, retail stores, artsy movie theaters, and lively crowds.

The intensive programming effort continued, but midway through the winter, Proulx realized that he could not successfully finish the Kwik-Chek program in interpreted BASIC—the program had grown too large. He had worried from the start about using BASIC for Kwik-Chek but had not felt comfortable overruling Cook (and Fred Gibbons from SPC, who had advised Cook) on the best language to use. Having poured so much effort into BASIC already, Proulx could not start over in a better language, and so he and his two programmers had to convert their work to the faster-running compiled BASIC, putting them weeks behind schedule. The additional delay only doubled Proulx's determination to finish the program.

As Stanford's spring quarter approached, the engineering team had made up for lost ground, but Proulx was not ready to turn Kwik-Chek over to anyone else so that he could return to school. Unfortunately, however, Stanford had warned him at the start of winter quarter that he would be allowed no further deferrals in his master's program. So Proulx faced an agonizing decision: Intuit or the Stanford master's degree, for which he would have to immediately return full-time to school.

Proulx made the choice with surprising ease. Convinced of Kwik-Chek's ultimate success, the idealistic and determined Proulx called Stanford's Computer Science Department and told them he was not coming back for his master's degree. Proulx had one course left to complete his bachelor's degree; during spring quarter of 1984, he returned to Stanford three afternoons a week to fulfill this last requirement while concentrating on finishing Kwik-Chek.

Proulx's decision to stay relieved Cook and LeFevre. Once Proulx decided to stay, LeFevre stopped focusing on operations, put on his marketing hat, and turned to the P&G imperative he shared with Cook: systematically developing a complete understanding of customer needs. As Proulx continued programming, LeFevre and Cook decided on three marketing goals for Intuit: (1) understanding fundamental consumer needs in personal finance, (2) designing a complete solution to meet these needs, and (3) making the solution intuitive to use.

As LeFevre thought more about these principles, he realized something critical for customers: the real-world checkbook metaphor that Proulx and Cook had used when creating the user interface was only the first step in making the software easy for novice users. To develop an "end to end" solution, LeFevre took this ease-of-use principle one step further by arguing that the ideal solution for personal finance would also include paper checks that users could print on their home printers.

Unfortunately, though, the then-ubiquitous dot matrix printers were not intended for check-sized documents, and few users would be able to figure out how to install check-imprinted paper in their printers to print checks correctly. But LeFevre still believed that the best product for users required a paper check design that would work every time any customer tried to print one.

When LeFevre explained this to Proulx, Proulx took the challenge characteristically to heart. Working through the night, a sleepless but elated Proulx returned the next morning with a way to get a computer to automatically verify that a user had installed blank checks correctly in a dot matrix printer. This ingenious solution, eventually earning Proulx and LeFevre a patent, would allow Intuit to meet user needs throughout the billpay and check-writing cycle.

Solving the printer problem inadvertently led Intuit into the supplies business that would become vital to its survival by providing a recurring profit stream. The supplies business (consumers' checks and window envelopes) became the "razor blade" for the software "razor." After Proulx designed the paper and printing specifications for checks, LeFevre chose a check and envelope supplier and worked out the business arrangements for Intuit to sell checks to its customers.

LeFevre, intent on achieving ease of use, decided to test the program with prospective customers. He set an audacious goal for the first version of the product: A complete PC novice should be able to install Kwik-Chek and print a check within fifteen minutes. To succeed, LeFevre believed that Kwik-Chek had to beat the pen from day one. And so, in the first instance of the usability testing that later became standard industry practice, LeFevre recruited people off the streets in downtown Palo Alto and timed their Kwik-Chek usage with a stopwatch. After every test, Proulx and the other programmers worked to improve the program.

Eventually, paying a bill with Kwik-Chek took half the time of doing it by hand.

Again focusing on customer ease of use, Cook and LeFevre chose not to use a technical writer for Intuit's manual. Instead, they recruited a "How-to" book writer from *Sunset,* a West Coast home and garden publishing company, Susan Schlangen, to use plain English and accessible instructions to write the first Intuit user manual.

Schlangen, along with LeFevre, then recruited her fellow members of the Palo Alto Junior League, most of whom had never used PCs, for the program's final round of prelaunch testing. In the tiny offices crammed with desks, tension ran high as the seven-member Intuit team carefully observed the doyennes of Palo Alto society. LeFevre timed each against the fifteen-minute goal. Proulx, Cook, and LeFevre took copious notes, observing where the women got stuck. Would the software meet LeFevre's ambitious goal for quick initial use?

Even though the inexperienced users took, on average, seven minutes just to locate the Enter key on the keyboard, the timing results elated the Intuit team: Almost all still made Intuit's fifteen-minute goal for installing the software and printing out a check. The computer novices heaped compliments on the Intuit team, exclaiming over the software's usefulness and general ease. The Junior League members also tested competitive products. Even PC whizzes struggled for up to five hours before they printed their first check. Novice users simply gave up in frustration.

By early summer 1984, Cook, Proulx, and LeFevre believed wholeheartedly that the Kwik-Chek program would save users time and effort over all alternatives. The software allowed consumers to write checks, maintain the check register, and add up income and expenses. Packaging and marketing messages for the software would showcase these features and benefits.

Cook and LeFevre took the final steps toward readying the software for launch by designing the product's bright and prominent packaging. In a nod to P&G's Tide laundry detergent, they chose bright orange for the software's box. They took package mock-ups to software stores to see if the boxes "jumped" off the shelves and grabbed shoppers' attention.

Inside the bright outer sleeve of the packaging, a box held disks, sample checks, a manual, and brochures. The back of the package had a flap that opened to reveal screen shots of the software saving time and simplifying finances. The headline announced, "Easy to use because it looks and works just like your paper checkbook!" The packaging also included testimonials from ordinary users recruited to test the software, including, "I love it. It saves so much time." "It's a piece of cake!" "It's so fast and easy and I've never used software before."

LeFevre's usability testing had validated the Intuit team's hard work. Faith in the business concept had been confirmed by the Junior Leaguers' enthusiastic responses. Proulx and his programmers had nearly completed the final tweaks to the software. Cook and LeFevre had created packaging and marketing, and LeFevre had ordered boxes, manuals, and diskettes in quantity so that the tiny company could fulfill orders for its software. Now, all the company needed was enough money for a retail launch.

CHAPTER 3

OF DOLLARS AND DOUBTERS

I n 1982, Scott Cook marveled over how little marketing his wife's company needed for new products: If Software Publishing Company, for which Ostby was a marketing manager, put a new product on the shelves, it flew out the door, no fanfare required. But in early 1983, Lotus upped the ante with what was then a staggering launch advertising budget of $3 million. Lotus 1-2-3, an innovative spreadsheet product, met instant success. Microsoft, still a modestly sized software company with 476 employees, followed suit with its release of Word 1.0 for DOS in late 1983. Its $3.5 million marketing campaign included demo diskettes inserted in *PC World* magazine.[1]

Cook, Proulx, and LeFevre observed these splashy launches with some dismay. Based on these lofty sums, Cook and LeFevre estimated that Intuit needed $2.5 million to launch Kwik-Chek successfully into the retail markets. With that kind of money, Intuit could create enough demand through advertising to persuade retailers and wholesalers to stock the product. With Kwik-Chek nearly completed, at least they could now demonstrate their software and ideas. The Intuit trio created a presentation aimed at venture capitalists and began to make the rounds.

Everyone was talking about personal computers (PCs) in 1983, and venture capitalists had already invested a record amount of money in high-tech companies. The market saw more initial public offerings (IPOs) in 1983 than any year since the late 1960s. In 1984, though, the PC industry slowed dramatically after nearly seven years of incredible growth and hype. Venture capitalists' investments fell by more than 25 percent after tripling the year before.[2] Media outlets were quick to proclaim the end of the PC era.[3] And high profile software companies tanked without ever shipping a product, making millions of venture capital (VC) dollars evaporate with them. The overall market for VC went from hot to frigid nearly overnight—not a good omen for the struggling Intuit team.

Aside from such market conditions, other factors worked against Intuit in its pursuit of funding. Venture capitalists did not generally believe in PCs for homes and joked about recording recipes or balancing checkbooks on them. Cook had heard that even Don Estridge, president of IBM's Entry Systems Division, had said at a Big Blue personal computer fair in 1983, "For the average person, the excitement of buying a PC evaporates very quickly. The same question keeps coming up: what do you do with it? My wife can't think of any reason at all to use a PC."[4]

The title of a *Forbes* magazine article from October 1983, echoed the prevailing view: "But what do I use it for?" The article asked, "Could it be that the home computer market is approaching saturation at a time when less than 6 percent of all the households in the U.S. own one?" It went on to quote a computer consultant: "There are really a limited number of people in a company now who benefit by all of the power a personal computer makes available. How many people, after all, do spreadsheet analysis? How many need both to write reports and manipulate numbers? The average executive with a personal computer uses it less than three hours a week, and almost half the people who own personal computers use them one hour a month or less. And most don't use anywhere near the full capabilities of the software." The article concluded by arguing that, "the all-purpose computer, like the all-purpose motor, may prove short-lived—a dinosaur."[5]

Also working against Intuit was its team's lack of experience in the software industry. How could venture capitalists believe that a college student and a former fat salesman had developed a killer product? Since highly experienced teams had failed to launch programs, venture capitalists would not bet on the inexperienced trio, even though their product was nearly complete. The final factor was the team's intention to use the money mainly in advertising and marketing to support a retail launch. In 1984, venture capitalists would not even consider using their investment dollars to support an intangible such as marketing.

And so, during spring and early summer 1984, Cook, Proulx, and LeFevre met with more than twenty VC firms, and every venture capitalist rejected their pitch. Not even one firm asked them for a second meeting. This utter failure dismayed the hardworking Intuit team.

One evening in the company's main room, shared by all seven employees—Cook, Proulx, LeFevre, Schlangen, and the three assistant engineers—Cook put down the phone after the company's twentieth rejection call from a VC firm. LeFevre buttonholed him: "Scott, we've got to change our strategy. If we can't get funding from venture capitalists, then we get it from someone else. Who else has money? Rich people, that's who."

"Do you know any rich people?" Cook asked.

"Just two: My former CEO at Velo-Bind, Terry Groswith, and my father-in-law, Heinz Cook."

With bated breath, LeFevre and Cook left to pitch Intuit to the two wealthy men. The signs looked good: Groswith, an inventor who created processes for making disposable medical gloves and instant hard-bound books, knew and trusted LeFevre. Kwik-Chek impressed Heinz Cook (no relation to Scott Cook), a highly successful salesman who also trusted his son-in-law, LeFevre.

After Cook and LeFevre met with both men, they agonized every time Cook's phone rang in the tiny office. Finally, Cook fielded questions from Groswith and then Heinz Cook. Greatly relieved, he learned that both men chose to invest. Cook's parents had also put money into the fledgling venture. By the end of summer 1984, Intuit had netted $151,000 in friends and family "angel" investments—enough to pay salaries and rent for a while, but far from their original $2.5 million goal. How could they stretch this small sum into a launch?

QUICKEN IS BORN

Despite the funding challenges, Cook finally scheduled Kwik-Chek for launch in October 1984. By late summer, the company had still not agreed on the product's final name, and its indecision threatened to delay launch. At lunch one day, Cook walked down bustling University Avenue to a local Stacey's bookstore and spent more than an hour poring through dictionaries and thesauruses. Finally, he found a word that captured the time saving at the product's core. He dashed back to the office.

"Everybody, listen—I've got it. I've figured out the name." Everyone looked up. "The name for our program is . . . Quicken."

Silence. Finally, Proulx spoke. "Er—isn't that when a pregnant woman starts to feel her baby move?"

Cook had preferred the word's more mainstream connotations, like *revive, stimulate, hasten,* and *come to life.* He snapped back, "Yeah, Tom, that's one meaning, but another is to speed up and to give life. That's what our product is going to do, speed up people's finances, give them back a part of their life. That's why Quicken is the perfect name." LeFevre tried to convince Proulx that the name would grow on him, but still Proulx thought Quicken sounded awkward. The company, however, had run out of time. With much ambivalence, Kwik-Chek became Quicken.

Cook's conversations with retailers had confirmed why Intuit's $151,000 could not support a retail launch. Earlier in the summer, he had met with software sellers in Los Angeles. One store had an office with a large one-way glass window looking out on the retail floor. Directly in front of the window was a big bin full of boxes of software with a sign marked "Huge Discount Closeout." When Cook asked the store's manager whether he would stock Quicken, the manager replied, "See that bin out there? Those are the products that *I* decided to sell. Now, I'm only stocking products that *customers* tell me to sell. If enough customers come in and ask for your product, then I'll stock it."

Other retailers echoed his refrain, telling Cook only advertising would make customers ask for his product. A retail launch required a big advertising budget to generate that demand. The paltry sum of $151,000 was nowhere near enough.

So Cook, Proulx, and LeFevre devised plan B: Launch Quicken by generating good press and forming partnerships. Even without advertising, the team believed that Intuit might not need so much money if Quicken got great press that made customers demand it from retailers. Since Bain and P&G had discouraged it, Cook had never talked to the press before. But Terry Groswith told Cook about Silicon Valley public relations (PR) guru Regis McKenna, and Cook headed back to Stacey's to study McKenna's principles and strategies.

McKenna's PR strategy included meeting with key "influencers": industry analysts and mainstream journalists. In fall 1984, Cook made appointments with more than a dozen such Silicon Valley figures, including celebrity analyst Esther Dyson, editor of an industry executive newsletter called *Release 1.0* and frequent conference speaker. He also met with journalists from magazines including *Forbes* and *American Banker* to show off Quicken.

Cook believed that before these influential people would endorse Quicken, they would have to understand the customer's needs and competitors' shortcomings in the personal finance software market. Like the venture capitalists, most of the influencers he courted would come to the meetings with a knee-jerk preconception: they ridiculed checkbook software products and saw no reason to use them.

Cook carefully choreographed these face-to-face encounters. He arrived with the portable computer of the day—a heavy Compaq "luggable"—loaded with Dollars and Sense, the leading competitor. Cook invited his audience—typically several people sat in on his demonstrations—to send up its most technically savvy person to do the simplest task: write and print a check. Technophiles, even engineers, would struggle to make the software work. When they surrendered, Cook would switch to Quicken and invite the least technically savvy member of his audience to write a check without peeking at the user manual. Within three to five minutes, every person could write a check— the software was that intuitive.

Cook knew from these sorties that his product could "wow" people and that words never worked as well as the comparison demonstration. But even though his demonstrations succeeded, Cook worried that a strategy relying on the press might fail. And so, he decided to take the demo strategy to everyone else he knew in the hopes of persuading his contacts to invest, recommend, or simply buy a copy of Quicken.

While at Bain, Cook had consulted with Wells Fargo about home banking, on which Bank of America had lost a lot of money. Cook realized that Wells Fargo might conceivably market Quicken to its customers as an interim home banking solution. Cook seized on the idea as a viable way to expose customers to Quicken, since Intuit was too cash-strapped to afford the advertising blitz that would persuade retailers to carry the software.

When Cook showed Quicken to a group headed by Bill Zundt, his former client at Bain and the current president of Wells Fargo Bank of San Francisco, Quicken's technical simplicity underwhelmed the bank's technical representative. But the Wells Fargo employee who was familiar with Quicken's competition elated Cook by saying, "You guys have a great product, and you're trying to reach customers whom we already have. Maybe you should talk to us about distribution."[6]

And so, Wells Fargo Bank became Intuit's first marketing partner. LeFevre decided that Intuit's contract terms for banks would be a 50 percent payment upon order/contract signature and the remaining payment upon delivery of the software. Cook sold Wells Fargo one thousand units, and Intuit, with great relief, embraced a bank distribution strategy as it deposited Wells Fargo's check.

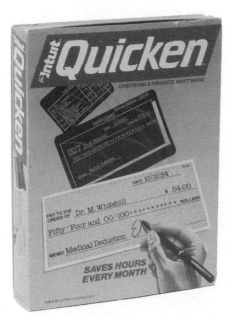

FIGURE 3-1

Quicken 1.0 for DOS personal finance software in 1984 used a bright orange Tide-inspired package. Cook brought several marketing innovations to Intuit from his Procter & Gamble days.

Source: Courtesy of Intuit.

Quicken 1.0 for DOS launched in October 1984 (see figure 3-1). Selling for $99.95, the software received a surprising amount of fanfare. Wells Fargo, the company's sole distribution partner, set its PR staff to cover the partnership launch. The new relationship got several favorable press plugs, and local television news crews covered the launch event. Intuit's seven employees, significant others, and Wells Fargo colleagues were jubilant that night in the basement of 540 University Avenue, celebrating with appetizers, drinks, and a toast from Cook.

Cook expected the good press to jump-start Intuit's retail sales, but after the initial flurry of congratulatory phone calls from friends and relations, the phones remained obstinately silent. Tension grew in the small office. Retailers ignored Quicken, pushing competitors like Managing Your Money, Dollars and Sense, and dozens of other products that were already on their shelves. The few stores that did want to stock Quicken couldn't find any distributors that carried the product, as all had turned Cook down.

No advertising, no distributors, no orders for Quicken—a crushing disappointment, particularly for Cook.

Late one night, several days after Quicken's launch, Cook observed glumly to LeFevre, "So much for the serendipity of knowing Zundt. We'll never get stores to carry Quicken this way."

LeFevre regarded Cook steadily, a little surprised at just how frustrated Cook sounded. "We just have to keep trying. We don't have retail distribution right now," LeFevre admitted, "but we do have one bank carrying our software. Maybe we can interest other banks, and distribute Quicken through banks all over the country."

So Intuit focused on the bank channel. Wells Fargo introduced Cook to other banks, including Bank of Hawaii. Tim Farr, an assistant VP in Honolulu who ran the Intuit deal, brilliantly led the Quicken sales effort. Instead of fulfilling orders only though an 800 number service, as Wells Fargo was doing, Bank of Hawaii bought enough Quicken in January 1985 to put several copies in each branch. As a result, Quicken was sold in more retail outlets (bank branches) than any other software product in the islands. Within six months, Quicken was second only to Lotus 1-2-3 as the top-selling software product in Hawaii. "A few more banks like that one," thought Cook, "and we've got it made."

QUIET PANIC

Wells Fargo had signed on as a partner in October 1984, and Bank of Hawaii signed on in January 1985. While Proulx worked on specifications for a version of Quicken for the Apple II computer and LeFevre concentrated on operations, marketing, and human resources, Cook spent the first months of 1985 trying to sign up more banks to distribute Quicken, offering each bank exclusive distribution in one to three states. Cook had contracts in front of five different bank managers, but as months came and went without a single signature, Cook and the rest of Intuit suffered.

By April, Intuit had burned through all the revenue from Wells Fargo and Bank of Hawaii as well as Cook's savings, his Bain retirement funds, money from his parents, and the $151,000 from angel investors. Never dreaming that he would not receive VC funding, Cook had blithely run up all his charge cards and lines of credit on his house. Now, struggling with the reality of his huge personal debt, he spent ever-longer hours at Intuit's cramped headquarters, trying to figure out how to make Quicken successful.

Cook's marriage suffered from the financial and emotional strain. His risk-averse wife worried about their financial future and chastised Cook for leaving Bain. Ostby's doubts, which grew worse as Intuit's financial promise declined, were a source of constant friction and stress in their relationship.

LeFevre had reached the miserable conclusion that Intuit was going to run out of cash. He tried to talk to Cook about the dire situation, but Cook would hear nothing of it. Cook listed the bank deals that might close, insisting that some would come through. LeFevre countered that bank sales cycles were too long and that the unfortunate writing was on the wall.

On the last day of April 1985, LeFevre said, "Come out to lunch with me, Scott; we have to talk."

At Round Table Pizza, LeFevre continued, "Scott, it's over. After we pay folks today we only have $385 in the bank and no firm prospect of cash coming in, except the little bit we are making from supplies orders. Do you know what bankruptcy looks like?" Cook shook his head. "Let me tell you, it's not pretty." Cook had believed that a bank contract, with its 50 percent deposit, would save them from financial ruin. Stunned, he now realized that it wouldn't. His personal finances were in shambles. His parents had trusted him with their hard-earned money. His marriage was suffering. Now the business had run out of cash and might fail. A quiet panic came over Cook. What could they do? How could they keep the dream alive without losing everything?

CHAPTER 4

SURVIVAL 101

On the first day of May 1985, Scott Cook called together the puzzled employees of Intuit. As they clustered around the makeshift receptionist area in the tiny basement office, Cook bluntly told them the bad news: Intuit could no longer pay salaries, beginning that very day. "This isn't a layoff," he emphasized quietly to his staff as he stood, hands jammed in pockets, before the small group. "I'd *like* everyone to keep working. But I'm sure some of you have to earn money, and the unfortunate truth is that we just can't pay you right now."

Cook paused, looking down at his shoes, then continued. "I really hope you do decide to stay. We need to work together to turn this around. When more banks sign up to sell Quicken . . . ." Cook looked away again, his mouth twisting bitterly. "I'd like to meet with each of you individually to talk about this. But now I've got to go meet with my marriage counselor. The only thing more important to me than Intuit is my marriage."[1]

As Cook's footsteps on the stairs died away, employees exchanged stricken looks. After months of waiting, they no longer expected any banks to sign. This seemed the end of the road. And Cook's personal turmoil on top of the company's failure daunted Intuit's mostly young and inexperienced staff.

Twenty-two-year-old Virginia Boyd, an Intuit employee for only two weeks, listened to Cook's quiet announcement in disbelief and anger. The sister of Tom Proulx's longtime girlfriend Barbara Boyd, Virginia Boyd had quit her job at radio station KNBR to work for $7 an hour to assist COO Tom LeFevre. Why on earth had they hired her if they were going broke, she wondered. They must have known they were running out of money. Boyd had initially rejoiced at getting the Intuit job. Now, she lamented. What should she do?

Other employees were more swiftly decisive. Within an hour, Proulx's programmers had resigned; later that day so did Tom LeFevre, acting COO and VP of marketing. LeFevre explained, "Scott, you don't need my skills right now, and you can't afford me, either." He began looking for other work, though he continued helping Intuit in his spare time.

Tenacious Proulx stayed, never doubting that Intuit would survive and that Quicken would ultimately succeed. Employees, he believed, just had to endure long enough for more people to discover Quicken. Intuit's research data proved that the overwhelming majority of people wanted to save time handling their most mundane financial tasks. What's more, Intuit's analysis of competitive products confirmed that Quicken was the only one that could deliver.

Once consumers saw Quicken and understood how much time it would save, Proulx knew that they would buy it. "Of course we're going to survive and be successful," he told his colleagues. "Quicken is good; we've done our research and know what consumers want. Nobody else in the market does what we do. We just need to wait it out."[2] Proulx's idealistic confidence in the research data affirming that Quicken would save people's time, as well as his ability to live as cheaply as a student, kept him at Intuit.

His convictions swayed Virginia Boyd and Susan Schlangen. When Boyd spoke with her parents about the situation at Intuit, they counseled her to honor her commitment to the company—

regardless of whether Intuit reciprocated and paid her for her time. So, perhaps naively but resolved to stay the course, Boyd remained without a cash salary. The company's tech writer Schlangen, by now friends with both Proulx and Boyd, also stayed, supported by her parents.

By mid-May 1985, Intuit was left with four employees—Cook, Proulx, Boyd, and Schlangen—with LeFevre as a some-time advisor. The company strategized about how to survive the starvation times. LeFevre gave Boyd, now de facto head of all operations, a list of which bills to pay on time, which to pay late, and which not to pay at all. They discussed the art of stretching payments without incurring reprisals and the importance of pre-senting the company as prosperous to the outside world. The company's survival depended on customers' confidence and on the release of its next product, an Apple II version of Quicken.

Wells Fargo and Bank of Hawaii had agreed to buy copies of Quicken for Apple II upon its release, and Proulx worked fever-ishly to complete it. Cook had interested Apple Computer in in-cluding Quicken in its December holiday promotion if Proulx could finish the software on time. The prospect of bank pay-ments, the small amount of revenue from the orders for checks and supplies, and the sheer determination of Intuit's remaining foursome kept the company alive during the summer of 1985.

But each of those four struggled intensively. Boyd thought, "What can I do to make sure this doesn't fail? Basically just an infinite amount of work." She juggled creditors and the minus-cule bank balance that dipped to as low as $51.95, fueled only by the trickle of supplies orders.

She paid rent and phone bills on time, but creatively delayed all other payments. She returned the rental furniture. (The four employees used product case boxes as desks and folding chairs from Proulx's parents.) To avoid eviction they told their anxious landlord that they were redecorating and waiting for new furni-ture. The team tried not to feel too desperate.

When Wells Fargo acquired the bank where Proulx's girlfriend Barbara Boyd worked, she gave the defunct stationery and memo pads to Intuit. The company maintained only four individual phone lines and a fax, and Proulx programmed on old, slow machines.

The company's health insurance policy at the time was, "Don't get sick." Life insurance? "If any employee passes away, then we can pay out $1.50." When Cook wanted to meet with one of the three others alone, because the office afforded so little privacy, they went for a walk. The more intensive the meeting, the longer and faster the walk. Employees joked that Cook's walks were the "health club membership" that kept them fit to do massive amounts of work.

For several weeks, Cook did not discuss compensation with the three employees. Conscious of his personal stress, employees hesitated to confront Cook. Eventually, Proulx insisted on a meeting to discuss the only currency left to Intuit—equity. Cook renegotiated stock agreements, and Boyd, the only hourly employee, found herself working in shares per hour, not dollars per hour. Cook and Proulx came to an agreement as to Proulx's new share of company stock. It was a lean and frustrating time for all the employees.

Magical moments occasionally lightened the load. One day Boyd opened a thick envelope and found multiple check orders from an accountant in New York City. "Isn't Robert Vaughn an actor?" she asked herself as she processed the day's first checks order from a customer. She did not recognize the names on the next two checks, but she definitely knew those that followed: Barbara Walters and Yoko Ono Lennon. Boyd spun around in her chair and called out, "Yoko Ono's using Quicken!"[3]

The weeks passed with agonizing slowness for Cook, who was facing personal purgatory. He had sunk everything into Intuit. Quitting now meant failure: he would lose his net worth, his self-worth, and possibly his marriage. Being unable to pay his valued employees humiliated him and violated all his principles.

Cook tried to be positive as he hung on with a grim determination, his resolve rooted in the dreadful prospect of spending the next decade alone, working to repay his investors—including his father. "Things could not be better!" he regularly exclaimed to callers, prompting eye rolls from the other employees at the disparity between Cook's public face and the truth. Cook felt the team was depending on him and had cast their hopes on his dream, his vision. He knew the others didn't view themselves as employees but as apostles and true believers. Seeing the dream crumble away devastated him.

LIGHT AT THE END OF THE TUNNEL

Proulx labored to finish the Apple II version while Cook tried to coax other banks into selling Quicken. Weeks passed, with Virginia Boyd dodging creditors and pinching pennies. Bent on saving money, Boyd examined every element of Intuit's cost of goods and decided to forgo the expensive packaging and resize the manual once the current supply ran out. The program disks and other collateral would be stuffed into the manual before the team shrink-wrapped it. This inelegant but practical packaging would cut Intuit's cost of goods nearly in half—if the company could survive to ship the Apple II version.

Proulx's conviction of success buoyed him, but the tireless Proulx devoted endless hours to programming and needed help. Around this time Cook met Eric Dunn, the Bain consultant who had taken over his clients when he'd left, at a social function. Dunn mentioned that he programmed in his spare time and offered to pitch in to help Proulx.

A Harvard M.B.A. with a passion for software and a strong aversion to television, Dunn had rarely followed convention. His father, a professor of medical anthropology and epidemiology at the University of California, San Francisco, specialized in tropical diseases, so Dunn had spent some of his youth in exotic locations.

Besides attending elementary school in Marin, Dunn lived for two years in Malaysia, arriving in Kuala Lumpur on the first day of the Six Day War.

When he was ten years old, Dunn's parents divorced. Dunn spent his middle school years at the Princeton Day School in New Jersey where his mother was an administrator at the Institute for Advanced Study. When he reached high school, Dunn decided to follow in his father's footsteps and attended Phillips Exeter in Exeter, New Hampshire. From there, he joined forty-three of his prep school classmates at Harvard.

Fond of applied mathematics, Dunn chose to study physics at Harvard, though by his junior year he was enjoying computer programming classes more. Dunn's first program was a music compiler that put him, for a brief moment, on the leading edge of digital music technology. After college Dunn spent a few colorless years at IBM in New York before returning to Harvard for an M.B.A. "I thought I should throw the deck up in the air again and see if I could pick a better card," he later reflected.[4]

After completing his M.B.A. in 1983, Dunn got married. The Stanford Law School had accepted his wife, so the couple moved to Palo Alto, California, and Eric Dunn joined Bain & Company, where he coincidentally worked on Western Digital, the client Cook had landed just before leaving Bain. Proximity to the high-tech industry reawakened Dunn's interest in programming. He began working on a calendar utility program and dreamed of starting his own company to sell it. But Borland Software of Scotts Valley, California, preempted him, releasing Sidekick—a calendar plus to-do list and notepad—in a blitz of advertising, in 1984. Despite this disappointment, Dunn remained keen on software and start-ups.

Predictably, Dunn soon grew restless at Bain. As a boy, he had appreciated straightforward rules and had followed them, harassing his mother if she exceeded the speed limit. The many gray areas of consulting—selling additional engagements and surreptitiously gathering competitive data for clients—troubled the straight-laced Dunn. He was ready for a change.

One of Dunn's friends at Bain roomed with Scott McNealy, CEO of Sun Microsystems. At a party in April 1985, Dunn leaned on his friend to introduce him to Scott. After meeting McNealy, Dunn whispered, "Not *that* Scott, I mean the other one, Scott Cook, the software guy." Dunn had heard rumors of his Bain predecessor's new enterprise. Dunn's friend knew the erstwhile Bain employee, and happily obliged.

When Dunn met Cook, he showed Cook his calendar program. Even though Cook couldn't apply the calendar to Quicken, he saw in his fellow Harvard alumnus a man of intelligence and resourcefulness. Dunn, tall and rumpled, wore metallic-framed glasses and exuded an earnest geekiness. Clearly, the Bain employee had a passion for technology and an articulate, knowledgeable grasp of the software industry. So Cook jumped on the opportunity to enlist Dunn as a "friend of the firm," convincing him to perform the quality assurance testing on the new Quicken for Apple II. As the company struggled during the summer of 1985, Dunn troubleshot Quicken for Apple II as a favor to Cook.

By August 1985, Proulx had finally completed the Apple II version of Quicken, and Dunn had tested it. Once the disks and manuals were duplicated, the company shipped hundreds of units to its two banking customers. Since the banks paid Intuit as soon as the software shipped, Intuit immediately earned several thousand dollars from these shipments.

Receiving checks from the banks marked a change in Intuit's fortunes. With the Apple II version, Intuit had finally created a consumer product for a machine targeted to home users. (PCs were used primarily for business, but the Apple II appealed to at-home technologists.) Apple had created thousands of fanatical fans, just the type of users that might embrace Quicken since its ease of use and intuitive approach fit so well with Apple's appeal. Apple and Quicken were natural partners.

And in contrast to the business-oriented IBM PC magazines, the magazines published for Apple II users eagerly profiled new and useful home products, and Quicken for Apple II met much fanfare. *A+ Magazine* heralded "The Quicken Breakthrough" in January 1986. "Finally, a check writing program that may make itself indispensable to you."[5]

Apple Computer gave Quicken a helpful nudge by including a coupon for a reduced-price Quicken in every Apple II box, the promotion Cook had arranged. Apple's holiday advertising campaign materials listed twelve great reasons to buy an Apple II, and one reason, with a picture of the product and the company's toll-free order number next to the listing, was Quicken. With its Apple II version, Intuit had finally tapped into the kind of enthusiasm needed to make Quicken a household name.

Other successes soon followed. After months of nit-picking contracts and delaying signatures, one Indiana bank, Fort Wayne National Bank, finally signed the Quicken contract they'd been delaying. Two weeks later, Shawmut Bank of Boston signed its contract, and four weeks after that, United Colorado Bank in Denver joined suit. By late 1985, Intuit had distribution contracts with five banks. Cook realized that his own inexperience with the banking industry had cursed his efforts: He had finally discovered that banks made unusual expenditures only at the beginning or end of their fiscal years.

To ship the Quicken for DOS and Apple II versions to Intuit's new partners, Virginia Boyd instituted a fun gathering that became an Intuit tradition: packing parties. She invited friends and relatives to Intuit's tiny basement office to assemble, shrink-wrap, and pack hundreds of copies of Quicken in an evening or a weekend, sometimes cramming as many as twenty people into the small space. She arranged for pizza or sandwiches from the nearby Togo's, an Intuit staple, to feed the hungry crew, each of whom tried to work faster than the person beside him or her in the makeshift assembly line.

Cook, somewhat distant from the other employees, did not usually join these parties, but Proulx delighted in working so quickly that he far outstripped the worker downstream; then, he would drum his fingers in an exaggerated fashion, impatiently—and teasingly—waiting for the "bottleneck" person beside him to catch up. Both productive and festive, packing parties increased Intuit's growing bonhomie, especially since the need to assemble software for shipping so tangibly evidenced additional sales. Even when sufficient product had been packed, employees often lingered in the festive atmosphere, chatting and laughing together.

In October, Cook and Proulx delightedly reinstated salaries for Intuit's four employees. They also decided to pay holiday bonuses in December 1985, as recognition for the dedication of the employees who had worked without salary for six months and saved the company from doom. When Cook handed out the bonus checks, Boyd just stood there, looking at hers. "Are you sure we can afford this now?" asked the operations convert.

The lean times had left other marks. Intuit had survived via exceptional frugality, and every employee knew it. Cook and Proulx resolved to continue the company's careful spending habits and to demand that all employees spend responsibly. The bonuses they paid in 1985 continued, and every time the company paid its employees a bonus, Cook made a point of reminding employees that they, too, owned part of Intuit and should treat the company's money as their own.

In a marked turnaround, by fourth quarter 1985, Intuit, still focused on frugality, became profitable and cash-flow positive. Shipments to banks yielded revenues long before Intuit had to pay suppliers for cost of goods sold. Customers prepaid for check and supply orders, and the company had sixty days to pay Deluxe, their checks supplier. Direct sales of Quicken for Apple II grew with the increased marketing by Apple Computer, and Intuit's success finally looked possible—not assured, but a long way from the $51.95 checking account balance of the previous May.

Although Intuit had only four regular employees, Eric Dunn continued to help the firm, and Tom LeFevre provided occasional counsel to Cook. By late 1985, Dunn, still fascinated by high-tech in general and tiny Intuit in particular, agreed to moonlight further for the company. First, he wrote a utility that corrected a bug in Quicken for DOS. Then, he programmed the Quicken Transfer Utility that exported Quicken data into Lotus 1-2-3 files; when this useful program shipped in January 1986, Cook and Proulx paid Dunn with a small amount of stock. Later that year, Dunn joined Intuit as a regular employee.

After his M.B.A. and years at Bain, Dunn did not want to become a mere "programmer" at Intuit, reporting to the junior Proulx. While taking the leap into a start-up attracted him, Dunn insisted that his new job title reflect his seniority and experience. After some discussion, he and Cook settled on the more conventional CFO title to reflect Dunn's M.B.A. and consulting background, even though programming was his primary responsibility at first. Dunn's prep school background dictated that he always wore a tie to work—quite different from Cook's khakis and Proulx's jeans. He never, he said later, wanted to be mistaken for "just any programmer."

In April 1986, Cook pitched Quicken to Mellon Bank in Pennsylvania. A forward-thinking banking executive there wanted Quicken as the cornerstone of the bank's online efforts, and Mellon signed on as an Intuit distribution partner. However, on the plane back from the successful pitch, Cook reviewed new sales data from the banks currently selling Quicken. Unfortunately, with the sole exception of Bank of Hawaii, none of the banks sold many copies, even of the popular Apple II version. Cook returned to California, dug deeper into the figures, and realized that the banks had not been successful at reselling Quicken, for themselves or for Intuit. Devising a new way to get Quicken in front of potential buyers became Cook's top priority.

Though the company's original distribution strategy was faltering, its finances were glowing. Expenses remained low, even with Dunn and a new receptionist and customer service rep, Peggy Smith, on the payroll. Sales of software and supplies were increasing and every month the company's bank balance grew. Intuit even had a new product, a set of spreadsheet templates called the Tax Reform Analyzer that Cook, in a bizarre departure from his management role, wrote himself in a weekend. Tax laws had changed dramatically in 1986, and Cook, initially for his own use, designed a Lotus 1-2-3 calculator that made it easy for people to see whether their taxes would go up or down because of the new laws.

With so few employees, after the Apple II release most of Intuit focused on operations and order fulfillment. Answering phones, assembling boxes, shipping software, and processing check orders took the majority of every employee's time. Even Dunn and Proulx had significant operations responsibilities and spent less time programming than just working to keep the company in business.

THE BIG BET

The company had survived an exceptionally lean period, but even though sales grew, Cook and Proulx realized that true success— that is, mass-market adoption of Quicken—still lingered tantalizingly out of reach. And so, when Borland Software Company created an unusual direct marketing blitz for its Turbo Pascal and Sidekick software products, which were not widely available in stores at that time, Cook and Proulx paid careful attention. Might this be the way to leverage their high-volume dreams into reality?

Traditionally, software companies sold products through wholesalers who stocked retailer shelves. High-tech advertising, after the Orwellian Macintosh ad that ran once and only once during the 1984 Super Bowl, emphasized image and concept above all else; retail salespeople educated interested consumers about specific products. Cook had found the Macintosh ad entertaining but not particularly effective at convincing customers to buy. His P&G training made him more intrigued with benefits-oriented advertising that ran in periodicals such as *PC Magazine*. To replace the role of retail salespeople and teach customers about their products, Borland took this benefits-oriented advertising one step further and ran wordy, persuasive print ads, the likes of which the industry had never seen.

Advertising directly to consumers was untried and risky. But Borland, founded in 1983 by flamboyant entrepreneur Phillippe Kahn, routinely took such risks. Turbo Pascal's quick placement on best-seller lists proved that Kahn's bet had paid off and that Intuit might reach high volumes by embracing the same strategy and selling directly to consumers. Borland's ads not only drove customers to buy directly from Borland, but also brought them to retail stores asking for its products. These requests eventually engendered widespread retail distribution for Turbo Pascal.

Intuit had built up $100,000 in savings, but still lacked the funds for a traditional retail launch, in which consumers, persuaded by massive advertising, would request Quicken at stores in sufficient number to entice wholesalers to stock and distribute the product. And so, Cook, Proulx and Dunn mulled over Borland's example. Cook sketched out a marketing campaign aimed at selling Quicken directly to consumers that marked a complete departure from the traditional wholesaler distribution model he'd absorbed at P&G.

Then came the really big decision. Intuit had a fixed amount of money. Should the company test direct marketing, or should it just go for broke (possibly literally): assume that the approach would work and spend its entire nest egg? Cook consulted with Proulx, Dunn, and Boyd, the de facto management team.

"Testing will make us miss the holiday shopping season, and that's when people buy a lot of software," observed pragmatic Dunn.

"Borland was very successful," said optimistic Proulx. "Let's go for it! Let's either go out in a blaze of glory and get on with our lives after three and a half years of struggle, or grow big. We don't want to continue existing as the living dead."

Proulx's "blaze of glory" resonated with the others, and so Intuit decided to bet its entire net worth on a $125,000 direct advertising campaign, thus committing every dollar it expected to earn by fall. If the direct ads failed, the company would be bankrupt—again.

Cook wrote the critical ad under the tutelage of Bill Mirbach, a direct marketing guru who had been his colleague at P&G. Headlined, "End Financial Hassles," the ad used Borland's text-heavy strategy to persuade customers to buy Quicken. Cook selected *PC Magazine, InfoWorld,* and *A+ Magazine* for their relatively low cost for reaching PC-owning households, and he bought the placements for the advertisement himself.

In a phone call with Cook, LeFevre, who was still advising the company, worried that direct marketing might not suffice, even for a product that outshone competitors. And so Cook and Proulx doubled their bet: They decided to up the ante by halving Quicken's price from $99.95 to $49.95, positioning Quicken as an "impulse buy."

Based on customer comments during his technical support duties, Proulx also recommended that Intuit remove Quicken's copy protection—the code that prevented people from copying Quicken for free—to please consumers who hated that feature and to promote Quicken's use as broadly as possible. Proulx believed that people who copied Quicken from friends would get hooked on the product and pay for later versions. Though this flew in the face of prevailing wisdom, Proulx convinced Cook that increasing adoption, even via illegal consumer copying of the program, would build market momentum. Years later, Geoffrey Moore would cite Quicken as a case study for moving to a mass market—"crossing the chasm"—by encouraging its broad adoption.[6] Cook, Proulx, and Dunn concluded that Quicken's lowered price would sufficiently offset the piracy risk, especially since customers were clamoring for removal of the copy protection.

Even as the Intuit staff was gearing up for direct sales, Cook continued to pursue retail distribution, so that customers who saw

Quicken's ads would be sure to find the program in their local software stores. He remembered that wholesalers would stock only products that retailers requested and that most retailers requested products based on customer inquiries. With the new advertisements and Borland's success as an example, Cook believed he could now make a case to persuade wholesalers to stock Quicken.

Cook's first conquest among wholesalers was SoftKat, a small distributor whose president, Alan Gleicher, agreed to carry Quicken at the insistence of a mutual acquaintance of his and Cook's, a marketing executive for the New York–based Computer Factory chain. The retail chain Babbages also agreed to stock Quicken because Cook's former boss at Bain had founded the retail chain and wanted to support Cook.

Then Cook turned to the bigger guns. He had already met with an executive from the largest wholesaler, SoftSel, about its Dollars and Sense program for personal financial management that now competed with Quicken. When Cook first approached SoftSel about distributing Quicken through its usual acquisition channels, SoftSel turned him down.

But Cook had a history with SoftSel; one of the senior managers there had once tried to hire Cook away from Bain. Rather than persisting with the normal SoftSel channels, Cook turned to his contact within the company. This creative networking approach worked, and a few weeks later SoftSel agreed to distribute Quicken.

By late fall 1986, the company's live-or-die campaign was ready: direct-marketing magazine ads, a much-lowered price, wholesale distribution, and no copy protection. "End Financial Hassles—$49.95," cried the full-page ads to run in PC and Apple magazines. The black-and-white ads had paragraphs of informative copy, lists of customer testimonials, and a toll-free telephone number for ordering directly from Intuit (see figure 4-1).

For two days after the first ad was due to hit, Intuit's six employees found it difficult to concentrate on work. They braced themselves for a flood of calls—or a drought that would end the

FIGURE 4 - 1

Quicken Magazine Ad Copy, 1986

End Financial Hassles. $49.95

Who doesn't want to rid themselves of the hassles of paying bills, managing finances, and keeping records? Finally, there's software so fast and so automatic that time and hassles evaporate.

Quicken Eliminates Time & Hassle. You don't have to labor over routine finances any longer. Quicken is the breakthrough software that eliminates the hassles of the routine financial chores you do every month.

- Automates bill paying. Eliminates rewriting the same checks every month.

- Instantly organizes financial records. Eliminates errors.

- Categorizes expenses automatically for business, taxes, budgeting. Eliminates manual bookwork.

- Reconciles your bank statement for you. Actually finds and fixes mistakes.

- Transfers your finances into your own AppleWorks spreadsheets. Automatically gives you custom-tailored reports, P&L's, budgets, and much more.

For Every Business & Home. Quicken works with any account from any bank, S&L, or credit union. It's the only system recommended by major banks across the U.S., including Wells Fargo, Shawmut, Mellon, Texas Commerce, Bank of Hawaii, Manufacturers National, First National of Maryland, United Banks of Colorado, Fort Wayne National, Fairbury State, and FirsTier Banks. No modem is used.

Critics Hail a Breakthrough.

"Thanks to Quicken, I'm automating my personal checking account. I've never seen such an easy-to-use manual or software that's so simple to use."

— Martin Blumenthal, *inCider Magazine*

"With the power of AppleWorks so readily available, it's more than good—it's indispensable. Home and small business checking software used to be too expensive, too hard to use, and too rigid, and it took too long to use. Quicken has changed all that."

— Ken Landis, *A+ Magazine*

"Now there is a program that truly saves time when it comes to paying bills and keeping track of tax-deductible items, and that program is Quicken."

— *Parents Magazine*

"Until now you might have been hesitant to consider using a personal computer system to balance your checkbook. Hesitate no longer! Quicken is more than a checkbook-balancing program."

— Cynthia Field, *InfoWorld*

"Extremely simple and fast."

— Esther Dyson, *Release 1.0*

"The area of checking and small account management has been mo⟨ for me. Many products promise more than they deliver or deliver only ⟨ of labor. Quicken is a wonderful exception to the otherwise bleak land

— Richard Katz, *UCLA PC Users Newsletter*

Call 800 624-8742.

Source: Courtesy of Virginia Boyd.

company. They had bet their future; would the gamble pay off? On the third day they got their answer: Intuit's phones started ringing like crazy. "It's so exciting! I can't believe how many people are calling us to buy Quicken—we're going to become a top seller," predicted a jubilant Boyd.[7]

"Finally," agreed Proulx, his persistent sanguine attitude rewarded. Cook, who had again faced down the specter of financial disaster, now could chirp, "Things could not be better" with real conviction to the various well-wishers who phoned.

And sales continued to build through the holiday season. Direct magazine advertising results tripled the Intuit team's wildest expectations, with the best ads generating revenues up to double their cost. In November, the company took one hundred orders in a single twenty-four-hour period, the most Intuit ever had, and celebrated with a champagne toast.

To keep the company staffed, half the company took the three days before Christmas off, with the other workers taking three days vacation after Christmas. Proulx was first into the office on the morning of December 26, and as he was unlocking the front door, he could hear the phones ringing. Lots of people had been given PCs or Quicken for Christmas, and many had questions about purchasing or installing the software. By half past eight, the technical support and sales phones were ringing off the hook.

Intuit had no phone system, only two U.S. 800 numbers and one for California. Intuit had leased some used cubicles earlier that year and set them up in a T shape in the office. Phones were ringing in all the cubes, and Proulx ran back and forth saying, "Intuit, please hold," "Intuit, please hold." After half an hour, Proulx grabbed the phone on Cook's desk as he was running by and took twenty seconds to call Eric Dunn, whose home was closest to the office (and who was supposed to be off that week). "Eric, the phone's ringing off the hook. Get in here right now," he pleaded and hung up.[8] Though the phones shrilled all day, Proulx thrilled to the racket: Intuit had finally made it to the mainstream.

CHAPTER 5

UNDER-PROMISE, OVER-DELIVER

Basking in the glow of Intuit's sales success, Tom Proulx and Eric Dunn decided next to rewrite Quicken's Apple II version for the ProDOS platform, the new operating system for Apple IIs equipped with hard drives as well as the standard 3.5-inch floppy drives. Anticipating only about five weeks of work—porting the program to a new platform rather than rewriting from scratch—the company informed its customers in February 1987 that the new version would be available in March. Though such preannouncements were common in the software industry, Intuit had never before tried one.

Quicken's sales volume also provided Cook with leverage to approach other distributors and the growing retail chain Egghead Software. Since October 1986, Quicken had appeared on the Soft-Sel Hot List (the equivalent of a best-seller list for books) almost every month. Using such sales charts, as well as the ever-increasing number of retailer inquiries, Cook closed distribution deals with Egghead and the remaining major software wholesalers in early 1987. Finally, customers could buy Quicken at most retail software outlets across the United States.

Intuit no longer hovered on the brink of insolvency, but its executives' decisions about what products to develop and how to distribute them still profoundly affected the company. The more

Intuit gained, the more it had to lose, and Moore's Law—the doubling of computer processing power every eighteen months—accelerated its pace.[1] Intuit faced rapid technical and market changes: Increasing hardware muscle and decreasing prices enticed many companies to create useful software applications leveraging technology's increasing power.

Quicken's success fostered big dreams at Intuit. Cook and Proulx realized that sustained victory for Quicken meant leading the financial software market across all platforms. To accomplish this, the company had to master improving machines, proliferating platforms, widespread distribution options, and evolving competitors. The ProDOS Apple II version became the first of a series of company wagers on evolving technology.

Struggling to meet the release date they had announced for Quicken for ProDOS Apple II, Dunn and Proulx quickly ran up against their own inexperience. Myriad technical challenges, from program compiling to adjusting to Apple's new hard drives, caused delays. Thousands of customers had ordered Quicken upgrades after the preannouncement, and as April approached with no program release, they began calling Intuit about the status of their orders. The increasingly frequent ring of the phones in the tiny office dismayed the two programmers.

So as not to disappoint their waiting customers, the twosome, cooperative partners as much due to their complementary differences as to the goals they had in common, worked around the clock to complete the new version. On the final weekend of March the prolific, pragmatic Dunn and the perfectionist, well-trained Proulx conducted a marathon debugging session. They became so weary that they traded off thinking and typing: One of them mindlessly manned the keyboard while the other cogitated and dictated what to type. After a few hours, trusting each other's skills, they switched roles. Fueled by pizza, sandwiches from Togo's, and caffeine, they continued for sixty hours straight.

Throughout, Dunn, the only Intuit employee to regularly sport neckwear, wore a green-striped tie that grew more wrinkled and dirty as the hours passed. By the end of the intense and difficult weekend, they were ready to release the product. Flying in the face of common software company practice, Proulx, Dunn, and Cook agreed that Intuit would never again preannounce. As for the soiled green tie, Dunn gave it up as irreclaimable.

Cook, Proulx, Dunn, and Boyd made the critical decisions for Intuit at this time, often meeting at Cook's favorite fast-food restaurant, Taco Bell, where Cook would fascinate Boyd by downing a single taco in three bites. The modest Cook, focused on sales, marketing, and general management, had never given himself a title, but by this time Proulx, leading the engineering efforts, called himself VP of engineering. Dunn, who programmed and handled some finance and administration duties, retained the CFO title, and Boyd worked as director of operations.

The all-nighters pulled by Proulx and Dunn convinced Cook that Intuit needed more staff. To find new employees the Intuit team members combed their personal networks, and the company also began running "Help Wanted" newspaper classifieds. Every hopeful interviewed with all of Intuit's six employees to ensure a prospect "fit," both in terms of job skills and cultural values. Keeping with the team's insistent customer focus, applicants had to demonstrate an explicit customer orientation along with the required skills and values.

Cook interviewed everyone who joined Intuit and became infamous for his provocative questions. He believed that theoretical interviews, like case studies, were not effective predictors of employee performance. Instead, he focused on past accomplishments and the prospect's entire perspective on how he or she had achieved them. Character and track record trumped bullet points on a person's résumé. Cook commonly asked interviewees, "What one thing did you contribute to this project that nobody else did?"[2]

As it added staff, the frugal company deliberately avoided overhiring. Before the company recruited any employee, the management team all had to agree that they saw the need for additional

help. Cofounders Cook and Proulx resolved to avoid laying anyone off, ever.

Intuit most urgently needed engineers to work on its proliferating platforms. Proulx posted fliers around the Stanford computer science building and, after in-depth interviews, hired two
talented grad students. Intuit couldn't afford both right away, so
Karl Reese joined in June and Eric Shenk later that summer.
Their offers included stock options, the phenomenal upside of
which was not yet widely understood. "It's risky to work for such
a small company," Shenk summed up the opportunity to his
mother, "but I think it will be fun."[3] Intuit also added support
personnel: first a technical support representative, then a supplies
clerk, and then an operations-and-manufacturing manager. Other
employees joined in customer service and accounting, and the
company's total headcount grew to thirteen by the end of 1987.

After releasing the Apple II version, Proulx and Dunn turned
to Quicken for DOS, whose current version had been shipping
for almost two-and-a-half years without any improvements. This
time BASIC clearly would not suffice; hardware advances and improved Quicken features would overwhelm that language's capabilities. So Proulx and Dunn, along with their new engineers,
started from scratch to write the Quicken 2.0 for DOS version in
C, a more powerful and flexible programming language.

To capitalize on the strong Christmas retail selling season,
Cook urged the programmers to ship version 2.0 by fall. During
summer 1987, Proulx and Dunn led the small engineering team
to rewrite and improve Quicken, adding enhancements that customers had requested, via comment cards and interviews, to make
it easier to track and analyze income and expenses: Quicken's
categories, split transactions, transaction groups, find/go-to functionality, and improved reporting. They also worked to make the
program faster and more robust.

Meeting their goal, the engineering staff completed Quicken
2.0 for DOS by September 1987. For a six-week stretch, they
worked exhausting one hundred–hour weeks; on the final night

FIGURE 5-1

Virginia Boyd dressed up as CFO and technical maverick Eric Dunn for Halloween, standing next to the real Eric Dunn incognito, 1989.

Source: Courtesy of Virginia Boyd.

diehards Proulx and Dunn pulled yet another all-nighter. After turning the master disk over to production at seven o'clock the following morning, they fell into chairs at a nearby hotel restaurant. Half an hour later, no one had taken their orders. They were rumpled and unshaven—and the upscale restaurant wouldn't serve them. "We've just produced the world's greatest software, and we can't even order breakfast!" Proulx huffed.[4] "Let's go to the donut shop."

Quicken 2.0 for DOS gratified Intuit employees by selling quickly. Momentum was growing along with the headcount, and old-timers rejoiced at Intuit's increasing prosperity. The company's tiny offices bulged at the seams, and Dunn began looking into other nearby suites. That fall, a retail chain, Egghead Software, advertised Quicken on the radio for the first time; all work halted in the tiny Intuit offices the first few times a radio station broadcast the ad.

As the company grew, operations again began stressing the four-person management team. Tom LeFevre had remained on Intuit's board of directors and had provided helpful ideas throughout the company's lean period. Cook and Proulx needed LeFevre's operations and management expertise, so they invited him to rejoin Intuit as COO. Still sold on Intuit's premise and now more convinced of its future, LeFevre returned.

Some core employees greeted LeFevre's return with annoyance, which surprised Cook. Boyd, in particular, resented that LeFevre had deserted them in their time of need but was welcomed back as her supervisor. Cook couldn't dismiss the concerns of passionately loyal and devoted employees, but LeFevre had the necessary experience for a company in Intuit's growth stage as well as a long familiarity with Intuit and its products.

Cook and Proulx wanted buy-in from every manager and worked hard to press the case for LeFevre, eventually winning Boyd over. LeFevre needed Boyd's support because she was to assist him as he took over operations, supplies, customer service, and technical support. Proulx scaled back to overseeing just engineering, and Dunn managed finance and administration (and the programming responsibilities he never really dropped). Cook continued to oversee marketing, sales, and general management.

Apple had released its Macintosh in 1984, and Mac users became known as the most fanatical computer users ever. Intrigued by the computer's hype and its graphical user interface, Dunn bought a used Macintosh XL at a garage sale in early 1987 for two hundred dollars. Dunn quickly convinced Cook and Proulx to create another version of Quicken, this one for the popular Macintosh.

Several Quicken competitors had embraced Apple's new Mac platform, with Survivor Software's MacMoney leading the way. Dunn, for an engineering shortcut, decided to depart from Intuit norm and try to acquire MacMoney to convert it to Quicken for the Mac. Survivor Software (based in Inglewood, California) turned Dunn down, but another competitor, State-of-the-Art in Costa Mesa, California, had produced an adequate program that it would sell to Intuit for ten thousand dollars. The management team, now including both LeFevre and Boyd, debated, and Dunn convinced the others that the engineering time to be saved by the acquisition justified the expense. So Intuit purchased the code along with access to its programmer, and Dunn set about converting it to Quicken for Mac.

With software versions for all the leading platforms, Intuit's profits were growing. Cook's life both at work and at home benefited. Ever since he'd left Bain to start Intuit in 1983, Signe Ostby's salary had kept the family afloat, and Cook had disciplined himself to a Spartan existence. In the spring of 1987, for the first time in four years, Cook finally felt comfortable enough to buy something that he didn't really need. He'd been in Washington, DC, for a meeting, where he came across an electronics store and indulged his lust for a CD player. Spending money on this nonessential item signaled an end to his days of financial desperation.

THINK FAST, ACT FAST

The company's status also registered with Eric Dunn, but his satisfaction evaporated the Monday after Thanksgiving. That day, the first day of December 1987, started well; sales were brisk on Quicken 2.0 for DOS, several additional people had been hired, Quicken for Mac was progressing well, and employees were anticipating their first real holiday party the next weekend.

As soon as Dunn entered the office, Intuit's technical support representative, Leslie Coe, pounced. "Eric, we've gotten several calls this morning about an error. Whenever customers try to record a transaction in Quicken for DOS, they're getting the message, "Get_Cache." Can you check it out?"[5] Dunn raced to his desk, but when Quicken launched perfectly from his machine, he turned to his normal business.

Then Coe came back. "Five more calls. And I get the error on my computer, too. Something must be going on." Puzzled, Dunn went to Proulx's adjacent desk and tried recording a transaction in Quicken. There, he encountered a blank screen with the message "Get_Cache" instead of the familiar Quicken recording beep. Dunn felt the first cold fingers of panic.

But why wasn't his computer producing the error? Dunn examined his machine carefully and realized that the internal clock on his computer was incorrect—it gave a date of November 30. With a feeling of doom, Dunn corrected the date on his computer and tried again: "Get_Cache" appeared instantly. Dunn and Coe went through the company, trying Quicken on every computer they had. Every computer with an accurate date gave them the error.

Dunn began troubleshooting. From the tech-support calls he realized that anybody using floppies encountered the error, which helped him figure out the underlying cause: The date stamp routine that he'd written to prevent people from overwriting newer data on their floppy drives had a bug. No one could record data for backup on a floppy disk using Quicken any more.

Once he'd diagnosed the technical problem, Dunn enlisted Proulx in a fix-finding frenzy. Twenty-four hours later, after they'd devised and tested a fix, Intuit's dozen-plus employees, waiting anxiously to help solve the problem, went to work. About twenty thousand customers had installed Quicken 2.0 for DOS; with little discussion the executive team agreed that every customer deserved a program fix immediately, whether or not they had called in. That meant that Intuit had to produce twenty thousand fix disks as quickly as possible. Intuit's normal supplier could only duplicate about twelve thousand disks in a three-day period. So everyone at the company began duplicating disks to produce the additional eight thousand necessary.

The engineering staff devised some awkward yet creative ways to increase disk-duplicating productivity. With their six computers both on and below the desks, they worked out a method where they could each duplicate about forty disks per hour by using both their fingers on some keyboards and their toes on others to begin the copy command. They got into a rhythm, and the engineers managed to make several thousand disks in their fourteen-hour days.

Managers produced a letter to send with the disk; everyone stuffed mailers for customers. No one at Intuit begrudged the time. A bug like this, for a company of Intuit's size, could spell disaster. Every employee had a personal stake in fixing the problem, realizing that, once again, the company teetered at the brink of failure.

After a brief conversation, the executive team agreed that Intuit needed to publicly own up to the bug. They reasoned that doing right by customers included being honest when the company had done something wrong. Cook called distributors and asked them to stop shipping Quicken until Intuit could replace the stock with fixed versions. The company also issued a press release describing the problem and its solution.

For the entire week following Thanksgiving, everyone at Intuit focused on fixing the problem. By Friday evening, they had completed twenty thousand packets for mailing. Dunn piled them all in his car and drove to the San Francisco airport post office, the only one open late on a Friday night. As he heaved the sacks onto the loading dock, a great weight lifted off his shoulders. He'd been sickened when he'd realized the scope of the problem, but he was pleased that Intuit had focused on fixing it. No one had looked for blame, and no one had reproached him. That, he thought, was remarkable. And the bug had provided the first real opportunity to prove Intuit's "under-promise and over-deliver" mantra to employees and customers alike.

Intuit's tactical response to this crisis situation grew out of its modus operandi: doing the right thing for customers. The entire Intuit team put its customers first. If they did not treat customers well, they believed, then they might lose their customers' loyalty, and ultimately, the company.

The company's response did not go unnoticed by customers or the industry. Customer satisfaction and loyalty actually increased after the date bug fix. Team Intuit had turned a huge problem into a strategic opportunity. They had averted disaster, earned customer goodwill, and crystallized a sense of the prevailing company culture. To acknowledge errors, be accountable, fix the problem, and never shrink from treating customers right became the pillars of the Intuit way.

DEAD ENDS AND DEATHMATES

Even before the date bug, Intuit's perpetual struggle to succeed wearied Cook, and the stock market crash of October 19, 1987 aggravated the toll. Although the economy bounced back fairly quickly, Cook suffered a crisis in confidence; the date bug exacerbated his self-doubt, and the record stock market devaluation made his continuing personal debt even more burdensome. "Should I continue to struggle with this company?" he wondered. Cook confided in his trusted friend from business school, Peter Wendell, a venture capitalist at Sierra Ventures: Selling Intuit to another company would enable him to pay his debts and relieve his stress.

"Selling is a huge mistake," Wendell responded. "Intuit has come out of its lowest point. Its profitability validates its business model."[6] Wendell believed that Cook had positioned Intuit for great success and that only Cook could lead the company there. He persuaded Cook to stay with the company. Eventually Cook's mood brightened and his confidence returned as he saw Wendell's logic. Cook recommitted himself to the company and to his vision of improving the way people manage their finances.

In its March 1988 issue, *PC Magazine,* the industry standard, included Quicken as number ten among its regular rating of best-selling software programs. By August, Quicken became the number one consumer software product, an astounding rank for a company that had nearly bankrupted itself three years earlier.

Also in March 1988, Dunn finished Quicken for Macintosh with the functionality of the DOS version and custom check-art and memos. When Dunn completed the programming, Intuit faced another decision. Should the company take the low-risk path of releasing Quicken for Mac, with no marketing, or should they go full bore, with direct marketing ads? "Let's not risk the money, let's just see if anyone bites," cautious LeFevre argued. Cook countered that the company should take what it had already proved worked in the DOS and Apple II worlds and apply it to marketing the Mac product.

Cook prevailed, and Intuit released the Mac version with a large direct-advertising budget. Mac users took to the program, which won the coveted Eddie award from *MacUser* magazine. Quicken for Mac became the Mac software market leader within days. The successful Mac project marked the first time Intuit had developed a product from acquired code and the first win on a platform that had already had a reasonable competitor.

Even with its newfound successes, however, Intuit's culture was still marked by its earlier near-bankruptcy. "Intuit thinks of itself as the little guy, with low awareness," new engineer Eric Shenk observed. "Even though we're number one, we still feel like we are vulnerable."[7] Intuit was particularly conscious of its well-known competitor, Managing Your Money. But when Managing Your Money Lite was released in 1988, Intuit saw that MECA still had no idea why Quicken succeeded. Even in its "Lite" version, Managing Your Money's unnecessary complexities still confused and frustrated customers. For all its humility, Intuit focused fiercely on solving problems for the user, and that customer orientation strengthened along with the company.

Intuit had shifted away from banking distribution in 1987, yet Cook and Proulx believed that the company should somehow work with banks to gain access to their large numbers of customers. So, Cook dusted off a product that Proulx had first created in 1986, an automatic reconciliation service for banking customers, called Accuret. For a fee, customers could sign up to get an Accuret diskette monthly in the mail that would automatically enter and reconcile that month's bank statement into Quicken. In those days before the Internet, banks could market the Accuret service to their customers as a means of electronic statement download. Accuret launched in fall 1988 with the First Interstate Bank of California.

In a 1988 article in *American Banker* magazine, Cook evangelized for Accuret: "It is a 20-to-1 speed improvement over doing it by hand. That equals the difference between driving and walking to Boston, 60 miles per hour versus 3 miles per hour. Few new technologies have brought about an improvement of this magnitude." Cook added more statistics to buttress his point. "The jet plane is only three times faster than the propeller plane. Federal Express is only two to five times faster than the regular mail. A word processor is only seven to eight times faster than a typewriter."[8] Despite Cook's enthusiasm for the service and its promise of another way to save time and hassles, it never became a success. Intuit's partnership with banks proved as elusive as ever.

Not discouraged by such dead ends and relentless in its desire for growth, the Intuit management team decided to risk another technology gamble, this one with a much higher cost. In early spring 1988, Dunn and Proulx met with Tandy Corporation, the Fort Worth, Texas–based electronics manufacturer. Tandy wanted to encourage software development for its DeskMate graphical operating system, which lacked application software. The corporate owner of the more than seven thousand Radio Shack electronics stores nationwide, Tandy offered enticingly widespread distribution. To reach Radio Shack's customers, Intuit agreed that tackling a DeskMate version of Quicken was another engineering priority. Tandy promised to purchase $1 million worth of Quicken for DeskMate for its Radio Shack stores.

The DeskMate—or "DeathMate" as the engineers came to call it—development effort did not proceed smoothly. Tandy's operating system was complex and buggy, and building an application atop it was very difficult. In addition, Tandy, primarily a hardware company, did not well document or support its software operating system.

The hours spent on Quicken for DeskMate development surpassed those spent on previous products. Some engineers kept a blanket and pillow or sleeping bag under their desks because they rarely made it home during the week. When Tom Proulx asked what kind of office furniture Intuit should purchase for engineering, the engineers requested futons. "Sometimes at night I just sit at my computer and cry," Eric Shenk told his mother. "I am so, so tired but I have to keep working."[9]

One morning Tom Proulx surprised Virginia Boyd by asking, "Can you take me home?"

"Sure, as soon as I make one more phone call," said Boyd, "I'll meet you at my car in a few minutes." When she reached the parking garage, she asked a fellow employee, "Have you seen Tom?"

"He's throwing up in the bathroom," came the response.

When Proulx approached, he paused, stuck his head in the bushes and vomited. Then he lay down on the ground, mumbling, "I just need to rest."

"Should I call an ambulance?" Boyd asked. Proulx refused, insisting that Boyd just take him the eight blocks to his apartment.

When they arrived, Proulx was sick again. "Please—just let me rest," he said. "But don't leave me."

Boyd telephoned her sister, Barbara—Proulx's girlfriend. "Come right home," she said. When Barbara Boyd arrived she found Proulx passed out on the bathroom floor. He had been throwing up blood. Virginia Boyd immediately called for an ambulance, kicking herself for not overruling Proulx and taking him to the hospital.[10]

The paramedics carried Proulx out of the bathroom and stuffed him into an inflatable suit to increase his blood pressure. The last the Boyd sisters saw of Proulx before the paramedics whisked him away, he was pushing away a hand holding a syringe—Proulx didn't care for needles. The ambulance siren shrilled as Proulx was transported to the Stanford Hospital.

CHAPTER 6

A CUSTOMER
EVANGELIST CULTURE

A s soon as they heard about Tom Proulx's illness, Eric Dunn and Tom LeFevre rushed to the Stanford Hospital, where they learned that Proulx had a bleeding ulcer and had lost a third of his blood volume. Bent on making a scheduled vacation to Europe, Proulx had feared that he would not finish in time. He had told Eric Shenk that he would just "kill himself" to get DeskMate done, and the two had ignored the clock and the concept of a workday. Even his illness did not slow Proulx's workaholic tendencies: Within a day of entering the hospital he asked for—but did not receive—his computer so he could keep working.

Proulx's physical implosion was a wake-up call for the company. No longer could Intuit rely on one person to heroically save the day; individuals couldn't work themselves into the ground. The executive team realized that Intuit needed depth and breadth to distribute projects across a team and that employees would benefit from living more balanced lives. Doing right by customers was still critical, but not to the point where employees were doing wrong by themselves. The company's "survival mode" approach had to change.

After Quicken for DeskMate shipped in January 1989, the team evaluated development opportunities facing Intuit with a more critical eye. Apple had lost its leadership position in the desktop market despite the innovative 1984 Macintosh. IBM PCs and "clones" made by Compaq, Dell, and others made up the lion's share of the home PC market, and DOS claimed an 85 percent share of operating systems. Even though Quicken was carried in Radio Shack's thousands of stores, Intuit never sold more than the initial $1 million's worth of the DeskMate version of its software to Tandy. As internal debates raged about whether to develop Quicken for other emerging platforms—including the competing OS/2 and Windows—the management team resolved to be more strategic about development choices given Intuit's limited resources. Betting on the right technology became a critical task for the company.

HIGH-GEAR HIRING

Part of the development conundrum involved how to hire, train, and deploy new employees. From thirteen employees in 1987, Intuit had grown to more than thirty in 1988 and one hundred in 1989. It was staffing up so quickly that operations struggled to keep pace. And there was still no systematic approach to adding new employees; the company relied on Cook's "rapidly fill the need only after identifying gaping holes in the team" approach.

Now, Intuit's executive team realized that part of strategic planning involved more systematically hiring and training new employees. Reacting only to urgent holes in current responsibilities meant Intuit perpetually struggled to keep up. The company needed a more thoughtful, deliberate approach to adding employees in its environment of explosive growth and rapid evolution.

Burgeoning growth also meant that founding team members had to start giving up responsibilities. Convinced by Dunn and LeFevre that his attention was too fractured, Cook started by hiring a director of marketing. John Monson, a former marketing manager at Software Publishing Company (SPC), had impressed Signe Ostby, so Cook invited Monson to his house for an interview.

Puzzled by the invitation to Cook's home, Monson made his way down the long multilot driveway in Woodside, searching for Cook's address. Entering the nicely appointed ranch house, newly purchased with Ostby's stock options and a large mortgage, Monson raised a brow when Cook suggested they have their interview in the swimming pool. Since Monson had not brought swim trunks, Cook provided a spare pair that fit a bit too tightly on Monson's tall, athletic frame. Sunlight glinted off Monson's reddish brown hair and mustache as the men made their way out to the pool.

To test Monson's problem-solving skills, Cook asked him to figure out how to stand on a beanbag chair (a remnant of the Cook family's lean times) in the pool. Cook knew that if Monson squished every bean in the bag to the sides, he could stand in the middle. Monson pushed the beans to the sides but couldn't quite make the chair float with his weight on it. Despite a drenching, Monson returned for additional interviews and demonstrated a thoughtful, analytical approach to solving problems. Impressed by the company's potential, Monson accepted when Cook offered him the director of marketing position.

Drawing on his SPC experience, Monson began his Intuit tenure by outlining specifically how the marketing department would contribute as the company developed new products. Most of the software industry equated marketing with marketing communications, but from his experience at P&G, Cook defined marketing more broadly at Intuit: Product managers would act as product business managers, overseeing income statements and all aspects of building the business. Cook and Monson agreed that Intuit's product managers had to act as champions for their products, embodying the voice of the customer not just for product development and marketing communications but also for technical support, and overseeing the critical feedback loop between technical support and the product team.

In April 1989, Monson hired the company's first official product manager from Migent Software Company in Lake Tahoe. Mari Baker had been a product manager for a software program

67

called In-House Accountant and had also done technical writing and quality assurance (QA) testing there. Baker had seen a job listing and landed an interview with the help of Tom LeFevre's wife, whom she knew from Stanford (Baker entered Stanford at the tender age of sixteen). In March, Baker interviewed at Intuit from 9 A.M. to 7 P.M. with no breaks for meals; she received an offer at the end of the marathon. Even though the intensity of the interview session surprised Baker, the Intuit team's energy excited her. Baker joined Intuit to plan the marketing launch for the company's upcoming Quicken 3.0 for DOS and 1.5 for Mac versions.

Throughout the 1980s, Cook had made the sales calls for Intuit. The company sold Quicken directly to large retailers Egghead and Software, Etc; independent stores (which made up 50 percent of sales) bought software through distributors such as Ingram Micro D and Merisel. Cook personally called on the large retailers and wholesalers to manage the relationships and to maximize sell-through to retail customers. Believing that Intuit's success depended on retail, Cook worked with distributors to devise promotions and create sales materials.

Having Cook run Intuit's sales department gave the company an edge. Software companies of the time typically compensated their sales managers based on the sales made to retail distributors, without regard for returns. This commission scheme created a conflict of interest that encouraged salespeople to "stuff the channel"; in other words, to sell far more to distributors than would eventually be sold to consumers, in order to make their quota, even if that meant product would be returned later. Cook's focus on *sell-through*—retail purchases made by end consumers—differentiated Intuit from most other software companies working with wholesalers.

Ultimately, the demands of the growing company made it impractical for Cook to handle these distribution relationships himself, and so he began searching for someone to run Intuit's sales department. After thirty unsuccessful interviews, Cook asked a buyer at Egghead Software to identify the best software salesperson he knew. The name that came back was Steve Katz, an educational software salesman who at one time had sold movie videotapes to retailers. Cook interviewed Katz for three hours over the phone. Cook then invited Katz for an in-person interview, which Katz later characterized as the toughest interview he'd ever had. Over dinner at a Japanese restaurant, Cook questioned Katz relentlessly, hardly giving him time to eat his sushi.

Katz, a sharp, likable, and quick-talking thirty-two-year-old, did not strike Cook as a typical schmoozy sales guy. The compact, energetic Katz, who had spent years managing sell-through, point of purchase displays, and channel management in the software and video movie businesses, impressed Cook with his marketing and distribution savvy. After additional interviews, Katz joined Intuit in May 1989. Unlike other software salespeople in the industry, Katz's incentive matched that of every other employee at the company: shares of Intuit's stock.

In line with their more strategic approach, Cook and the rest of the executive team also wanted to hire someone to develop product ideas beyond Quicken; they did not want Intuit to be a "one-product wonder." Early user studies revealed that nearly half of Quicken's customers used the program for small business accounting, but in its initial focus on survival, Intuit had ignored these customers. In late spring 1989, Cook met Sam Klepper, a Bain & Company alumnus who had written him asking for an internship to gain experience before going to Harvard Business School. After running the interview gauntlet, Klepper joined Intuit in June 1989 and began to research the small business market, seeking a follow-up product to Quicken.

While Cook added sales and marketing employees, Proulx beefed up the engineering staff, adding programmers to support the company's proliferating product versions for different platforms. As Proulx added staff, he fretted that Intuit could not keep up with so many necessary development efforts. And so, he decided to speed up product development across many software operating systems by developing a core of standard programming code that could be used across all platforms—a significant technical challenge at the time. By mid-1989, after the new Quicken versions for DOS and Mac launched, the engineering team concentrated on this core development effort, code-named "Bedrock."

The experiences of new hires in the technical and nontechnical areas of the company couldn't have been more different. In marketing, since workload demand still outpaced hiring, new employees had great responsibility—and great freedom—in their new roles. New hires largely set their own priorities and decided how to achieve them; Intuit did not write defined job descriptions or standardize processes. The company expected new marketing employees to take initiative and be resourceful; creativity was encouraged, and training was on-the-job.

Baker's experience on arriving at Intuit typified those of marketing employees. She immediately immersed herself into the Quicken launches, with frequent late nights and constant juggling of duties, and her guidance came from the series of urgent meetings she held with Monson and Cook to solve problems. Her first office in a hallway gave way to her second office in a closet. Baker brought her sleeping bag to work and pulled hours just as long as the engineers.

In engineering, though, Proulx hired team members for specific projects and skills; the discipline of engineering required greater coordination than did marketing. The technical groups created standard processes like the QA bugs database to create consistent bug tracking and evaluating. Every technical employee learned how to rate bugs in the database for severity and impact so there was a consistent way to prioritize bugs. Training for engineers, too, occurred on the job.

With such a rapid pace of hiring, the company quickly ran out of office space. Since office space in downtown Palo Alto was expensive, Dunn decided to search elsewhere. In adjacent Menlo Park, Dunn found two attractive buildings; one at 66 Willow Place, previously occupied by *Sunset* magazine, and the other around the corner at 155 Linfield Avenue. Dunn signed leases for

FIGURE 6-1

Intuit's employees proudly posed in front of the company's new building at 66 Willow Place in Menlo Park, California, in 1989. Intuit moved into the building the day before a magnitude 7.0 earthquake rocked the Bay Area.

Source: Courtesy of Virginia Boyd.

both buildings and in October the technical support group was the first to move into the Willow Place building (see figure 6-1).

The new quarters elated the tech support team, as did their new $250,000 Aspect call system that handled incoming phone calls. The elation lasted nearly twenty-four hours—until the Loma Prieta earthquake, measuring 7.0 on the Richter scale, rolled through the Bay Area. Despite the damage elsewhere, Intuit's new and old offices alike, to the relief of its employees, stood firm.

CREATING APOSTLES

Even without the formal training programs that more mature companies like P&G offered employees, Intuit ensured that new hires understood the company's Holy Grail: a happy customer. During the company's whirlwind growth years, Cook concentrated fiercely on keeping everyone at Intuit customer focused. He quizzed prospective employees about their view of customers and pitched Intuit as a company "revolutionizing the way people manage their finances." Intuit managers insisted that the company's goal was to make a real difference in the lives of ordinary people.

Beginning with the Apple II version, Intuit had included a postage-paid "Customer Suggestions" postcard in every box of software it shipped. The completed cards circulated throughout the company; everyone read customers' opinions, and, in the early days, combined virtue with necessity by taking turns fielding technical support calls. Cook trained employees to record feedback and questions received during these calls, and this information helped shape product development even as LeFevre hired a professional technical support group.

As the company grew larger, all of Cook's personal instincts and professional experience continued to convince him that everyone at the company must thoroughly understand what people needed and wanted from Intuit's products and customer service. How, he wondered, could Intuit establish a "customer evangelist culture" that would endure for the long term? Cook and Monson began devising several new ways to institutionalize regular contact with customers throughout the organization.

Drawing from the P&G playbook, Intuit instituted "Follow Me Home" research in 1989, in which members of the marketing and engineering staffs followed willing, first-time customers home from software stores to watch them install and use Quicken. The Intuit escorts solicited feedback and answered questions. The powerful experience of watching new customers in their own homes taught engineers and marketers the precept *We Are Not Our Customers* and the critical corollary *We Have to Make Quicken Even Easier to Use.*

For Intuit's growing technical support group, the key phrase was "Do Right by Customers." Customers judged all of Intuit by its tech support: Intuit's goal was not only to answer questions and learn where products could be improved but also to "create apostles." Technical support's mission was to treat customers so well that their delight moved them to tell five friends about Quicken.

Proulx developed a database order-entry system to track Quicken registration cards, customer comments, and direct sales customers. The system disseminated customer information throughout the company; no one was allowed to be ignorant of customer feedback. Meanwhile, Monson concentrated on customer input collected firsthand. From the time he joined Intuit he regularly picked five of the returned Quicken customer suggestion cards distributed in the product and called those customers himself to get feedback.

Taking Monson's idea and melding it with the company's earlier practice, Cook instituted another Intuit requirement: By 1989, to ensure firsthand customer contact for all employees, everyone in the company answered customer service and support calls for at least four hours each month, increasing to twelve hours a month when the company launched new products. This one-on-one customer experience augmented the technical support staff and provided a strong cultural bond across the company.

Employees, particularly new hires, initially resisted the assignment, intimidated by the direct contact and resentful of the time required. But most employees warmed up to the idea after speaking directly with customers because of the thrill of solving real customers' problems. Also, employees frequently saw Cook, Proulx, and other executives answering customer calls right beside them. Cook jotted notes from these calls in a little notepad that became ubiquitous, recording ideas and observations for the product teams.

Even though he couldn't quantify it, Cook believed that the immersion of all employees in customer contact shaped their intuitive decisions, and the "guts" of the company became more aligned with the needs of actual customers. "Total customer alignment" did not come from third-hand reports or management exhortations, but from talking to customers one-to-one. Cook told his employees, "No matter what your business problem is, talk to your customers or prospects in depth. Listen intently. Some of the biggest wins in business are the paradigm shifts that do not come from current wisdom. Those major wins only come from bathing yourself in and swimming with the customer. Reorient your priorities and view of the world to what the customer really wants."[1]

Meanwhile, Intuit expanded market research to better understand prospective customers, basing product, marketing, and customer service decisions on solid studies. The company conducted focus groups across the country to understand consumers' difficulties in managing their money and the anxieties their finances aroused. Employees observed consumers at software stores to understand their shopping habits and the importance of product packaging. Intuit measured its technical support quality, speed, and courtesy against tech support from its competitors, and studied every element of its advertising and marketing materials.

To create an on-site usability lab, Intuit recruited Judee Humburg, who had managed such labs at Hewlett-Packard. Intuit's new lab had a soothing décor with blue, purple, and teal colors, comfortable furniture, and attractive artwork displayed on the walls. It also featured one-way mirrors, one big focus group room and smaller lab rooms, audio recording, and video cameras that recorded not only the computer screen but also the user's face, the keyboard, and the mouse. The lab was conveniently located in Intuit's offices so that product teams could walk over and observe sessions. Engineers delighted in seeing for themselves where customers fumbled with their program because the fumbling pointed the way to product improvements.

The company also created a Quicken customer advisory panel, a creative group of loyal Quicken customers. Intuit marketing and engineering managers met with this panel every other month to get feedback on new products, new features, or whatever else the company needed to learn. Engineers and other team members attended these meetings and listened intensively to the panelists about features in development. These repeated personal interactions with customers galvanized team members. Now, they felt a personal responsibility for getting things right for these customers who had a face to them.

By the end of 1989, many employees believed that the secret to Intuit's success was the customer evangelist mindset that pervaded the company. Everyone at Intuit embraced Cook's belief in figuring out what customers wanted and driving the company to deliver it. "If you blow that," Cook argued, "it doesn't matter what else you do. You must invest in R&D to build superior products based on a superior understanding of customers. This is Intuit's fundamental advantage."[2] Unlike many software companies, Intuit saw technology not as an end but as a means to the end goal of improving customers' lives.

The customer focus paid off. Intuit revenues grew from $6 million in 1988, to $18 million in 1989 and $33 million in 1990. Not only the marketing and engineering departments bulged; from 1988 to 1990, personnel increases in the technical support and customer service departments kept pace. The company was still producing and shipping its own software products, so manufacturing muscle, too, also grew rapidly. Intuit had become a rapid-growth company with increasing momentum and credibility.

Intuit's holiday party at the Quadrus restaurant on Sand Hill Road in 1989 gratified its founding team. The company's revenue had just tripled, and for the first time the executive team approved a rather lavish party, with chilled shrimp and an open bar. Boyd put together a retrospective slide show with sentimental photos, including one of the team enjoying a champagne toast in December 1986 to celebrate one hundred Quicken orders in a day. The crew delighted in the party's gourmet food and wine; for weeks afterward Boyd teased Dunn about his affection for the endive hors d'oeuvres.

Heading for home the next day, Proulx and Cook bumped into each other in Intuit's parking lot—the egalitarian company did not have reserved parking spaces for any employees—and gazed at the beautifully lit Menlo Park building that housed their growing company. Through the windows, they could see dozens of hard-working employees. "Wow, this company has made it," Proulx said to Cook. "Look at these lives that are wrapped up in Intuit's fortune. We've really built something here."[3]

CHAPTER 7

CROSSING THE CHASM

I n the early 1990s, no other software company had anything like Intuit's National Sales Tour. When Intuit launched a new version or product, most employees who weren't tied to the phones (i.e., tech support and customer service) traveled to retail stores all over the country to train store salespeople on the new product. Retailers enthusiastically welcomed these visits. One Midwestern retailer remarked, "Most companies just send salespeople to visit us, but you guys send real people." A retailer in Florida told Intuit: "My Microsoft District Sales Manager only lives about two miles from my store, but I only know that by rumor. I've never met him. Intuit sends me salespeople, engineers, and even top management. It's great."[1]

Intuit worked hard to make its retail outlets feel like partners. The National Sales Tour helped mitigate the "channel conflict" (the inherent clash between its vigorous retail sales strategy and the company's aggressive direct-marketing effort) that resulted from Intuit's unusual two-pronged distribution strategy. Retailers already happy with Intuit because of Quicken's extremely low return rate liked the company even more after a National Sales Tour visit.

The National Sales Tour provided another employee cultural touchstone, a unique job experience that helped tie workers together. To save costs, employees traveled to stores near family or friends and stayed with them. The National Sales Tour also brought employees closer to customers and shopping experiences, again reinforcing Intuit's customer-centric orientation. Intuit engineer Lun Yuen observed: "My code is there on the shelf, at the front lines. Seeing it there and the enthusiastic response of the retail sales teams convince me that my work really matters."[2]

Scott Cook argued that the National Sales Tour gave Intuit an all-important "sense of the merchant." "During the early 1900s," he asserted, "mom-and-pop grocery stores were at the heart of the typical American town. These local store owners knew their customers' names, favorite grocery items, and tastes. Mom-and-pop merchants had not only an understanding of their customers' current needs but also an uncanny ability to anticipate their future needs."[3] Cook insisted that Intuit develop this intensive customer intuition.

MARKETING MUSCLE

The National Sales Tour was only a small part of Intuit's overall marketing machine. Advertising, another important part, flourished under the rigorous testing that Cook and John Monson required for every ad. Concentrating on benefits-oriented print advertising that sold Quicken directly to consumers, marketing communications manager Tanya Roberts, a tall, athletic working mother hired in 1990, meticulously tracked sales responses from every test and control ad to evaluate specific ad elements.

Friendly, sometimes frazzled, Roberts correlated response rates for ads in different magazines, as well as overall design, placement, message, copy, special offers, mail versus 800 numbers response, and other variables. Employees gravitated toward Roberts' nurturing style; at stressful times she'd buy boxes of See's chocolates to boost team morale. With Monson's encouragement and Roberts' support, Intuit's marketing team experimented, learned from mistakes, and did not fear errors.

The obsessive Cook, now infamous at Intuit for his "Good enough—isn't" mantra, often rewrote managers' ad copy just before deadlines to ensure ads followed clear communication principles. One workday, the copy for a new ad was due to production at the end of the business day. Cook met with two marketing managers at five o'clock that evening to approve the final copy. Instead of rubber-stamping the ad, Cook proceeded to mark up and edit the copy dramatically, chewing on his tongue and concentrating intently while redoing hours of work in minutes. Though the marketing and production team sweated bullets as time passed, they (barely) met their deadline with Cook's improved copy.

Eventually, Intuit's direct-marketing expertise extended beyond print. The company experimented with direct-response radio, even trying Rush Limbaugh as spokesperson after he waxed enthusiastic about Quicken on the air and his loyal talk-show listeners called Intuit in droves. The resulting Limbaugh ad generated so much controversy inside and outside of Intuit, however, that marketing quickly dropped it. And radio, with its time limitations and lack of visuals, couldn't match the success of the copy-intensive, visual ads that worked well to sell Quicken.

Despite the company's advertising blitzes, Intuit management learned in a 1990 study that Quicken was on the radar of fewer than 40 percent of PC-owning household prospects. And so, Intuit tried direct-response television, a medium never before used by a software company. The company bought cost-effective "remnant" advertising time, typically slots late at night that television stations hadn't sold. Even though only about 23 percent of U.S. households then owned PCs, the company found that direct-response television sold more copies of Quicken than print ads. Through television, Intuit extended Quicken's brand recognition, boosted awareness among PC owners, and increased sales.

Intuit also experimented with promotions. Its "Try-before-you-buy" offer allowed customers to use Quicken free for sixty days. If customers liked the software, Intuit charged them after the trial period ended. If they didn't like it, they didn't have to buy it or even send it back. Intuit charged a small, nonrefundable shipping and handling fee to cover its costs for this successful effort.

Trade shows became another Intuit marketing vehicle. At Comdex, the largest computer show cum Las Vegas bacchanal, Intuit staffed a creatively designed and noisy booth and passed out Quicken buttons. The booth featured life-size photos on the walls of people standing in line to buy Quicken at a retail store. Intuit employees wandered around the show; if they spotted someone wearing one of their buttons, they yelled, "You've just won a FREE box of Quicken!" Users loved the freebies; Intuit loved the attention.

When an internal study found that word-of-mouth recommendations generated more than half of new Quicken sales in the early 1990s, Intuit seized every opportunity to prime the pump. The "Cult of Quicken" contained a polyglot but loyal—even fanatical—customer base, and these avid customers often recommended Quicken to their friends, neighbors, and family members. Intuit incorporated customer stories into Quicken advertisements and the company's recorded lore. "This is easy!" one testimonial said. "I went kicking and screaming to a computer. But one look at that screen and I could see right away where to go." Another customer stated, "With Quicken I'm in control. I love it. This is one year I have absolutely no knot in my stomach about spending. With Quicken, I always know where my money goes."[4]

To increase this devotion to Quicken, Cook, Proulx, and other employees regularly attended computer user group meetings. User group members were typically early adopters and technology fanatics who formed clubs to share information about their beloved technologies. They tried new products and experimented to realize the potential of their PC hardware and software. User groups were good forums not only to solicit product feedback but also to influence an even wider sphere because these evangelists might tell others how Quicken had changed their lives or describe unexpected uses of Quicken, like tracking airline miles or cataloguing a baseball card collection.

Unusual Quicken stories did not just arise out of user groups. One day, when Proulx answered the phone in tech support, a Quicken user called just to say thanks because Quicken had saved his marriage. Another time, on a Saturday, Proulx was startled by a call at home. Answering the technical question, Proulx then asked if the customer knew he had called Proulx's house. "Oh, sure," the customer said. "I looked in the manual, saw your name listed, and called directory assistance." Affable Proulx chuckled at the customer's tenacity.

Intuit's marketing machine played an integral part in its product launches. Whenever a new version came out, Intuit marketing geared up its activities. In addition to managing advertising, public relations, and upgrade mailings (offering new versions to current customers for a reduced price), marketing worked internally with the rest of the company to prepare them for launch. Marketing worked with product development to train technical support and customer service on the new versions and with finance to forecast sales volumes for operations to use in planning.

Marketing also planned company launch parties and product team "ship trips" to places like Napa Valley or Hearst Castle. During one memorable ship trip to Disneyland, the Quicken for Mac product team stayed until the amusement park closed at midnight. Too tired to head back to northern California, the motley crew tried several nearby inexpensive motels before finding a room, possibly because innkeepers objected to one of the engineer's long, scraggly beard, which he had vowed to shave only after the product shipped. The close-knit team of six elected to share one room, although an engineer grumpily slept under the coffee table because there weren't enough beds. After the impromptu overnight stay, the team checked out the next morning, caught a flight back up to northern California, and went into work—in the same clothes they wore the day before.

Employees looked forward to wearing their launch T-shirts, each more garish than the last. One such shirt proclaimed its wearers "Fiscally Fit," while another touted the, "Faster, Easier,

Better" results of its new version. The positive momentum and energy Intuit generated during this golden era was palpable, especially to employees.

PRODUCTS TAKE FLIGHT

Customer devotion, retailer loyalty, and Intuit marketing and advertising led to success for Quicken. In summer 1989, newly hired sales manager Katz and product manager Baker had worked together on introducing Quicken 3.0 for DOS and Quicken 1.5 for Mac. Created from Eric Dunn's vision and architecture, Quicken 3.0 for DOS marked the company's technical maturity, breaking new ground with its advanced features and a robust file system; it transformed Quicken into a sophisticated piece of technology that no one could mistake for an electronic checkbook. This superior version of Quicken anchored the company's overall approach to its personal finance software that would endure for over ten years.

The new versions, packed with new features, were well received by such august reviewers as the *Washington Post*. "Quicken has been one of the best-selling software programs for more than a year," the newspaper raved in 1989. "The new version provides many new reasons for that popularity to continue."[5]

During the fall of 1989, Intuit became the second highest volume software supplier to retailers, trailing only Microsoft. The number of Quicken customers grew radically from twenty thousand in 1987 to 1.3 million by 1990. And in February of that year the Software Publishers Association presented Dunn with their "Best Consumer Software" award for Quicken 3.0 for DOS—one of the high points of his career.

To sustain this growth, Intuit had to release new products every year. However, in December 1989 company management realized that its engineering group's all-consuming effort to develop the cross-platform Bedrock technology left them too busy to develop new versions for 1990. Since Intuit, for the first time, had experienced a sales slowdown in late 1989, the potential revenue shortfall deeply concerned the executive team.

Mari Baker wanted Intuit to create Quicken 4.0 for DOS not only to allay the company's revenue concerns but also because she was trying to land Intuit's first OEM (original equipment manufacturer) deal. Baker was working to persuade IBM to pre-load Quicken, rather than its competitor Managing Your Money, on IBM's new family-oriented PS/2. To convince IBM of Intuit's size, Baker rousted every employee in the company from their desks one memorable morning in January. Grouping them together in front of the company's Linfield Avenue headquarters, she lined up the noisy staff for a picture in front of a banner saying, "Intuit: Ready to Support IBM," which she presented to her IBM contacts as proof of the company's significance and commitment.

Even though the IBM OEM price for Quicken was very low—Intuit would receive only $6 a unit versus $33 at retail—and might cannibalize other, more profitable sales of Quicken, the possibilities of locking out the company's key competitor and securing incremental new customers excited the Intuit executive team. IBM's lead-time for shipping during the holiday season required that Intuit ship its new product by the last day of August. The news that IBM had selected Quicken as its preloaded personal finance software elated Intuit and made certain a new Quicken version—despite the brutal schedule imposed by IBM's deadline.

Though he'd retreated from product development to focus on his CFO duties, Dunn, the company's unique programmer CFO, agreed to create Quicken 4.0 for DOS because he realized that no one else could work on it. Dunn and Baker planned an investments management feature in the new version to compete with Managing Your Money. And Dunn also wanted to build in electronic bill payment, a particular interest of his. Electronic bill payment was already available in a special version 3.0 "EP" (named to reflect the new electronic billpay functionality) of

Quicken for DOS, but was not yet available in the basic product shipped to retail stores.

As they struggled to meet IBM's deadline, Baker and Dunn developed a warm personal friendship. Baker, a tomboy, would regularly physically tackle her friend Dunn and wrestle him to decide issues of schedule and feature conclusion. "I never won," she acknowledged, "but I had fun trying."[6] Baker and Dunn worked as equals; each had fully internalized the perspective of the customer.

Baker's "do what it takes" approach and familiarity with software development pleased Dunn, and his respect for Baker's marketing perspective created a successful development environment. Together they created innovative product solutions to customer problems in record time. Though some engineers doubted that this quick and dirty approach would result in a high enough level of product quality, Dunn and Baker recruited a handful of helpers and created a successful version of Quicken in a very short time frame.

The tiny Quicken 4.0 for DOS product team attended off-site meetings together to promote team building and make major progress on product features. "Offsites" had become another Intuit cultural icon. One such team meeting in La Honda, in the hills between Silicon Valley and the Pacific Coast, featured a some-times-harrowing ropes course to cement team cohesiveness (see figure 7-1). Teams also met at Cook's friend Peter Wendell's house in Healdsburg, in the Napa wine country, to hammer out product specs and develop feature prototypes. Proulx and Cook often dropped in to help, recreation—including killer water volleyball and Marco Polo in Wendell's pool—and food abounded, and teams bonded tightly through these offsites.

Though the Quicken 4.0 for DOS schedule tested him, Dunn, with the occasional assistance of other engineers purloined from the Bedrock project, successfully delivered an OEM version of Quicken for IBM at the end of August and a retail version in September. The functionality of Quicken 4.0 for DOS pleased Dunn. Reflecting later, he said, "The evolution of Quicken from

FIGURE 7-1

The Quicken product development team enjoyed a ropes course team building offsite in La Honda, California, 1989. Product teams also went on "ship trips" to celebrate new product launches.

Source: Courtesy of Virginia Boyd.

the easiest-to-use, but perhaps least-capable product (1987) to the easiest-to-use and most-capable product (1991) marked a tremendous technical accomplishment, one that enabled Intuit to compete effectively against all comers."[7]

IBM's required quality assurance (QA) testing of Quicken intimidated Baker. She worried about IBM's reaction if it found the bugs Intuit had been forced by time constraints to leave in the product. Before she sent the release, she tried to set expectations for the QA process: "We have rapid response development; if you find problems let us know and we'll fix them right away."[8]

Fortunately, Intuit didn't need to worry. After their QA testing, IBM phoned and said, "We didn't find any problems. In fact, can we come out and learn about product development from you?" This response relieved Baker and Dunn and, since they knew of bugs, indicated somewhat perfunctory testing. IBM also offered Baker a tour of its usability labs and practices.

Quicken 4.0 for DOS launched in September 1990. In addition to a sales boost from the IBM OEM deal, Quicken 4.0 for

DOS was the most "bundled" product—that is, sold together with other software products for promotional purposes—in Intuit's history. For starters, Katz signed a deal with ChipSoft to package Quicken for DOS with the market-leading TurboTax tax preparation product. Intuit also bundled Quicken with Microsoft Works, despite Baker's unease about the formidable software company learning too much about Quicken that way. Quicken 4.0 for DOS was also sold packaged with the small-business-focused Lotus 1-2-3 version 2.2. With help from all the bundles, the new version of Quicken got off to a great start.

TO IPO OR NOT TO IPO?

Intuit's marketing success caused a flurry of interest among financiers. Investment bankers began calling on Intuit, urging the company to consider an initial public offering (IPO) of its stock. To avoid subjecting the company to the pressure of Wall Street, Cook and Dunn wanted to delay an IPO for as long as possible. But selling stock would ensure that the company's founders received a payout. Tom Proulx was buying an expensive new house, and all the early investors wanted to obtain liquidity and some tangible reward for their seven years of effort.

And so, the company's major stockholders decided to sell some of their own stock privately to venture capitalists to generate personal cash. (Intuit itself didn't need more cash because of software's low capital intensity and high gross margins.) For the first time since approaching the VC community in 1984, the Intuit executive team began looking again for outside investors.

As soon as the company put the word out, many venture capitalists expressed interest in the deal, despite the somewhat subdued VC environment in the aftermath of the 1987 stock market crash. Six years earlier, no venture capitalist would talk to Intuit; now, the phone just kept ringing with interest.

The biggest stumbling block to the investment round was a dispute, unknown to most of the employees, that had been brewing between Proulx and Cook. A VC firm, after interviewing the two founders, told CFO Dunn, "We might be interested eventually but you've got a serious problem: there's no agreement between the cofounders about the capital structure. We can't invest until this gets straightened out."[9]

Tom Proulx believed that in 1985, when he had stayed on with no salary and he and Cook had essentially restarted the company together, the two had agreed that the equity of the company would be reset to equal shares between them, except for a set-aside proportion to compensate Cook for initial capital investments in the company. Cook believed that Proulx had been fairly compensated for going without salary with the large, but not equal, equity grant he'd been given in 1986. For his part, CFO Dunn had never heard of any additional equity offer to Proulx. Cook and Proulx were at an impasse.

Peter Wendell, Cook's cohort from Harvard Business School and the founder and a general partner of Sierra Ventures, wanted to participate in the Intuit VC transaction. Wendell had befriended both Cook and Proulx during the company's early years, and they agreed to let him mediate. As an experienced venture capitalist, Wendell often encountered this kind of a conflict between founders. He talked with both men and did some independent research to figure out what was fair. Eventually, the company accepted his recommendation to award more shares to Proulx, who received a few hundred thousand additional shares to resolve the dispute and clear the way for the transaction.

Though more than a dozen venture capitalists expressed interest in the Intuit stock investment, the company quickly fixed on Technology Venture Investors (TVI) and Kleiner Perkins Caufield & Byers (Kleiner Perkins), two of the top-tier VC firms in Silicon Valley. The Intuit executive team wanted to add Burt McMurtry of TVI and John Doerr of Kleiner Perkins onto its board of directors, to add their experience in taking a company public to a board that lacked such expertise.

The venture capitalists' courtship intoxicated the Intuit team. One day, a group from Kleiner Perkins made its pitch. Vinod

Khosla, a founder of Sun Microsystems and now a partner at Kleiner, arrived in his red Corvette with other Silicon Valley luminaries. Intuit executives presented an overview of the company and gave a demo of Quicken on a giant Mitsubishi monitor. John Doerr then pitched Kleiner Perkins, saying the VC firm could add value with its *keiretsu* (a group of companies with interlocking operations or affiliations). Dunn marveled, "They all listened so carefully to our description of Intuit's prospects. Being courted by the leading VC company was amazing."[10]

Proulx did the due diligence (necessary background research) on Burt McMurtry of TVI. "I made lots of calls and almost everybody talked about Burt's strong ethics. I thought it was remarkable that ethics were so salient in his character that they were explicitly mentioned. Once I got to know him I saw why: Burt is one of the finest, most upstanding people you will ever know."[11]

Cook asked Gordon Eubanks, CEO of Symantec, about working with Doerr who was also on Symantec's board. Eubanks praised Doerr's contributions but warned that Doerr demanded detail. He told Cook, "With John Doerr on your board, who needs product managers?"[12] Scott McNealy, CEO of Sun Microsystems, also warned Cook that Doerr could be very hands-on.

Cook, ever the taskmaster, treated prospective board members just as he did prospective employees. To earn the right to invest in Intuit, Doerr and the other venture capitalists had to answer Cook's questions about what Intuit should do if Microsoft introduced a product directly competitive with Quicken. The slight, sandy-haired and intense Doerr also had to write an essay agreeing not to get too hands-on with product discussions. "I couldn't believe I had to write an essay and promise that I wouldn't interfere in product strategy!" said Doerr later.[13] Cook put the essays in a drawer and cleared Doerr and McMurtry to bid.

The actual funding process was a delicate dance. Venture capitalists calculated what they would offer per share—and hence, the value of Intuit—based on their estimates of its earning potential. Kleiner Perkins assigned a company value of $30 million; TVI said $60 million; and a late bidder, Accel Capital, said $70 million. Cook and Dunn let the companies compete against each other, managing to get most of the high valuation from Kleiner and TVI, the firms that Cook preferred because of the expertise that they would bring to the board. Intuit's final valuation of $65 million thrilled its executive team. The total investment was $12 million, $5 million each from TVI and Kleiner and $2 million from Sierra. Burt McMurtry and John Doerr both joined Intuit's board by the end of August.

After Intuit passed this milestone, the company faced new excitement: Microsoft called. A junior Microsoft product manager flew from Redmond, Washington, down to Menlo Park to talk with Intuit management about licensing the Quicken name for a personal finance product on Microsoft's growing Windows platform: "Microsoft Quicken for Windows." The concept intrigued some of the Intuit team because Intuit had no Windows expertise and no plans at that time to build a version for what they saw as a business operating system.

Monson, now VP of marketing, appreciated what Windows offered consumers, especially since it was now apparent that Microsoft was abandoning the OS/2 platform. He thought that a partnership with Microsoft might provide a shortcut to a Windows product. But Proulx hit the roof. He believed that Microsoft wouldn't offer what Quicken was worth and was trying to eliminate Quicken as a competitor on Windows.

What should the newly flush executive staff of Intuit do about Windows—and Microsoft?

CHAPTER 8

CRUSH MICROSOFT

I n 1981, IBM agreed to use Microsoft's DOS operating system in its first personal computer. Ten years later, Microsoft was closing its stranglehold grasp on the software industry; its 1991 revenues, up 56 percent over the previous year, hit $1.8 billion and the Redmond, Washington–based company employed more than 8,200 people.[1] These figures dwarfed Intuit's 1991 revenues of $44 million and its two hundred employees, but the companies differed in more than just scale: Each company's culture reflected the values and personalities of the men who founded them.

Gates loved technology; Microsoft's technical innovation imperative demanded brutally long hours from its employees. Intuit focused on serving customers well and tried to strike a balance between hard work and office fun, between jobs and personal lives. Gates' pragmatism ensured that Microsoft's operational efficiencies and processes outstripped Intuit's, while, under Cook's tutelage, Intuit had developed a better feel for marketing and listening to customers. Before 1990, modest, thoughtful Cook could often ignore Intuit's ineffectual competitors, but the confident and aggressive Gates had ensured that Microsoft competed effectively on several fronts.

Microsoft's size provided far greater resources to tackle adversity. Careful Intuit had never been in the federal government's crosshairs, but by 1990 the Federal Trade Commission had investigated Microsoft for antitrust activity, including Microsoft's bold requirement that PC manufacturers pay a royalty on every computer sold, even if it didn't use a Microsoft operating system.[2]

By 1991, Microsoft owned about 25 percent of the software applications market. The bulk of the company's profits came from operating systems; application products, which accounted for over half of Microsoft's revenues in 1991, were less profitable. But Microsoft did not yet dominate the three biggest office application categories—word processing, databases, and spreadsheets. Word-Perfect led the market over Microsoft Word. Microsoft had no database program to compete against Ashton-Tate's dBASE, and Lotus 1-2-3 was ahead of Excel.[3] In the smaller personal finance market, Quicken held an 85 percent revenue share and 69 percent unit volume market share of the personal finance category.

Intuit and Microsoft, though not yet direct competitors, were hardly strangers. In 1989, Microsoft's Jeff Raikes had approached Cook at a Software Publishers Association meeting. "We don't see a lot of companies we really respect," Raikes said to Cook. "You seem to be one that does things right. We might be interested in acquiring you. Do you have any interest in that?"[4] Cook told his executive team—then made up of Scott Cook, Tom Proulx, Eric Dunn, Tom LeFevre, John Monson, and the soon-to-depart Virginia Boyd—that having Microsoft look at acquiring Intuit was a high compliment.

The companies held preliminary discussions, and Intuit gave Microsoft its top-level financial reports. A month later Microsoft called back and said: "We've talked again with Bill Gates. We're so focused on Windows 3.0 and LAN Manager now that we can't tackle anything additionally. We just can't add you to our plate right now."[5] A little disappointed, Cook was also relieved that he would not have to consider a potential merger while Intuit was growing so quickly. As an end to the discussion, he proposed bundling Quicken with Microsoft Works. Even though he did not know whether Microsoft was friend or foe, Cook thought it worthwhile to befriend them just in case.

Months later, Microsoft returned with its Quicken licensing offer for the Windows platform. The discussions raged for several weeks. "They really like the Quicken brand name because it's so well known," Cook pointed out to the executive group. Microsoft proposed that it would build the product and license Intuit's brand name. Flatteringly, it also asked Intuit's advice on how to build it.[6] Despite Proulx's opposition to licensing, Cook continued the discussions, worried that Microsoft's so-far-amicable courtship could turn into a potential competitive threat.

Microsoft courted Intuit, pumping for as much information as it could get about Intuit's possible Quicken for Windows development project (which did not exist) while extolling partnering rather than competing. After a long-winded exchange of information, Microsoft abruptly made Intuit an unacceptable offer— a $7 per copy licensing fee for the use of the Quicken name on a Microsoft-developed product. Microsoft marketing managers Mike Slade and Laura Jennings told the Intuit execs, "If you don't work with us, we're going to win. Are you going to work with us or not?"[7] Enraged Intuit executives believed that Microsoft knew Intuit would never accept this lowball ultimatum.

Shortly after, a phone call cemented Intuit's fears about incipient Microsoft competition. Mike Maples, the head of Microsoft's applications division and one of the company's top executives, withdrew the licensing offer, telling Cook, "Our people have been talking about this partnership for months, but it's not going to happen. If we went alone, we think we'd get 60 percent of the Windows personal finance business. If you went alone you think you would. We will never come to agreement. So we've decided to go it alone and we've got a team developing it now."[8]

When Cook hung up the phone, his heart sank. How much had Microsoft learned from Intuit that they could put to use in their own product? He thought Intuit had been careful, but concern remained. Microsoft was entering Intuit's business and Intuit had next to nothing with which to compete. Their calculated risk not to jump into Windows development had turned sour. And worse, their soon-to-be competitor, Microsoft, knew exactly how far behind Intuit was. Intuit's Quicken for Windows project went from zero to number one on its priority list—the most urgent imperative Intuit had ever faced.

DOING WINDOWS

Originally, Proulx had started the Bedrock project to produce the first version of Quicken for Windows. Bedrock—conceived to develop a programming platform that would work across DOS, Macintosh, OS/2, and Windows—had fallen behind schedule, however, with Intuit engineering struggling to master the technical difficulties. When Cook got the call from Mike Maples, he realized quickly that Intuit could not depend on Bedrock to deliver a Windows version of Quicken.

Instead, he, Proulx, and Dunn began looking for an outside company that could. Software Transformations, Inc. (STI) in Cupertino, California, had successfully programmed in the new Windows environment and was looking for a high-profile client like Intuit to solidify its reputation as a software migration expert. STI had developed a library of Windows modules and presented a plausible case for getting the development contract. Dunn and Proulx concluded that STI knew Windows, and so Intuit gave STI a $1 million contract with a 2.5 percent royalty per copy sold. Proulx chose an Intuit project manager to interface with STI, gave over the Quicken source code, and then left STI alone to convert Quicken for DOS to Windows within a few months.

Dunn drew on Intuit tradition to assign the Windows project a code name. Dunn had code-named Quicken 4.0 for DOS "Ginger" after the *Gilligan's Island* character. Because Dunn did not have a television in his home, he recalled only older TV shows that he had seen in his childhood. Intuit employees teased Dunn mercilessly for his unfamiliarity with popular culture; despite the ribbing, the team assigned the code name "Professor" to the Quicken for Windows development effort.

Spurred on by the imminent competition with Microsoft, the company also decided to enter the international market. Microsoft sold well internationally, and Intuit scrambled to meet the upcoming competition on all fronts. Intuit already had Quicken customers in the United Kingdom, and so the company made the United Kingdom its first overseas target.

To test the Quicken concept, longtime comrades Dunn and Baker traveled to the United Kingdom in early January 1991. The brilliant Dunn and tomboy Baker had no industry contacts, just one thousand business names and one hundred Quicken user names. They visited software stores and randomly called prospective customers, just as Cook had done in 1984 to test the Quicken concept in the United States.

Reticent Dunn did not enjoy cold-calling random households and businesses and asking about their accounting processes. He and the persistent Baker had to telephone dozens of people for each completed interview, racking up a hotel phone bill of over one thousand dollars. But they were encouraged by their survey results. Increasing PC penetration and only moderate satisfaction with existing accounting solutions augured well for Quicken.

On the plane home, Baker assailed Dunn with her concerns about the Quicken for Windows development project. STI had fallen behind on interim deliverables and had not communicated the reason for the delays. The vendor seemed stuck in a pattern of "We are delayed" messages. Baker said, "This project is too important to Intuit to let slide." After hearing her concerns, Dunn promised to investigate.

The Windows platform intrigued Dunn, even though he had preferred the failed IBM OS/2. When he returned from the United Kingdom, Dunn and a senior Intuit engineer created a crude Windows interface for Quicken 4.0 for DOS, using the Windows graphical display interface to demystify the Windows platform. At the end of January, Dunn showed Baker the mockup, which, though rough, was fully functional. The contrast between this work of two weeks and STI's delays confirmed that STI was not engaging effectively. Intuit had a problem.

SWAT TEAM

By March 1991, Quicken for Windows anxiety began to build within the Intuit management team. They agonized that Microsoft must have been working on their competitive program even as the Goliath had offered Intuit the Quicken for Windows licensing deal. These delay tactics had given Microsoft a head start to market, convincing Intuit management that the company's survival was, once again, at stake. Regarded as a precedent, Microsoft's sound defeat of Lotus with its new Windows spreadsheet product, Excel, struck a note of doom.

Intuit believed that Microsoft would launch its competing product in the fall of 1991. STI had been working since the previous September and had produced nothing tangible. As Dunn focused on the Windows project, Baker took the executive team's urgency to heart. For the rest of 1991, she and Dunn lived and breathed beating Microsoft.

Numerous STI problems, including extremely slow progress on even basic issues, engineer turnover, and an overall lack of knowledge about the Quicken code that Dunn viewed as unacceptable, had convinced Dunn that the Quicken for Windows project would not meet its ship date. On March 21, 1991, after innumerable missed milestones, Dunn sent a letter to STI taking back the lead of Quicken for Windows development. He wanted to fire STI completely, but for expedience, he decided to work with them.

Before he sent the letter, Dunn had a heart-to-heart conversation with Proulx. Intuit's "go-to guy" for programming under pressure, Dunn told Proulx that he could fix the Windows debacle if it was worth his while. He set his price: a black BMW M5, with all taxes paid by Intuit. Proulx agreed. Dunn said, "Something needs to happen. I can do it, and I will do it. The car is not the primary motivation but it makes me feel like I'm not getting rooked—after all, I am handling international, CFO, investment bankers, etc., in addition to the programming. The car makes it all worthwhile."[9]

And so, Dunn and a handful of handpicked programmers took over the Windows development project. Proulx had hired Tim Villanueva, a former Hewlett-Packard engineer with significant Windows experience; Dunn roped him into the Professor project and assigned him the reports feature because of his Windows graphics and fonts expertise. Villanueva proved a perfect Intuit fit; his can-do attitude, aesthetic sense, and commitment to getting things right galvanized the team.

At first, the engineers programmed at Dunn's Palo Alto home while listening to opera CDs and eating Wolfgang Puck frozen pizzas. Then, Dunn and Monson planned an offsite the week of May 20, 1991 at Pajaro Dunes, a small beach town near Monterey, California, to escape from office distractions. The offsite delighted the SWAT team of engineers, who were eager to work uninterrupted.

At Pajaro the Intuit team occupied one large condominium, with five bedrooms to share. They brought their portable computers and used "sneakernet" (i.e., walking between computers with floppy disks) for connectivity. The team of eight coded and debugged all day long. Baker had arranged for a constant flow of delicious catered food, and the engineers slept from midnight to 8 A.M. and worked full-throttle the rest of the time for one week straight. The team went to Pajaro with a barely functional product and returned to Menlo Park with key pieces working.

For Dunn, this development period was marked by unbelievable intensity. Merging the Intuit and STI teams and code proved difficult. Dunn worked around the clock, thinking nothing of scheduling team meetings on Sunday evenings. He even missed paying his mortgage bill, too busy to read his mail. "Finishing Quicken for Windows was like climbing up the last five hundred feet of Mount Everest," Dunn remarked later. "Microsoft had a formula for destruction—they'd killed off WordPerfect with Word for Windows and Lotus 1-2-3 with Excel. Microsoft was applying that formula to us and if we failed, Intuit was finished."[10]

Intuit management agonized that the project would fail, that Dunn's Intuit and STI team might not be able to release Quicken for Windows in time. The Pajaro breakthroughs and management concerns convinced Dunn to schedule a second offsite for July. By then, engineers had completed the product's feature set, and the team dared to imagine that they might finish the Windows version and ship in the fall. Still, a lot of work—and a lot of bugs—remained.

The terrible aesthetics of STI's code offended the Intuit team, Villanueva in particular. During the second offsite, Villanueva told Dunn that he had enough time to refine the user interface (UI) for Quicken for Windows. Dunn disagreed. Villanueva said, "If I can get the UI done this week, will you go jump into the ocean with all your clothes on?" Dunn, believing Villanueva would never finish, took the bet. Before heading back to Menlo Park, a grumpy (though secretly pleased) Dunn jumped into the cold Pacific: Villanueva had worked furiously to win the bet and produce a more attractive UI.

At the second offsite, the Professor team completed an alpha version of their product. They focused next on fixing bugs. Microsoft's Excel had shipped with an Easter Egg, a hidden "signature" within a program put in by its amused programmers: a picture of Lotus 1–2–3's logo with lots of six-legged bugs scurrying around and eating it up. This play on the well-known buggyness of Lotus's software haunted the Intuit engineers, who wanted to avoid a similar industry indictment.

To efficiently test Quicken for Windows, Proulx arranged a "Bug-o-Rama," where engineering gave the rough code to many Intuit employees and challenged them to find bugs. An Intuit institution, the Bug-o-Rama had originally started out of necessity when the company didn't have a QA testing department. Years later, the event still helped to find some nasty bugs. The first employee to find a major bug that caused the program to crash was paid fifty dollars on the spot. One clever employee made nearly $1,000 that afternoon.

Baker's Quicken for Windows launch schedule called for a beta release on August 5 and a final manufacturing release in October. The all-important Comdex trade show was October 22, and Intuit had to finish Quicken for Windows in time for the show—and for Microsoft's upcoming release. Would Dunn, Baker, and the rest of the team be able to pull it off?

BEATING THE BEHEMOTH

In a 1991 board meeting, angry Proulx had proclaimed, "We will crush Microsoft." This statement of pure bravado sparked a meeting among Baker, Monson, Cook, and John Doerr from Kleiner Perkins, during which Baker proposed an audacious "Crush Microsoft" approach to match Dunn's programming feats in drama and effectiveness. Cook and Baker presented this Crush Microsoft plan at Intuit's next board meeting, with Cook drumming on the table for emphasis: "We're going after them, defending the space, and thinking about every piece of the puzzle to ensure that we are delivering against all of them—product, price, promotion, and placement."[11]

Cook challenged Baker to read everything about Bill Gates so that she could better anticipate Microsoft's likely strategy. "If you know everything about our competitor," Cook said, "then next you have to ask, what are *our* assets?" They agreed that Intuit's most powerful asset was its customer base and that Microsoft was likely to try to get to market first to "lock up" or grab all the Windows personal finance customers. Since Intuit knew that customers hated changing personal finance programs, the early mover advantage was a serious threat. Monson advocated aggression: "We can't give them an inch to maneuver in," he said.[12]

But what could Intuit do to convince customers to wait for Quicken for Windows since Microsoft's new product, called

"Money," would likely come to market first? Baker decided to break company tradition and preannounce the Windows product, something Intuit had not done since its terrible Apple II preannouncement. Baker hoped to convince customers to wait for the Intuit product by including an announcement in its DOS upgrade mailing to let its current users know that a Windows product was on the way.

The announcement in the upgrade mailing wasn't a typical Intuit direct-mail piece. Cook, Monson, and Baker had wondered how they could get retailers to stand by Quicken instead of recommending Microsoft's new offering to their customers. In a brilliant masterstroke, Cook decided to send Intuit's installed customer base to retail stores for the Windows product, instead of asking them to order their product directly from Intuit, by providing a $15 mail-in rebate coupon for Quicken for Windows software bought at retail stores.

This insightful move—the first time a software company had ever offered a rebate coupon—would capitalize on Intuit's superior retail relationships. Driving customers to retail stores would increase retailer loyalty and inflate Intuit's retail market share numbers. This strategy would also help dampen the huge upsurge in calls that swamped Intuit's phone centers every launch.

Cook, seeking the best information, as was his wont, brought in a former Microsoft executive for a strategy session. Cook asked, "What should we be doing as we're putting together this whole 'Beat Microsoft Money' approach?" The former Microsoft employee recommended that Intuit hire high-tech PR firm Wilson McHenry to handle public relations because Microsoft excelled at PR. Intuit's PR message reflected its strategy: "You know and love Quicken, so don't switch." Intuit wanted to ensure that Quicken users knew they didn't have to switch to get a Windows product. The company also announced its upcoming Windows version with posters and displays in retail stores.

To further please retailers, Baker led Intuit to slash its pricing. Since Microsoft Money would launch first, Intuit used its "second mover advantage" to set Quicken's price lower than Money's. Intuit set the distributor price for Quicken for Windows at $13 per unit (Quicken for DOS was at $30) and suggested a retail price of $59.95, the same as DOS, offering retailers a huge margin for Windows. For the first time the company also offered retailers discounts for ordering in quantity.

The company's defensive moves were complete. As expected, Microsoft released Money in September 1991, and all of Intuit held its breath. Would customers migrate to Money, handing Microsoft yet another market success, or would they wait and buy Intuit's Windows entry scheduled to release nearly two months later?

To the overwhelming relief of the company, customers patiently waited for Quicken for Windows. Retailers, seeing how much income they could generate with a little bit of patience, recommended that customers purchase the personal finance software package from the company whose software had the lowest return rate in the industry.

Stores began to create long waiting lists of people interested in Quicken for Windows. One store only ten miles from Microsoft's headquarters in Washington delighted Baker when she tried to purchase Money and was talked out of it by the retail staff. Most of the retail community advised customers to "Wait for Quicken." Intuit reaped the payoff for its new retail strategy and its years of National Sales Tours and customer interactions.

And Dunn's first look at Microsoft's product relieved him. Money had limited functionality—no investments, tax categories, dynamic data-exchange features, or electronic payments. Microsoft had, however, built a very nicely finished product with no perceptible bugs. It performed well, looked good, and had the Microsoft competitive trademark—an automatic, albeit awkward, Quicken data import so that Quicken users would be able to convert all their data to Money if they wanted to switch programs. Microsoft had moved quickly.

Baker reacted differently. She knew that Microsoft competed hard, looking at what their best competitors had done and delivering those features in what they created. Microsoft did not try to break new ground; it just tried to achieve parity. Baker concluded that Microsoft was Intuit's first competitor to really "get it." Money imported Quicken data, mimicked Quicken's user interface, and made it easy for users to switch.

Even though Microsoft Money imitated Quicken superlatively, Baker and Dunn believed that if they could release a decent product in the fall, Quicken would still beat it. Baker and the team relied on the fundamental differences between the two competing organizations. As Monson, VP of marketing, observed: "The things that distinguish us are engraved into our organizations. They copied us but Microsoft doesn't have the customer empathy built into the organization that Intuit has."[13] Monson felt certain that Intuit's customer orientation was superior to Microsoft's and that this would keep Quicken the market leader.

Baker agreed. She had observed Microsoft's usability labs while finalizing the bundle with Quicken and Microsoft Works the previous year. She recalled that Microsoft hired Ph.D. usability experts who ran the tests and then produced a report for the team. Microsoft engineers did not learn firsthand by observing customers interact with their software. In contrast, Intuit engineers loved to find problems with the software and treasured those "A–ha!" moments when they watched a customer get stuck and realized, "My God that's so obvious; we did that wrong!"

Intuit could utilize its superior customer insight and marketing expertise to beat Microsoft—if they could get the product released in time.

THE BEST COMPETITOR TO HAVE

After an astoundingly short seven-month development cycle, Intuit released Quicken for Windows in October 1991, just in time for the Comdex trade show. Retailers found it a great traffic builder; Windows provoked customer interest, and Quicken appealed to these customers. Many retailers took advantage of Intuit's pricing and advertised Quicken for Windows at only ten or fifteen dollars to bring in customers, using the product as a "loss leader" much as grocers might discount bread or milk to attract shoppers. After using Intuit's mail-in rebate, upgrade customers could practically get the product for free. Even after the release, some stores could not stock Quicken fast enough to meet the pent-up demand and had to keep waiting lists to track customers.

The day Quicken for Windows was launched, Proulx was on vacation. When he returned to the office, he found an employee expense report on his desk awaiting his approval. The amount was for about $85,000 to reimburse Dunn for his new BMW. Proulx's first reaction was, "Damn, I wish Eric had let me negotiate a lower price!" Proulx's second reaction gratefully acknowledged Dunn's heroics and agreed this company hero deserved his reward.

Quicken soundly and consistently defeated Microsoft Money. Intuit succeeded partly because Microsoft blundered: Microsoft initially priced Money too high versus Baker's aggressive Quicken for Windows price. Then Microsoft overcompensated and lowered the retail "street" price of Money to $9.99 as well as copying Quicken's rebate coupon. This strategy also backfired because it left retailers with almost no margins; Money ended up in clearance bins in software stores everywhere.

Mike Hallman, the president of Microsoft when Money was introduced and who later became an Intuit board member, said: "Money was such a small piece of Microsoft that it wasn't getting mind share, wasn't viewed as a strategic killer application like Excel or Word or Windows. It was just a part of the small group doing consumer stuff, a whole hodgepodge of stuff like games, really kind of a sideshow to Microsoft. Money wasn't getting appropriate resources or mind share and was never positioned strategically like Quicken for Intuit."[14]

PC Magazine published monthly retail sales reports, and Intuit's elation grew when Quicken ranked number one whereas

Money sometimes didn't even make the list. Even though Quicken for DOS still generated Intuit's largest unit and dollar sales, Intuit understood the strategic importance of beating Microsoft on the Windows platform.

Intuit continued to increase customer devotion. As the company released Quicken for Windows, Tim Villanueva perfected the one original feature that Microsoft had done better than Intuit: Money's "SmartFill," its feature that automatically filled in a field based on what customers had previously entered. Villanueva completed Intuit's version of the new feature by December, and Intuit decided to invest a little more in customer goodwill: about $2 million more. Intuit put QuickFill along with a few necessary but minor bug fixes into a Quicken for Windows release 1.01 and created a customer care mailer.

In January 1992, every registered customer received a free copy of the new version, a newsletter with tips and tricks, and special offers. In the 1.01 release, Intuit also addressed Windows 3.1 compatibility. By then, the company already had about three hundred thousand Windows customers, and the $2 million spent on the mailing consumed a large percentage of an $80 million revenue year. Customer satisfaction, however, climbed to above 90 percent in the "very" or "somewhat satisfied" categories, and the company deemed the expenditure a worthwhile investment in customer goodwill—another example of "under-promise and over-deliver."

Partway into the 1992 selling season, Intuit raised the distributor price for Quicken for Windows to $22 and later to $30 (at parity to Quicken for DOS), but the price increases did not stop Quicken's sales lead. At an all-employee meeting Cook made a point that became widely quoted: "At Intuit, five hundred people are totally devoted to personal finance software. But personal finance isn't Microsoft's sole focus. You can have confidence that we're going to listen better, work harder, and understand customers more. Against Microsoft, it's a battle to the end forever. We've got to keep moving forward."[15]

After the Quicken for Windows release, Intuit commissioned a package design research study of Quicken and Money. The results encouraged Intuit: The "Microsoft Money" name was good, but its bland blue packaging, awful. Observed Baker, "They could have beaten us in the market, but their version 1.0 products and marketing are never that great."[16] Quicken's packaging, refined through years of research conducted on actual shelves at stores and on mocked-up shelves in research labs, acted as a stop sign to capture consumers' attention and persuade them to pick up the box. The benefits-oriented copy on the back of the package worked to convince customers to buy.

Baker also initiated Quicken versus Money comparative usability testing. The studies measured the number of steps each program used to complete specific tasks, as well as the number of people who gave up on tasks. Intuit concluded from the research that Money had a lower error rate on ease-of-getting started, so the Quicken team worked to improve in that area. However, Quicken rated higher on ease-of-use for the things that people need to do frequently when managing their money, like writing checks and balancing check registers.

Armed with this knowledge, company executives went out on PR tours and did side-by-side comparisons with Money, showing the press that Money was not as feature-rich or well designed. "It would have been easy to be smug because our market share was so much greater," product manager Jacqueline Maartense said. "One month Money's market share was *negative* due to returns! But we didn't want to get lazy about it. 'Microsoft usually gets it right by version 3.0,' Mari often said, to keep our healthy fear alive."[17]

Indeed, Intuit did not rest on its laurels. Steve Katz, the company's sales director, hit another retail home run in the spring of 1992. He worked out a promotion with two large software distributors, Ingram Micro and Merisel, in which Intuit gave Quicken away to customers who purchased the new Windows 3.1 release. It was the hottest promotion in the industry, and, according to Katz, "my happiest moment at Intuit."[18]

Beating Microsoft Money was a triumph. From the launch party at a local comedy club, where product manager Maartense stomped on a box of Microsoft Money to the fervent cheers of Intuit employees, to the monthly sales numbers where Quicken consistently ranked first, the triumph over Microsoft intoxicated the company. Employees cheered to charts created by marketing showing Quicken for Windows, Quicken for DOS, Quicken for Mac, and even Quicken for the Apple II dramatically out-selling Money. Engineering produced a widely circulated Micro-soft Money box that they doctored to say "Mo' than 5 copies sold!!" Some months the only version of Quicken that Microsoft beat was Quicken for DeskMate.

On the strength of Quicken's success, Intuit became one of the most successful consumer software companies in the industry. Other companies came calling because they wanted to do pro-motions and deals with the market share leader. Intuit had truly "arrived," and even Microsoft acknowledged it: "Intuit has done a really fine job establishing the category. They have huge name recognition," acknowledged Charlotte Guyman, director of mar-keting for Microsoft's consumer division, in a *Los Angeles Times* arti-cle. More ominously, she continued, "We're realistic about how long it takes (to gain a foothold), but we're definitely committed."[19]

In the same interview, Guyman told the *LA Times* that Microsoft would have to be more Intuit-like to compete success-fully in consumer markets: "It's a different design process for us. It requires much greater dialogue upfront with our customers. It's a challenge for us to sell low-price-point products."[20]

The *LA Times* article credited Cook's fanaticism about re-search for Intuit's success: "Good data are the cornerstones of his management philosophy, which stresses the need to make deci-sions based on information, not on rank. He sketches an organi-zational structure in which the senior executives are not at the top of a pyramid, but rather at the center of a circle."[21]

"In a truly consumer-driven company," Cook told the *LA Times,* "decisions are based on data, so the person with the best data wins."[22]

For Eric Dunn it wasn't the *LA Times* article that signaled the new era at hand: "The moment I really realized that we were doing well was when Walt Mossberg wrote about us in the *Wall Street Journal* and said that Quicken was better than Money. Driving in to work after reading the *Journal,* I was on cloud nine. It was one of the highest points in my whole life."[23]

But one group remained aloof from the giddiness, isolated from the victory. Intuit's small business product development team struggled, and Dunn had just heard a rumor that Microsoft was about to release a business accounting package called Profit. How could Intuit ensure the same success against Microsoft in the small business accounting market as it had just achieved with Quicken in the consumer market?

CHAPTER 9

SIMPLE IS HARD

S mall businesses had first registered on Intuit's radar in 1985, but the company overlooked these customers for years. In Intuit's first survey of customer satisfaction, Tom LeFevre had included demographic questions—ages, incomes, and whether buyers were using Quicken for home finances, business finances, or both. Although 48 percent of customers answered, "Business or both," he and Scott Cook mistakenly dismissed this as a research glitch. The odd result just couldn't be true; Quicken's product and marketing had focused on personal finance consumers down to the garish bright orange color used on the package.

After Intuit launched Quicken for the Macintosh three years later, LeFevre commissioned a subsequent survey, and the "business or both" share proved to be no glitch: it registered again, at 49 percent. "This is beginning to bother me," Cook told LeFevre. "I wonder why businesses are using a home checkbook product?" The product contained a few small business features, but Cook was puzzled to discover how popular Quicken had apparently become in that market. "When you think about it, it makes sense," reasoned LeFevre. "Most small businesses are very small or even home-based. Their accounting needs are not that different from the accounting needs of households."[1]

Later in 1988, Cook's old business school friend, Peter Wendell, introduced Cook to entrepreneur Ridge Evers; Wendell and

Evers had become acquainted while picking up their children from a playgroup. Though Evers had never taken a software course in college, he told Cook about the business accounting program he had created. Resourceful Evers had written software programs since he was fifteen. "I hate accounting with a passion," he said, "so I taught the computer to do it for me."[2] Cook decided that Evers might be able to make Quicken even more appealing to Intuit's business customers.

Evers, a trim forty-one-year-old with wire-rim glasses and wavy graying hair, sported an affable charm and an intense, passionate manner. His deep laugh often roared down the hallways. Evers had a Stanford M.B.A. and many interests, including an olive orchard in Sonoma Valley with twenty-five hundred trees imported from Italy to make high-quality olive oil.

Cook did an impromptu phone survey of over a dozen Quicken business users and became intrigued with those users' descriptions of using Quicken to manage their businesses. And so, Cook asked Evers to work part-time to add more business features for these customers, including payroll, accounts payable, and business reports. Evers agreed, but said later, "Since I knew about business accounting, my personal goal from the start was to do a separate accounting program for Intuit. My putative goal was to create modules to attach to Quicken. I called the module approach perfuming a pig."[3]

Meanwhile, Cook had hired Sam Klepper in 1989 to help scope out Intuit's next big product, and, still intrigued by the survey results, he focused Klepper on developing an overall vision for small business. Klepper, a friendly, eager young man in his mid-twenties, began his research by obtaining a list of local small businesses from the Palo Alto Chamber of Commerce. He then phoned a sample of them, asking realtors, accountants, restaurant managers, and others about their current accounting practices. He asked questions like, "How do you do bookkeeping? What's frustrating about it? Is bookkeeping important to your business?"

Since he spoke to only a dozen or so people, his results were preliminary, but Klepper believed that a larger, quantitative study with hundreds of survey respondents would confirm his initial findings: Small business owners hated bookkeeping. Their three most critical tasks were payroll, invoicing, and paying bills, and they almost always kept their books by hand. They wanted to save time on bookkeeping, but existing accounting software only complicated the task.

Bookkeeping had not changed in nearly five hundred years; the Italian priest Pacioli had first described the double-entry book-keeping system in 1494.[4] Double-entry bookkeeping used complicated layers of records: transactions, then ledgers, and then trial balances. Contemporary software companies in the early 1990s based their programs on this complex accounting scheme—using debits, credits, double ledgers, posts, and closes. But Klepper's first study suggested this rigid and nonintuitive approach frustrated business owners.

To confirm his initial research, Klepper commissioned a national survey to determine exactly how much time and money small businesses spent on accounting. Klepper examined business owners' complaints about accounting and searched in particular for bookkeeping tasks that were costly and frustrating, as these would be the areas most appealing to customers seeking help. Invoicing and payroll met those two criteria.

The national survey results validated Klepper's initial findings. The research showed that most businesses were tiny: 85 percent of the ones surveyed had fewer than twenty employees, and 98 percent fewer than one hundred. These small businesses had no room on their payrolls for a trained accountant. Instead, the owner, the owner's spouse, or an office manager kept the books. This person had never taken accounting in school, didn't know a debit from a credit, and didn't want to learn.

Klepper presented these results to Cook and John Monson, and the divergence between what small businesses wanted and what business accounting software offered immediately struck them. Cook and Monson realized that the frustrations of managing small business finances closely resembled those of managing house-hold finances. Therefore, Intuit could take the same approach to helping small businesses that it had taken so successfully with Quicken.

"We are wrong about accounting," Monson told Klepper. "The best way for many small businesses to keep books is not by accounting—they *hate* accounting—but by Quicken."[5] Indeed, many businesses already used Quicken because its simple approach of automating routine tasks easily solved most business accounting problems—without those messy debits and credits.

This fundamental insight about what small business owners wanted caused a shift in considering how Intuit might meet businesses' accounting needs. Intuit's relentless consumer focus had blinded the company to a huge potential market. The company shouldn't just sell to consumers; it should have businesses right at the heart of its prospective customer list.

But how could Intuit best reach that largely untargeted business market? Cook wanted to add more business-oriented modules to Quicken. This, he believed, would be cheap, easy, and effective for current Quicken business customers—and it was already under way, with Evers' efforts. In contrast, Tom Proulx wanted to design a separate business-focused program to offer what small business owners wanted. A second, independent product would not only meet businesses' needs better, Proulx reasoned, but would also help Intuit become a more robust two-product company.

Evers had always favored the latter alternative. He argued that adding modules to Quicken would eventually lessen that product's appeal to its core market. "A software program can only take a certain amount of space—if you try to raise the ceiling at a certain point you bring the floor up to it. Quicken today is accessible to a broad range of people, but should Quicken be the cornerstone of everything?"[6]

Evers enlisted Klepper to lobby for the separate program approach and, with Proulx's support, convinced Cook and the rest of Intuit's leadership. The executive team, planning to leverage Evers' work as well as the Quicken 3.0 for DOS code base, authorized the development of a small business bookkeeping product, code-named "Snoopy" after the Peanuts character. And so, Intuit officially kicked off its small business product development in spring 1990.

KEEP IT SIMPLE

The Snoopy development team's organization reflected the pattern established by Mari Baker and Eric Dunn. Klepper served as marketing product manager, and Evers led engineering project development. Klepper channeled the voice of the customer, handled marketing, and acted as the product's business manager; and Evers, like Dunn combining the role of architect and team leader, moved the entire engineering team into a giant cubicle and allocated development tasks among four engineers.

Klepper and Evers, however, differed significantly from Baker and Dunn. Neither had worked together before, and neither had managed project teams. While Klepper's dogged intelligence helped Intuit analyze the small business opportunity, his background in consulting had not prepared him for developing a new software product. And Evers' enthusiasm for features and programming differed from Dunn's relentless pragmatism and prolific programming capability.

Intuit's previously successful model for product development had depended on experienced team leaders, and the company found it difficult to carbon copy that model. Team effectiveness weakened as the company launched multiple projects simultaneously with less experienced staff leading projects. The individual achievements of workhorses Proulx, Dunn, and Baker that carried early product development did not translate into systemic development success for other employees; Intuit could not sustain the lone ranger product development model of the past as the company grew larger and more complex.

Proulx, inexperienced at leading large teams, had established few standard processes that would work across multiple teams:

Intuit had no standard testing for QA; no documented release processes; no formal project management training. Engineering standard processes had not progressed beyond the company's bugs database. This lack of processes exacerbated Evers' and Klepper's relative inexperience; beyond informal interactions, the two had little organizational structure to rely on.

Still, the small business team had faith that it was getting the product right. Using Klepper's research, the team analyzed the most common business tasks and planned to make those jobs easy to do with their software. In Quicken, checks looked like paper checks, and its register looked like a paper check register. The small business team extended that concept to the things businesses needed: invoices would look like invoices, payments like receipts. The Quicken team's founding idea became the small business team's mantra: use forms, terminology, and metaphors that people already understand—instead of complicated accounting concepts that they don't—and people will love the product.

Because business customers needed useful information about their finances in a format they could comfortably and credibly share with banks, accountants, or lawyers, the team also focused on creating useful reports. Business financial information needed to be reliably accurate, and so the small business program would carefully track assets, liabilities, and income statement accounts and would create clear reports containing this information.

Navigation in the business product would be as intuitive as in Quicken. But the Intuit product would have the fewest features of any business accounting software on the market—no inventory, audit trails, calculation of finance charges, or point-of-sale accounting. For many businesses, this simplicity would provide a breakthrough in bookkeeping.

THE ELEPHANT IN THE ROOM

Despite its intended straightforwardness, project Snoopy encountered problems from the start. Making accounting simple turned out to be quite difficult. Evers told the executive committee that he estimated completion of the small business project in nine months, but later observed wryly, "We were correct in identifying the incubation as the gestation period of a mammal, we just got the species wrong—it was closer to an elephant [twenty-one months]."[7]

While Evers was initially excited to have access to the Quicken 3.0 for DOS code as a basis for Snoopy, he came to feel differently. Dunn had had to write Quicken 3.0 extremely quickly. His code was written for expediency rather than for clarity for engineers who might modify the code after him. Working alone or with a few familiar colleagues, he had not always used constant names and had written little documentation, keeping most of it in his brain. Only partly joking, Evers complained, "Eric, if 'Name 0 = 2,' then 'reformat hard drive' is not a productive command." The Quicken code was thus very difficult to extend, but once the team had begun by modifying the Quicken code, they felt they had to finish that way. "You always think," observed Evers, "that you're too close to the end to go back."[8]

Evers' entrepreneurial nature also complicated the team's job. Expectations for the product—from the company and from prospective customers—led the team to "feature creep." Though simplicity remained Snoopy's fundamental premise, Evers' enthusiasm for additional functions made it the most complicated software program Intuit had ever developed. Evers' continual stream of new ideas made the product definition a moving target, which meant the team blew one deadline after another.

The small business team also forgot a fundamental Intuit rule: "We are not our customer." Rather than focusing on the few tasks that most customers required, Evers, enthusiastic and strong-willed, found dozens of interesting features that he personally wanted to include in the product. Klepper could not resist Evers' infectious determination, and so the development team staggered under its impetuous leader's desire to make Intuit's small business offering the best possible.

As Jane Boutelle, an Intuit marketing manager, put it: "Most of the initial prospects were Quicken customers and their expectations were very high. There's quite a tug between wanting the product to be perfect (like Quicken, but better) but realizing at some point the team has to get the product out in the market. Ridge is a brilliant guy with so much vision. But he's not at all reined in."[9]

Despite Klepper's qualms about the length of product development, the young and inexperienced product manager could not force the team or its wayward leader to finish the product. Proulx, Evers' boss, also found it difficult to manage the fiery maverick. And as the rest of Intuit focused seriously on the Microsoft threat to Quicken, the Snoopy engineers became orphans, a small island of struggle amid a sea of company attention and effort directed toward Quicken for Windows.

As the initial Snoopy launch date passed with no sign of development wrapping up its work, Klepper came across a new software product called QuickPay, the brainchild of an individual developer named Mike Potter. The Intuit developers who reviewed Potter's product ironically conceded that Potter had done an outstanding job of hacking the Quicken code to add payroll functions. Evers had never completed the payroll module that he had joined Intuit to create, and so, as a way to appeal to businesses while the company worked to complete Snoopy, Intuit decided to license and release QuickPay.

Intuit engineering resisted QuickPay. Some resented Potter's windfall for an easy little add-on; they felt that their development efforts, which didn't result in any royalties, ranked higher in strategic importance to the company. Others hesitated to use code not developed at Intuit as a basis for an Intuit product, as Intuit had never before released a program "not created here." Nevertheless, Klepper, Monson, and Dunn persevered with negotiations and struck a deal with Potter.

Klepper and Monson scrambled to create packaging and marketing for the new product. Mike Potter earned a tidy sum, about $600,000 over four years, and Intuit introduced its payroll add-on to Quicken in May 1991, months earlier than if it had waited for Snoopy.

QuickPay, retailing for $59.95, shot onto *PC Magazine*'s top ten sellers list. The product kept lists of employee information like salaries, commissions, hourly wages, deductions, and exemptions. It also calculated federal, state, and local withholding taxes, union dues, Social Security and Medicare deductions, and other deductions defined by the user. High margins, low marketing costs, and rapid sales soon convinced everyone at Intuit to accept the buy (versus make) approach.

QuickPay included a subscription service that generated significant recurring revenues for Intuit. Potter had designed an option allowing business owners who bought QuickPay to acquire a tax table update every year to ensure that the tax rates used for calculating payroll deductions were accurate. Intuit initially charged $19.95 annually for this update. Almost every active user subscribed, but Intuit paid little to acquire the information contained in the tables, making the tax table service extremely profitable.

By mid 1991, with the inevitable distractions created by the licensing of QuickPay and the boundless feature enthusiasm of its leaders, Snoopy fell more than a year behind schedule. The project team felt demoralized and frustrated. The company's triumph over Microsoft in personal finance exacerbated the small business team's dysfunction. Arguments broke out among engineers and marketing, and the strain of trying to finish the project increased. Some team members began to doubt that they would ever successfully launch the small business product.

INTRODUCING QUICKBOOKS

As the product's release date slipped further, the team narrowed Snoopy's final feature list. The drive for product features transformed into a drive to finish the product as quickly as possible.

In late summer 1991, Klepper held a naming contest among Intuit employees to solicit clever names for the new product.

Engineer Eric Shenk won with the name "QuickBooks." Once senior management approved the product's name, marketing began creating its logo, packaging, advertising, and public relations launch plans. The team moved a tiny step closer toward launch.

Then, in fall 1991, Sam Klepper left Intuit to attend Harvard Business School. Klepper was fulfilling a long-postponed personal dream, but the team, which had become accustomed to Klepper's engaging style, suffered. Jane Boutelle became the next QuickBooks product manager, and she rushed to arrange the product's beta testing, which continued engineering delays had made difficult to schedule. Boutelle also created a marketing communications campaign for the QuickBooks launch and approved the final package and logo designs as the team struggled to complete a successful beta version.

QuickBooks' positioning messages differed from Quicken's because Boutelle realized that business owners felt differently about business finances than consumers felt about personal finance. Quicken's advertising contained an aspect of fun and excitement, a little bit of playfulness that would be jarring for business finances. Instead of fun, QuickBooks advertising emphasized that the software made easier a business task that people simply had to do.

Yet this ease created its own kind of joy. With QuickBooks, users did not need traditional double-entry accounting because calculation errors disappeared. A user could query his database and generate reports without any transaction posting requirements. QuickBooks represented an enormous increase in ease-of-use over traditional accounting programs. The QuickBooks marketing team worked to convey that business owners could do "real" double-entry accounting with their single-entry system that used plain English, not accounting jargon.

The marketing team designed two print advertisements before launch. One, a copy-intensive one-page piece, sold Quick-Books primarily to Quicken users by emphasizing its benefits and detailing its features. Cook and Monson patched together the copy for this ad in an airport. The other ad represented a departure for Intuit: to emphasize QuickBooks' difference from other accounting software, Monson approved a vividly-colored green and purple two-page ad in a mock *National Enquirer*-style layout featuring a bald lady who had pulled out all her hair trying to do accounting (see figure 9-1).

Cook also helped create the QuickBooks packaging. The team wanted to build on Quicken and its brand name but also wanted to differentiate QuickBooks, a difficult balancing act. QuickBooks' dark-green packaging and more professional look contrasted with Quicken's eye-catching red logo and large green dollar sign. The QuickBooks package used a slimmer font and set a more serious tone with its front package photograph of reports and invoices. The team revived the package flap on the box once

FIGURE 9 - 1

QuickBooks' launch ad featured a screaming bald lady with a mock National Enquirer *style headline, the worst performing Intuit ad ever.*

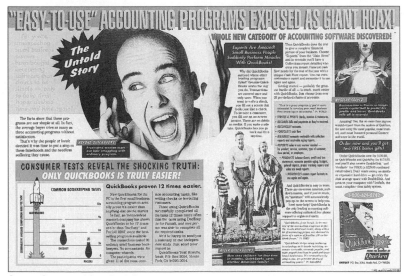

Source: Courtesy of Jane Boutelle.

used on Quicken's packaging to add more information to persuade shoppers who picked up a box to buy the software.

Cook vetoed a suggestion to use a dollar sign ($) for the s in the QuickBooks name as "too cheesy." Just before the launch Cook had a brain flash and pushed for calling the product "Quicken QuickBooks"; the team, believing that the name QuickBooks already linked the two products elegantly, overruled him. However, the team agreed to put a small Quicken logo on the QuickBooks package to ensure that customers understood the product's affiliation with Quicken.

Quicken had a suggested retail price of $59.95 with an actual street price of about $29.95 at retail stores. The leading business accounting program before QuickBooks' introduction, DACEasy by DAC out of Dallas, Texas, cost only $49.95, but several other business software products cost $130 or more.[10] Intuit's suggested retail price for QuickBooks was $139.95, resulting in a street price of about $89.95. Intuit positioned QuickBooks as a more robust and valuable product for small business owners who were, Intuit believed, willing to pay more than consumers.

Boutelle was pregnant, and departed for maternity leave in early 1992. She continued to oversee product management, hiring a consultant to function as her arms and legs while she stayed home with her new child and Intuit searched for someone to replace her. The product team completed its rushed QA testing in March 1992.

Intuit finally launched QuickBooks in April 1992. The long development death march had ended, and the company awaited the influx of sales reports.

Initially elated by the release, the QuickBooks team soon grew concerned about the number of technical support calls that QuickBooks engendered. As much as this unexpected trend worried the team, the rising number of calls complaining that QuickBooks had lost entire data sets truly alarmed them. What in the world was going on?

INDIGNATION AND INDIGESTION

As calls to technical support complaining of lost data increased, anxiety mounted. Aghast, the company realized that QuickBooks had launched with severe, data-destroying bugs. Though the bugs affected a minority of its customers, the news dismayed all of Intuit. The company had waited months for its new small business product, and now the team responsible for the delay had launched a product with serious flaws.

Hundreds of QuickBooks customers called in, truly irate. Many had lost critical invoice and receivable data and didn't know who owed them what. Some had to go without access to their accounting information for days on end while Intuit engineers struggled to solve the problems. Instead of building the Quick-Books business and moving it forward, Intuit had to focus on cleaning up the mess.

Intuit's concern about the QuickBooks launch increased as another, uncharacteristic blunder came to light: QuickBooks' initial ad campaign bombed. Customers told Intuit they liked the product's packaging, but not its first two advertisements. The single-page QuickBooks ad successfully converted only a few Quicken users; few non-Quicken users saw its appeal. The two-page bald lady ad fared far worse. Intuit ran that ad in *PC Magazine* with a circulation of one million readers and received only four orders. This lack of response stunned Intuit management; the company had never before experienced such an outright marketing failure.

Monson acknowledged, "The QuickBooks 'bald lady' ad is terrible. The hard part is that we can't say that QuickBooks is easy because no one will believe it. In the small business space, everyone is skeptical. We're trying to convey that QuickBooks has fundamentally redefined accounting software, but the bald lady ad has failed."[11] Cook wondered whether Intuit might have received more responses by running blank pages with only Intuit's 800-number, and the chagrined marketing team resolved to stick to Intuit's tried and true, trial and error approach for future ads.

Intuit marketing could fix the QuickBooks advertising problem, but the technical crisis remained. At the heart of the maelstrom, a newly hired employee struggled to overcome the QuickBooks disaster. Jay O'Connor, son of Supreme Court Justice Sandra Day O'Connor, began working as QuickBooks' new product manager in June 1992. During O'Connor's interview, Evers had acknowledged that QuickBooks had a bug, but the severity of the crisis stunned O'Connor when he arrived at Intuit.

O'Connor, thirty-years old and a newly minted Harvard M.B.A., brought an analytical mind and a perfectionist's approach to his new job. Growing up in a family of lawyers, O'Connor had learned how to debate an issue vigorously from multiple angles. O'Connor began working furiously to help solve the disaster. "Basically," Cook told him, "events like this can really cripple a business. If our first face to the customer is so compromised, we may never recover."[12]

Intuit's exhausted product team quickly figured out how to fix the bug but didn't immediately know how to repair corrupted data files. Unable to correct the software's error in one step, the engineers were forced to develop a phased strategy. Because Intuit required customer registration of QuickBooks within fifteen sessions or else the program stopped working, the company had accurate records of its customers' names and locations. The first step in fixing the problem was sending disks to all these customers to halt any new data-damaging transactions.

Drawing on its "Do right by customers" mantra, the company then addressed customers' damaged data. This painful repair involved deleting all infected transactions. The deleted records had to be reentered by hand, and some customers had many hundreds of impacted transactions. Intuit knew the bug affected only 5 to 10 percent of its customers, but it could not identify which 5 or 10 percent. So, the company announced that all customers could hire temps to reenter their transactions and Intuit would reimburse them for the cost. And Intuit's data recovery team grew to about twenty people.

As it had in earlier bug situations, Intuit bent over backward to help its customers. The company spoke frankly about the bug and accepted responsibility. In addition to the data recovery experts, Intuit hired forty tech support reps within a week and swiftly trained them all to answer the most urgent question from customers: "Where the heck is my QuickBooks data?" In all, Intuit spent more than $1 million to shore up technical support during the crisis.

QuickBooks marked the first company crisis in which, as much as Intuit employees wanted to pitch in and help, Quick-Books' complicated accounting and technical support barred them from doing so effectively. Gone were the days where the entire staff could answer technical support calls. Intuit had to rely on accounting experts to answer questions, whether related to the bug or to the program itself. For the first time in company history, talented generalists devoted to customers could not solve customer problems. Suddenly, *accounting* experts were what the company needed most. Accounting temps and independent contractors flooded in, driving up costs.

Over time, customer indignation lessened. The customers affected by the bug received the corrected program and, with or without Intuit's help, reentered their corrupted transactions. After the crisis passed, O'Connor surveyed customers. To his relief, he found that customers had very high satisfaction with Intuit; satisfaction had actually increased after this episode. Users told Intuit that the company had gone far beyond the call of duty; they had been treated professionally and appreciated the attention.

"During the crisis, senior management realized the seriousness of the situation," O'Connor observed. "Our set of very clear values determined our response: 'Do right by customers.' I had only just come into the company but I felt that value throughout the direction set by the senior managers. If you know that treating customers right is paramount, you can act on that."[13] This praise-worthy attitude, however, was not without cost.

For six months, QuickBooks team members spent the majority of their time cleaning up the QuickBooks bugs. Knowing that the problems cost customers real pain and Intuit lots of money and distraction increased the team's stress. Lamented O'Connor: "We had all been inculcated with the idea that our job was to delight customers, and here, instead of delighting all our customers, we had caused a chunk of them serious hassles."[14] The bug deeply affected morale on the QuickBooks team.

Despite the well-publicized problems with QuickBooks and the struggles of the QuickBooks team, the program gratified Intuit by debuting at number one in the business accounting software category, a position it has held ever since. In 1992 alone, the business accounting software category grew by more than 50 percent, and QuickBooks fueled 80 percent of that growth.[15] The overwhelming benefits of QuickBooks' shift to easier small business accounting overcame its development mistakes and launch missteps.

Quicken customers purchased slightly more than half the QuickBooks copies initially sold. Evers had cleverly designed QuickBooks to accept data seamlessly from Quicken data sets, so Quicken's installed base fueled sales. Intuit's retail relationships also paid off. Retailers, enamored of Quicken, recommended QuickBooks to customers. Intuit repeated its Quicken for Windows strategy and sent out an upgrade mailing that drove its customers to retail stores. Intuit targeted Quicken toward businesses with one to five employees, and QuickBooks toward businesses with one to twenty. Retailers recommended both solutions.

As the bug crisis passed, Intuit began testing new advertising. Eventually, Intuit discovered through experimentation that its most effective QuickBooks ads contained testimonials from customers. These ads featured pictures of real customers with quotes like, "Super-quick! A butt-kicking program! About time! Amen!" and "Easy! I haven't used the manual since I installed it!"[16] Not only did these ads perform well at generating direct sales, they also captured the rabid customer enthusiasm behind the product's success.

Even though the QuickBooks team dealt effectively with the embarrassing program bugs, and the product sold well, Intuit reeled under the continuing costs associated with fixing the bugs and handling QuickBooks' increased technical service demands. Even after Intuit fixed the bugs, the costs for supporting Quick-Books ran three to five times higher than costs for supporting Quicken. Longer and more numerous than forecasted, Quick-Books support calls severely impacted profitability.

The company grew rapidly with annual revenues of $80 million and 425 employees in the fall of 1992. But as a senior executive handed out profit-sharing checks at a quarterly meeting, he observed that the checks would have been much higher but for the million-dollar fix of the QuickBooks bug. The chastened QuickBooks team remained the underdog in the still very Quicken-centric Intuit.

It was then that Dunn heard the ominous intelligence that Microsoft was working on a Windows-based small business accounting product.

CHAPTER 10

PLAYING IN THE BIG LEAGUES

When Intuit heard rumors of Microsoft's intent to enter the small business accounting market, the company knew it needed to react quickly. But the QuickBooks competition with Microsoft differed from the battle over Quicken. First, QuickBooks' small volume relative to Quicken's in 1993 made it less critical to Intuit overall. Second, Intuit learned that an outside software company, Great Plains Software of Fargo, North Dakota, a specialist in higher-end business software, had created Microsoft's upcoming release, Microsoft Profit. Scott Cook was convinced that a Great Plains solution would rely heavily on difficult double-entry accounting. Nevertheless, Intuit scrambled to create a Windows version of QuickBooks, and a change in product development leadership helped the cause.

In 1991, Tom Proulx had focused intensely on the Bedrock project, but he had begun to question the project's ultimate success. While, under Eric Dunn's leadership, the Quicken 4.0 for DOS development effort had proceeded smoothly the year before, the Quicken 5.0 for DOS team struggled without Dunn— and with the continued drag of Bedrock. Beset by an overly ambitious product plan, the Quicken 5.0 team narrowly made its release date only after new engineers and Proulx himself scrambled to save the development. Facing annual releases of Quicken for DOS, Windows, and Mac and of QuickBooks for DOS, as well as the Bedrock project debacle, the product development department flailed. Proulx did not see how the engineering group could keep up with the ever-increasing demands.

Intuit's ever-growing engineering organization with its proliferation of projects did not play to Proulx's strengths. And the job of running such a large department, which had now grown to over sixty developers, testers, and technical writers, did not appeal to him. Proulx found his days consumed by endless meetings, reviews, and presentations. Other than his brief fling with the Quicken 5.0 for DOS team, Proulx felt far-removed from Intuit's products and began to dislike his job.

Always interested in other areas of the business beyond engineering, Proulx wanted to focus on something new. In particular, he sought to help Intuit identify opportunities to acquire products or companies, such as QuickPay, that would move the company forward more quickly. The biggest area of opportunity Proulx wanted to address was the tax software category. To help Intuit's bank strategy, he also wanted to lead an effort to create automatic credit card and bank statement reconciliation—a service for which he had developed a prototype in 1986. But first, he had to hire a new engineering leader.

After dozens of interviews, the executive team chose Steve Pelletier, a Harvard alumnus and experienced engineering manager, to lead engineering. The brilliant, intense Pelletier, with longish dark hair and trim beard and mustache, had worked from programmer up to chief technology officer at Interleaf of Boston. The fast-talking technologist impressed the entire company with his focus, intellect, broad product development experience, and passionate interest in Intuit's accomplishments. With the addition of Pelletier as VP of engineering, Proulx moved on to lead the new business development function for Intuit.

When Pelletier started, he held a meeting at a park near the Intuit offices, where he told the entire assembled engineering group that they should be proud of what they'd achieved at Intuit.

Pelletier, impressed by the "magic" factor at Intuit, knew that the company needed change but wanted to proceed carefully. "I had to avoid the baby and the bath water phenomenon," he said. "Intuit had been very successful—I knew the company had done lots right. Many times the bad things in an organization are a byproduct of the good. I wanted the team to remember the good things."[1]

Pelletier fretted over the often dysfunctional relationship between engineering and marketing. "What you want is impossible," engineering would tell marketing—but marketing wouldn't always heed engineering, promising features that the engineers struggled to deliver. And with its current dearth of processes, product development could not easily grow larger. The individual heroic efforts that had driven much of Intuit's development complicated further growth; engineers found building on the work of such prolific soloists as Dunn trying. "Incredible as he was," Pelletier observed, "Eric's remarkable achievements actively suppressed others' efforts, since people struggled to have the confidence to work around him."[2]

After getting more familiar with the company, Pelletier went to work. He standardized processes to make the engineering team more professional and introduced engineering mainstays such as change control, version management, QA rigor, feature teams, weekly engineering status meetings, and more systematic recruiting. These methodical practices helped the team operate efficiently and less ad hoc. Under Pelletier's leadership, Intuit began to gracefully manage multiple development projects. Pelletier also canceled the company's cross-platform Bedrock project—an unassailable mountain among many other hills to be climbed.

At the same time Pelletier focused on scaling product development, the company also hired a VP of technical support and customer service, Marsha Raulston, an experienced customer relations leader from American Airlines. Raulston added personnel, phone and computer technology, and new facilities to the customer call centers, ensuring that those critical support groups did not get left behind in the whirlwind of Intuit's radical growth.

With Raulston's leadership and training, the call center groups kept pace with Intuit's growth and increasing complexity.

AN ATTACK ON PROFIT

When, after several months at Intuit, Pelletier heard about Microsoft's upcoming entry into business accounting software, he worried that porting the problematic QuickBooks for DOS code to the Windows platform might not produce the best product. So he turned to another one of Intuit's dynamic duos for an alternate solution.

Mari Baker had recruited two friends and former colleagues, Craig Carlson and Dan Wilkes, to work as freelance engineers on the Quicken 4.0 and 5.0 for DOS teams. (Interestingly, Carlson had originally worked for his high school teacher on Home Accountant, the first popular personal finance software product and one of Quicken's early competitors.) Carlson, articulate and thoughtful, and Wilkes, shy and sharp, had created a business accounting software program sold by their former employer, Migent Software of Lake Tahoe, California. Called In-House Accountant, this Windows-based program—and Carlson's and Wilkes's dreams—had languished while Migent suffered financial difficulties.

Carlson and Wilkes, already highly respected Intuit engineers despite their short tenure as contract employees, bought the rights to In-House Accountant and marketed it from Carlson's living room while contracting for Intuit. When Pelletier began to consider QuickBooks for Windows staffing, Baker enthusiastically recommended the two engineers, knowing that they could be relied on to deliver good quality software on time and as promised. More important, their In-House Accountant program might provide a shortcut to a Windows program for business accounting.

But Pelletier had a dilemma: Did his concerns about using the QuickBooks for DOS code justify trying another approach?

Pelletier assigned two senior engineers to evaluate making Quick-Books for Windows, one analyzing what would happen if the team started with the QuickBooks for DOS code, and the other if the team started with the In-House Accountant code. Based on their reports, Pelletier concluded that In-House Accountant would provide a more robust, reliable basis for QuickBooks for Windows.

Carlson and Wilkes had cannily negotiated a significant cash royalty into their Intuit employment contracts in the event that Intuit chose to use the In-House Accountant code. CFO Dunn believed Intuit would not be well served by paying such a royalty in cash; he and Pelletier convinced Carlson and Wilkes to sell Intuit their code in exchange for valuable Intuit stock. Carlson and Wilkes then joined Intuit as regular employees.

Once Pelletier decided on the In-House Accountant code base, he assigned Carlson to manage QuickBooks for Windows' development with Jane Boutelle as marketing lead. At the same time, Evers' team upgraded QuickBooks for DOS. Intuit's small business products should continue to succeed so long as Micro-soft's entry was not too formidable.

Tall and athletic, Carlson brought solid, flexible code, strong engineering skills, clear customer understanding, and valuable people management and teamwork skills to QuickBooks for Win-dows' development. He and Baker had known each other since residing in the same freshman dorm at Stanford and the two shared a sibling-like bond. Although senior Intuit engineers were even more resistant to using the In-House Accountant code than they had initially been to QuickPay, QuickPay's success and the elegance of the In-House Accountant code eventually reconciled the team.

Under Carlson's and Boutelle's joint leadership, the Quick-Books for Windows team worked effectively to counter the new Microsoft threat. Senior management marveled at the calm, coor-dinated development and marketing activities. The QuickBooks for Windows project highlighted the improvements made by Pel-letier in the product development area as well as the talents of

Carlson and Boutelle. Despite the organized development process, Intuit management worried as Microsoft launched its Profit software months before Intuit could complete QuickBooks for Windows.

But Microsoft Profit never really got a foothold in the market. As Cook had foreseen, Profit embodied the traditional double-entry accounting Great Plains knew. Intuit exulted that the Profit team didn't get that QuickBooks' simpler paradigm better addressed customers' needs. The product generated lukewarm press references and user complaints about its sluggish performance and difficult interface.

In summer 1993, the QuickBooks product teams released the second version of QuickBooks for DOS and the first version for Windows, also called version 2.0 to signal to customers the advanced nature of the Windows release. New features introduced included improved financial reporting and QuickFill automatic data entry, which saved customers time entering transactions. Both products sold well upon release, building on the 50 percent growth experienced in the software accounting category in 1992.

In short order, Microsoft acknowledged defeat in this quarter by selling Profit back to Great Plains a year after its release. As Microsoft Executive VP Mike Maples admitted, "We were not successful at all. Profit tried to be almost too cutesy. It had a dashboard running your business with a lot of flashy colors and graphics. Small businesspeople didn't care about those things. QuickBooks captured the guy who was working from a checkbook metaphor and it was easier to get customers that way."[3]

THE RAMP-UP TO AN IPO

Though Intuit beat Microsoft a second time in the financial software area, the Redmond company's multifaceted assault on Intuit continued. Beginning in 1992, Intuit and Microsoft fought a heated battle over which personal finance software would be pre-loaded onto home PCs. For both companies, the burgeoning original equipment manufacturers' (OEM) channel provided an irresistible new customer acquisition opportunity.

Computer manufacturers found that offering valuable free software already installed on their machines attracted customers. Since many wanted to use their new computers to help manage finances, Quicken and Money were natural fits. Intuit first pursued the OEM channel with Quicken for Windows as a defensive move to keep Microsoft from loading Money on all PCs sold.

But Microsoft's DOS and Windows agreements with PC manufacturers gave it a head start in negotiating to lock up the OEM market. In response, Intuit developed a stripped-down version of Quicken, Quicken Special Edition, for the OEM market. It contained the key features that drove customer satisfaction in early use.

Creating the Special Edition was only Intuit's first salvo. The marketing group analyzed customer lifetime values and argued that Intuit should be willing to pay PC manufacturers to preload Quicken on machines because eventual upgrade and supplies purchases made customers profitable, despite cannibalization. In the three years from 1991 to 1994, Intuit dropped its OEM version price to PC manufacturers from $7 to just over $1 per copy.

Though the virtual giveaway of the software made many at Intuit queasy, the company regarded its OEM strategy as an essential defensive move against Microsoft. Once customers used and liked a finance software product, Intuit reasoned, they would have little reason to switch and, it was hoped, would eventually buy upgrades, paper checks, automated services, and QuickBooks.

The OEM battles eventually stabilized with both Microsoft and Intuit preloading their software on about 40 percent of all home PCs sold. OEM deals became a leading source of new customers for the company.

As Intuit's attempts to own its domestic markets succeeded, the company's international efforts, seen as another essential part of the company's strategy, gained momentum. Dunn had established a small U.K. office in early 1992, which had successfully launched Quicken 6.0 for DOS in the United Kingdom in the fall of that year. But when Microsoft Money's 2.0 launch announcement in 1992 touted Microsoft as the first U.S. company to release personal finance software in France, Germany, the United Kingdom, and Canada, Intuit knew it had to catch up.[4]

In March 1993, British citizen and product manager Roger Bass launched Intuit's German operation in Munich. Bass set out to create a more localized version of Quicken than Microsoft had introduced there—Microsoft's Money product had infamously shipped with U.S. checks, infuriating the German press. After Germany, Bass moved on to France to open another office. Intuit's initial successes in the United Kingdom and Germany encouraged executives, and the company envisioned huge successes from these international software efforts even though the European market's financial complexities strained Intuit's developmental resources both internationally and at home. For example, German consumers did not use checks to make payments as often as they used authorized bank transfers between accounts. Sales results confirmed Intuit's optimism: Wherever Intuit launched, Quicken almost immediately outsold Money despite Microsoft's superior international distribution system.

Domestically, Quicken product development continued on the annual fall release cycle that Proulx and Dunn had established. In the fall of 1992, Intuit successfully launched new versions of Quicken for the DOS, Windows, and Mac platforms. Pelletier's leadership ensured that the company achieved its annual multiple version introductions.

However, despite Pelletier's new processes, Quicken 2.0 for Windows contained a serious running balance bug that incorrectly calculated checkbook balances for some users. Had it followed its past model, Intuit would have automatically provided a new release to all registered users, not just to those who requested the product fix. The estimated cost to send new diskettes to all users exceeded $1 million.

For the first time, Intuit managers, led by the experienced Pelletier, balked. The cost would devastate Intuit's bottom line—and thus jeopardize the company's potential initial public offering (IPO). Despite the possible hit to customer satisfaction, Intuit management decided not to send a new release to all users, instead responding only to customer complaints. This shift in policy, weighing the economics as carefully as the customer satisfaction outcomes, became Intuit's new standard in addressing software bugs.

Pelletier strongly advocated a dollars and cents approach to business decisions. In Intuit's early years, engineering had fixed almost all the product bugs they learned about—even those unlikely to impact customers—as a matter of policy. Under Pelletier, engineering analyzed the impact of a bug on users and weighed the benefit of the fix against both its cost and the risk that fixing the bug would create more problems. While this line of thinking made practical sense, some engineers felt that the tradition of "doing right by customers" suffered.

The company's transition from pleasing customers at all costs to pleasing customers within reason—and counting costs—foreshadowed its becoming a public company. Like many other software executives, Cook had always hoped to offer Intuit stock for public trading even though he worried about the possible effects of a Wall Street orientation on Intuit's culture. Though he and the executive team had briefly debated going public when they'd looked for financing in 1990 and again in mid-1992, they had decided that Intuit at that time lacked the track record and discipline needed for consistent public success.

Now, with multiple successful products, an international strategy, a strong senior management team, and a full-time (finally) CFO in Eric Dunn, Cook and Proulx believed that circumstances favored an Intuit IPO. Intuit had proved it was more than just a one-hit wonder, and 1992 finished strong for the company. All the products that Intuit had released performed well with at least a 75 percent market share, and all garnered industry awards and favorable reviews. Intuit products accounted for half of the top ten productivity applications on *PC Computing*'s and *Computer Reseller News*' best-seller lists. And the QuickBooks team celebrated when the product received *PC Magazine*'s prestigious Editor's Choice and Best of 1992 awards. The company's revenues and profits had increased steadily and reliably every quarter for the last five years. Intuit finished 1992 poised and ready to pull the trigger on its own IPO.

CHAPTER 11

GETTING THE PUCK ON THE ICE

Every Silicon Valley entrepreneur dreams of selling his or her company's stock in a public offering. Intuit executives had weighed taking this momentous step for more than two years. In early 1993, Tom Proulx, who had urged the company to hold its private financing round in 1990, believed the time had come to secure more liquidity for the company and its senior officers. Going public would create a new form of currency to acquire other companies, and Proulx knew this was the best way for Intuit to get into the tax software business. With Scott Cook's support, the Intuit board decided in January that Intuit should become a public company. Using his well-known Silicon Valley phrase, board member John Doerr put it, "Let's get the puck on the ice."[1]

To ready the company for this eventuality, CFO Eric Dunn had been running the company's books, for the prior two years, as though Intuit were already public. He, Cook, and Proulx had felt that Intuit would benefit from practicing the discipline required by the financial markets. Since the company's finances glowed, the management team prepared for its IPO by generating the required documents and creating the traditional "road show" presentation for investment houses.

Since 1990, investment bankers had wooed Intuit management for a chance to take the company public. Board members

Doerr and Burt McMurtry had helped many other companies go public and advised Intuit to hire Morgan Stanley as the lead investment banker for the transaction. The other leading investment bank of the time, Goldman Sachs, was Microsoft's banker and a Redmond partisan. After meeting the Morgan Stanley team, Intuit adopted the recommendation.

Once Intuit formed its IPO team, the company swept up their Morgan Stanley representatives into an orgy of documentation preparation. Proulx and Dunn, back to working ferociously long hours in tandem, created a draft of the materials necessary for the IPO in only two weeks; the fact that Intuit was financially "clean"—with a simple capital structure, no litigation, and no significant acquisitions—helped streamline the effort.

Once Dunn and Proulx finished the initial draft of Intuit's prospectus, they moved into the edit phase. Confounding their attorney and the Morgan Stanley bankers, Intuit shattered arcane traditions and innovated the revision process. Instead of sitting around a conference table, marking changes on a master copy by hand, the clever duo insisted on editing the documentation interactively, using laptops and projectors. Later, the Morgan Stanley bankers told Dunn that Intuit's progression from decision to go public to first trading day (fifty-nine days total) was the fastest they had ever seen.

Intuit's prospectus reflected its usual under-promise and over-deliver philosophy. The company's profit ratio amounted to an unimpressive 10 percent of revenues pretax in fiscal 1992, though profitability had increased by January 1993. Dunn did not want Intuit to go public facing unrealistic profit expectations. So the company's prospectus said profitability might fall even lower because of money invested in international markets, automated financial services, and launching QuickBooks.

When Morgan Stanley lead banker Frank Quattrone saw the unimpressive projections, he reacted negatively. "I thought you were supposed to be an emerging growth company—not a submerging growth company," he growled.[2] At the risk of a lowered IPO price, Intuit refused to budge in its conservative portrayal.

Once the team finished Intuit's prospectus in early February, they sent a copy to the Securities and Exchange Commission (SEC) and the company entered its "quiet period," the government-prescribed time during which a company about to go public can make no public comment so as not to influence its public stock price. To ensure that the inexperienced Intuit executives made a good impression on Wall Street, Cook hired a road-show coach to work with the IPO management team on its presentation.

THE ROAD SHOW

Two weeks later, the team hit the road. Intuit's executives and investment bankers traveled to a dozen cities to pitch the company's prospects to prospective institutional investors at securities firms across the country.

The road show went well, although it began with some consternation on the part of Morgan Stanley. As they checked in at the San Francisco airport, the team of investment bankers claimed their first-class seats at the gate. Then Cook arrived and checked into his seat in coach class. After eyeing Cook's boarding pass, the Morgan Stanley group grudgingly got back in line to switch their first-class seats to coach, (un)fortunately still available. The Morgan Stanley team spent the flight grousing about their cramped accommodations.

During the road show, Intuit presented a compelling IPO case. The presentation emphasized Quicken's 75-plus percent market share across all three major platforms—Windows, DOS, and Macintosh. What's more, customer satisfaction was so high that 52 percent of Quicken users bought because someone had recommended it to them.

Intuit touted its IntelliCharge service and Quicken-branded credit card as important signposts to the company's electronic future. The IntelliCharge service, when used with the Quicken credit card, allowed customers to save time by automatically downloading precategorized credit card transactions into Quicken.

Launched by Proulx in 1992, the service had gained over fifty thousand users, not significant financially but important strategically. The business' proven results demonstrated that Intuit had the technology, marketing, and partnering know-how to make an impact in electronic finance.

Morgan Stanley scheduled the last road show meeting the day before the IPO in New York City, on March 11, 1993. More than fifty funds managers and major investors attended. After the final meeting, the bankers paid Cook back for the coach class seats by procuring a gaudy pink limousine to chauffeur the embarrassed Intuit team to a celebratory dinner.

The day before the IPO, demand for Intuit stock appeared to be greater than supply, predicting success for its IPO. And so, while riding in the ostentatious pink limousine, Quattrone raised the IPO price, initially projected at twelve to fourteen dollars per share, to twenty dollars, believing that Intuit's good prospects, with market-leading brands, millions of customers, and consistent growth and profitability, warranted the higher pricing. The tremendous growth and seemingly unlimited potential of the PC market increased Intuit's attractiveness.

Intuit went public on March 12, 1993, with an IPO price of $20 per share. It closed for the day at $31.75, up almost 63 percent, a successful opening.[3] Intuit had completed an important rite of passage.

On the day of the IPO, Cook—who garnered close to $5 million by selling 240,000 shares and held additional stock worth some $140 million—made a routine sales call to a New York client before flying back to California, still in coach class.[4] He refused to let his new wealth affect his priorities. Dunn—now worth nearly $10 million—caught up on some much-needed sleep on the plane. When they returned to Intuit, they found employees excited about the company's success and their stock options' increased value, but otherwise largely unaffected. For most of Intuit, the IPO was but a natural step in the company's evolution, and it didn't change their day-to-day work.

WOW VALUES

Cook was pleased that his employees remained grounded and relatively indifferent to Intuit's IPO, but the company's rapid evolution concerned him: How could he ensure that Intuit's culture remained focused on core values rather than stock values?

To address this concern, Intuit executives called an unprecedented all-company meeting two weeks after its IPO. The meeting arose from an effort that began in late 1992, when Cook and Ridge Evers, the former QuickBooks team leader, reflected on the state of the company. After the QuickBooks launch, Cook had asked Evers to create an engineering calendar to show the company's development priorities. But Evers could not come up with an acceptable calendar because he couldn't get consensus on project priorities. When he pushed harder for agreement, Evers realized that Intuit had not defined criteria to evaluate the alternatives that would determine its future direction.

The lack of development criteria was not the company's only Achilles' heel. By 1993, facing burgeoning growth and opportunity, the company writhed with growing pains. Intuit's executive team stultified rapid action by insisting on approving all strategic and tactical decisions as well as all hiring. Because Intuit management still believed in consensual decision making, they worked hard to get complete buy-in from employees, further slowing forward progress. Operations consistently struggled with the practical demands of growth, and increasing staff and product complexity forced the company to let go of some of the early practices that had brought it closer to customers: employee customer contact hours and manufacturing packing parties.

Into this strained culture came employees like Jim Heeger, recruited from Hewlett-Packard to run the supplies business at Intuit. Thoughtful Heeger quickly came to lament the executive committee's "pedagogical discussions about particular issues that didn't relate to the real world" and its slow decision making.[5] The executive team did not delegate; for example, when Heeger tried to hire an assistant, he found that the form to authorize new employees had to be signed by every member of the executive committee (Cook, Proulx, Dunn, Pelletier, and Monson). "Guys, this isn't gonna work," Heeger railed. "This isn't scalable. It can't be a group grope every time you want to do this kind of thing. We have to trust our managers."[6]

In the face of the accelerating speed of the company's progress, its consensus routines imposed a huge strain on senior executives. This strain also caused personal relations among some of the executives to fray. Proulx and Cook, frequently diametrically opposite in approach, often could not agree in team meetings. And the stress increased as Evers pushed for strategic criteria.

And so, Intuit began searching for a strategic planning process that would aid executive decision making and help the company move more gracefully forward. The Silicon Valley elite celebrated Intel for its planning processes, so Intuit hired Proulx's former college roommate, an Intel strategic planner, to advise. Intuit executives, following the example of Disney and American Express, also decided to create a company mission statement to ensure that decisions aligned with corporate values. The result was the "Vision, Mission, Operating Values, and Achievements" initiative (VMOVA).

Cook wrote and distributed a memo to all employees to explain the VMOVA effort. "Why are we doing this? The reason is simple: to stay successful in business and make Intuit a better place to work. Intuit has experienced phenomenal growth in sales and number of employees. Often, as companies grow larger, it becomes increasingly difficult to keep growing at a rapid pace, to maintain communications between departments, and to keep focused on a common goal. Rifts can develop, different departments can develop different value systems, and goals can become decentralized. This type of breakdown has led to the demise of many companies today."[7]

On March 25, 1993, Intuit closed down for the day and rented part of the San Jose Convention Center. Jim Collins, Stanford business school lecturer and eventual coauthor of 1994's best-

FIGURE 11-1

Scott Cook with employees at companywide VMOVA meeting to develop Intuit's vision, mission, and operating values statement in 1993. The entire company closed for the daylong event.

Source: Courtesy of Intuit.

selling book, *Built to Last,* appeared as keynote speaker. Collins gave a rousing speech to kick off the VMOVA meeting, praising Intuit for making this project a top priority (see figure 11-1). As an example of a mission statement he invoked President Kennedy's goal of sending a man to the moon and back by the end of the 1960s. That mission statement, like all great ones, was clear, measurable, and "a BHAG—a big, hairy, audacious goal."[8]

After Collins's talk, employees organized into twenty teams of about twenty-five people each, with facilitators recording the discussions and hanging up butcher paper all around. The teams generated "signpost" words to describe Intuit; the most common one was *revolutionize.* Cook recalled:

> *Having the whole company involved, wrestling with everyone's thoughts made the process new, better, and fresh—far better than if the executive team had just done it themselves. Five hundred minds that cared deeply were thinking about Intuit's values and mission. They also emerged from the process engaged and committed. People could see their own handiwork and felt a*

143

sense of ownership. But that's not why we did it. We did it because involving employees in creating their mission was the right thing to do.[9]

Over the next few months, the VMOVA team processed the contributions received during the offsite meeting. In one session, Tom LeFevre articulated that Intuit wanted to "Wow" its customers. Dunn insisted, "Customers are important, but integrity and ethics are our number one value because they are the most crucial for a company. If you can't get that right, then don't go on to number two. Just stop."[10] Cook thought that something needed to capture the importance of great employees: "People are the root cause of Intuit's success."[11] "It's the people" became another explicit Intuit value.

After weeks of follow-up work, the VMOVA team released its final document (appendix). The forward-looking document began with the company's vision for the year 2010 and stated Intuit's fundamental mission of change: to "revolutionize how people manage their financial lives." And it described Intuit's ten most critical operating values:

1. Integrity without compromise

2. Do right by all our customers

3. It's the people

4. Seek the best

5. Continually improve processes

6. Speak, listen, and respond

7. Teams work

8. Customers define quality

9. Think fast, move fast

10. We care and give back

CHAPTER 12

A TURBO-CHARGED INTUIT

A s the company completed its VMOVA process, Tom Proulx embraced his business development role. Now married to his longtime girlfriend, Barbara Boyd, Proulx, thirty-one, had made enough money on his Intuit stock to retire. But Proulx had believed since 1989 that Intuit should be in the tax business. By 1993 he was certain that, had Intuit entered the tax business earlier, the company would have paid tens of millions of dollars less than if they entered now. The stalwart Proulx considered Scott Cook's resistance to a tax strategy Intuit's most significant strategic blunder and determined to correct it even at the higher cost to the company.

Proulx got turned on to tax in 1989, when Dan Caine, founder of Legal Knowledge Systems, approached Proulx to try to interest Intuit in his tax software, Ask Dan About Your Taxes. Proulx had lobbied to acquire this software, but Cook resisted. He worried that adding a tax preparation product to Intuit's software lineup would reduce Intuit's focus on its core finance products. Although Cook acknowledged that tax and finance complemented each other, the complex and unforgiving nature of the tax business scared him.

Tax software's intense seasonality in upgrades and customer service seemed too daunting, even though the software's annual obsolescence created a potentially profitable necessity for customers to upgrade. Cook knew that at tax software companies, if the product missed its deadline, the company died. The IRS wouldn't wait for bug fixes or software upgrades. And Cook knew that Intuit had an uneven track record for on-time delivery. Though Mari Baker and Eric Dunn supported Proulx, no one was able to persuade Cook.

After Intuit spurned him, Caine had moved on to MECA, the creator of Quicken's main competitor at the time, Managing Your Money. MECA eagerly added Caine's tax preparation product to its lineup, signing an exclusive marketing licensing agreement. Beginning in 1990, MECA changed Caine's product name to TaxCut and bundled it successfully with Managing Your Money.

UNFORGIVING COMPETITOR

Even with its new name and partner, TaxCut could not outsell the leading software for personal tax preparation, TurboTax. Created by San Diego–based ChipSoft, TurboTax had originated from an engineer's desire to automate his own taxes. Mike Chipman had worked as a scientific programmer for twenty years before creating TurboTax, which took him only three months to write. The entire program contained nine thousand lines of Pascal code, and in 1983 Chipman and his wife Evy launched ChipSoft to market it (figure 12-1). The Chipmans priced TurboTax at $65, compared to $200 and $300 for competitors' programs, because they wanted as many people as possible to buy it.

ChipSoft's market success resembled Intuit's. TurboTax took off despite fierce competition from fifteen other tax preparation products. The Chipmans placed a tiny 1½-by-1-inch classified ad in *PC Magazine* containing a toll-free 800 phone number; its unexpected success caused their bedroom phone to awaken them every morning by six o'clock. Tagging along with a friend at the Comdex high-tech trade show, the Chipmans casually dropped

FIGURE 12-1

ChipSoft cofounders Mike and Evy Chipman.

Source: Courtesy of Intuit.

off a copy of their program at the *PC Magazine* booth. Luckily, *PC Magazine* was in the midst of writing up a big review of tax software programs and chose TurboTax as its favorite.

After two years of tripling sales, ChipSoft in 1989 moved to its own offices in a San Diego office park and began hiring more staff. TurboTax gained momentum, and ChipSoft expanded to maintain its market share lead. In 1990, ChipSoft earned $19 million in annual revenues and suffered severe growing pains. Mike Chipman's experience in engineering and Evy Chipman's in teaching did not prepare them for managing such a fast-growing organization. Realizing their limitations, the Chipmans decided to seek professional help.

Putting most of their company stock up for sale, they found a buyer who could help ChipSoft reach the next level of growth: Warburg Pincus, a mid-sized New York investment bank, bought the Chipmans' shares for $25 million and took over ChipSoft, installing Chris Brody on the company's board. Brody, a New York insider, immediately hired a new CEO, Charlie Gaylord. A professional manager from the oil trading and transport industry, Gaylord, a bluff man in his forties with a broad, gap-toothed smile, prized ChipSoft's profitable, annually recurring revenue stream. Gaylord fine-tuned ChipSoft's business strategy and helped the company execute that strategy for growth.

To help lead ChipSoft, Brody hired media expert Bill Harris as president. A trim, clever Harvard M.B.A., thirty-three-year-old Harris had spent ten years in New York running news magazines such as *US News & World Report.* Harris grew up in an intellectual household; his inventive doctor father pioneered artificial hip technology. Fascinated with the intersection between media and technology, the articulate and energetic Harris saw TurboTax as an early example of interactivity coupled with domain-specific information and logic. Unlike Intuit, ChipSoft employed more tax experts to create the tax content for TurboTax than software engineers to write the program. Harris said, "ChipSoft is half interactivity, half information publishing—a superrich combination of both."[1]

Gaylord and Harris formed an effective partnership. Gaylord, the more experienced business manager, oversaw operations and company strategy; Harris's ideas, persuasiveness, and presentation skills lent ChipSoft vision. Together, they transformed ChipSoft from a family-run business into a well-managed, professional company with clear lines of decision making and authority.

Gaylord and Harris foresaw that the Windows platform would transform the PC market, and the Mac already had a devoted customer base. But TurboTax could run on neither. The old-school ChipSoft development team had been satisfied with its DOS-dependent TurboTax and wanted nothing to do with Windows or Mac. As Harris's first big move, he persuaded Gaylord that if ChipSoft would not develop a TurboTax for Windows product, it would have to buy the market share.

ChipSoft soon acquired SoftView Corporation of Oxnard, California, with its 95 percent share in the Mac market. Its software, MacInTax, incorporated a graphical user interface like Windows, so buying SoftView increased ChipSoft's expertise and gave the San Diego company a faster way to develop a Windows tax product. After its SoftView purchase, ChipSoft led market share for personal tax software in Mac and DOS.

Although it made sense in business terms, the SoftView acquisition proved difficult for ChipSoft in human terms. Many SoftView employees quit because they didn't want to move to San Diego and because many of them held disdain for ChipSoft's DOS development platform. The struggling ChipSoft nearly failed to release the next version of MacInTax. Gaylord and Harris grappled more with integrating SoftView into the rest of the company than they had with buying it in the first place.

Even given the SoftView integration debacle, Gaylord and Harris couldn't resist contemplating a merger with Intuit. In mid-1991, they approached Cook: Intuit and ChipSoft each led the market in their categories, had complementary products, and would have greater retail clout together.

Intuit and ChipSoft had already briefly courted, agreeing to counter the Managing Your Money–TaxCut promotional bundle by bundling their products together at a discounted rate for the holiday selling season. While the promotion succeeded in increasing sales and shelf space, the end-of-season product returns from retailers associated with unsold packages of TurboTax, to which ChipSoft was accustomed, came as a rude shock for Intuit. Unprepared for this effect of tax software seasonality, Intuit managers, who took pride in Quicken's low return rate, resented ChipSoft for the returns. In 1991, Cook continued to be wary of the tax business. And he did not want Intuit distracted from its battle with Microsoft.

So, Gaylord and Harris, rebuffed, returned to San Diego to pursue other options. They took ChipSoft public in February 1992 to position the company for other acquisitions and to help replenish cash reserves used to cover SoftView's inadequate working capital. The IPO netted a modest cash reserve of about $40 million.

By the time ChipSoft went public, Gaylord and Harris had established a professional and somewhat hierarchical management method. Harris and Gaylord were both from the East Coast, and their styles reflected that stratified business environment. The unforgiving nature of the tax business, which forced ChipSoft managers to make quick, firm decisions in order to stay on schedule, heightened this management perspective.

But no matter how buttoned-down Gaylord and Harris were, ChipSoft's rigid tax deadlines created an engineering culture of semi-managed chaos. Near catastrophe occurred with each new bug to fix and every looming deadline. Engineers crunched each October through January; Christmas vacation didn't exist. If ChipSoft missed a shipping deadline, it missed the entire year. This "do or die" environment further increased ChipSoft's autocratic management style.

Gaylord and Harris did succeed at bringing order and discipline to ChipSoft's marketing department to garner direct customer purchases and renewals. Beginning with a solid customer database, Harris transformed ChipSoft's direct marketing into a magazine-like department, using test-and-control cells to discover the most effective combinations of mailings. After testing with premiums, postcards, newsletters, fold-overs, and other types of mail pieces, ChipSoft used seven mailing waves during the tax season with astounding results: more than 90 percent of TurboTax customers renewed annually.

ChipSoft also counted tax accounting businesses among its customers. ChipSoft's ProTax professional tax business began when accountants bought the consumer version of TurboTax. Reacting to that opportunity, ChipSoft expanded on its code base to build a ProTax version of its software, creating two distinct businesses and sets of customers. Having two versions allowed ChipSoft to amortize development costs over a larger customer base and undercut competitors on the price of a professional tax product. ChipSoft made up to one thousand dollars annually from each of these higher-margin customers.

After its IPO, ChipSoft acquired several other small companies with expertise in electronic tax filing. With these acquisitions, ChipSoft gained engineering and professional tax prep experience, but it also gained new organizational and technical problems. ChipSoft's development platforms proliferated, and multiple code bases made for a messy programming environment. Multiple environments led to multiple tax coding teams led to multiple headaches.

So Harris decided on an ambitious move: to build a new cross-platform technology for all of ChipSoft's products. "In packaged software, the guy with the market share and volume wins," Harris argued. "High fixed cost, low variable cost—so the biggest guy wins. We need 50 percent plus market share in every segment, even if it kills us. How can we avoid getting killed? We'll build the next generation of software: cross-platform, consumer, professional and business, all jurisdictions for federal and various states, multiple types of tax."[2]

ChipSoft managers were less confident that cross-platform code could be achieved. Failures littered the track record of companies who had tried. Microsoft, Symantec, Intuit—all had futilely attempted to create a multiplatform code base with Mac and Windows. ChipSoft also had to support DOS—its tax renewal imperative meant it had to succeed on all three platforms. Despite the concerns, Harris insisted on mounting a cross-platform effort, and ChipSoft engineering dove in. During the extensive development period, ChipSoft struggled to keep TurboTax and MacInTax as the market leaders.

While the multiplatform project distracted ChipSoft engineering, the competitive landscape for personal financial software started to settle. TurboTax and Quicken led their markets, followed by TaxCut and Microsoft Money. Then, in early 1993, an investment banker ruptured that equilibrium by inviting ChipSoft and Intuit to bid on MECA Software at MECA's upcoming sale.

MECA MADNESS

MECA Software needed cash. Its stock price had tumbled because of stalled growth, and it had never been more than marginally profitable since its IPO in September 1990. Its anxious management team, led by CEO Dan Schley, had decided their only option was to sell.

Intuit and ChipSoft both wanted MECA. Both competed against MECA: Intuit's Quicken faced off against Managing Your Money and ChipSoft's TurboTax battled with TaxCut. Both also led in these markets with shares greater than 60 percent. Proulx from Intuit and Harris from ChipSoft decided to pursue MECA using the same rationale: Whichever company won the bidding battle had a way to enter the other's market overnight and had great leverage for any later negotiations they might have with each other.

But Intuit had an advantage that ChipSoft lacked. Although Intuit wanted to buy MECA, Proulx, in a flash of crafty brilliance, prepared his company for either success or failure. Unbeknownst to the other parties, Proulx orchestrated a behind-the-scenes coup to ensure that Intuit would win even if they lost.

MECA still had a marketing license with Dan Caine of Legal Knowledge Systems, who intensely disliked archrival Chip-Soft. Caine believed that Harris wanted the TaxCut rights to kill his product so that TurboTax would be the undisputed leader. In contrast, Caine and Proulx had maintained a collegial relationship ever since the creator of Ask Dan About Your Taxes had first approached Intuit in 1989. Caine had never sold the engineering rights to his code or to his Newton, Massachusetts–based company to MECA; MECA merely marketed TaxCut via its licensing agreement. So, Proulx decided Intuit needed those engineering rights *before* the MECA sale.

In the week prior to the MECA sale, Proulx and Caine agreed to a sale price for Caine's engineering rights and sealed the deal with an over-the-phone "handshake." Shortly thereafter, Caine called Proulx back and said he had just heard that Gaylord was on a plane, coming out to see him at eight o'clock the next morning. Caine had met earlier with Harris, who wanted the engineering rights to TaxCut in addition to the marketing rights that MECA owned. Even though Caine didn't expect to change his mind, he wanted to hear what Gaylord had to say.

When he heard about Caine's meeting with Gaylord, Proulx worked fast to lock up a deal before Gaylord arrived. Proulx knew how persuasive and charming Gaylord could be and worried that his oral agreement would not survive Caine's face-to-face meeting with Gaylord. So at six o'clock that evening, Proulx called Intuit lawyer Gordy Davidson and said, "We're doing a deal tonight." Proulx phoned Caine and said, "Dan, we're going to paper our deal tonight, and the deal we're going to give you will be a better deal if we sign it before 8 A.M. than if you wait until after you talk with Charlie. We'll still love *you* and we'll still want to do a deal with you, but it won't be as good. This is a blue light special. Call your attorney; it's going to be a long night."[3]

Proulx had learned a lot since his long-ago "blue light special" days (he'd worked at Kmart as a stock boy in high school). Through Intuit's ten-year history, Proulx had been involved in all major business decisions and had fine-tuned his business judgment. He'd absorbed the on-the-job business training like a sponge. This experience, and Proulx's natural ability to use it, informed the elaborate negotiations and machinations he adopted to get Intuit into the tax business.

Proulx did not want to acquire Legal Knowledge Systems outright, which would have been hard to do so quickly. Instead, he wanted a deal that Intuit and Legal Knowledge Systems could dissolve—but only if they jointly agreed. So he proposed a contract in which Caine gave Intuit a "call" option to acquire his company, and Proulx gave Caine a "put" option that allowed him to force Intuit to acquire Legal Knowledge Systems. Only if both parties later agreed not to go through with it could the sale of Legal Knowledge Systems to Intuit be stopped.

Caine, his lawyer, Proulx, and Davidson worked through the night, and after multiple revisions and several telephonic meetings with the Intuit board, the final option agreement was signed at 4:40 A.M. PST, or 7:40 A.M. EST, twenty minutes before Gaylord was to arrive on Caine's doorstep. When Gaylord arrived, Caine turned the exasperated Gaylord away.

Proulx's ingenious arrangement prevented ChipSoft from acquiring the engineering rights to TaxCut regardless of the outcome of the MECA auction. If ChipSoft's acquisition of MECA succeeded, ChipSoft would own only marketing rights to Tax-Cut, not the critical engineering code. And per the terms of Legal Knowledge Systems' marketing license, if ChipSoft failed to market TaxCut, they would be in breach of the agreement and would lose their exclusivity, allowing Caine to market TaxCut either on his own or with another marketing partner, presumably Intuit. Proulx felt confident that Intuit could not fail at the MECA sale regardless of the outcome.

MECA held its sale in a Connecticut hotel Easter weekend 1993. Though rumor claimed Microsoft would bid, only Chip-Soft and Intuit vied against each other. Proulx, Cook, and Dunn brought an attorney and an investment banker; Gaylord and Harris represented ChipSoft. Initially managers from both companies felt awkward as they met, but since ChipSoft and Intuit had previously bundled their products together, the executives knew each other and overcame the discomfort.

MECA's investment bankers had told Proulx that the sale would not be an auction: Intuit and ChipSoft should make their best offers and then the MECA board would decide. Accordingly, Intuit offered stock worth about $63 million, and ChipSoft came to the table with $60 million in cash.

After the presentations, MECA's investment banker pulled Proulx aside in the hallway to say that the MECA board was leaning toward the ChipSoft offer because it was all cash, but that if Intuit could raise their offer a bit he thought the board could be persuaded to accept Intuit's offer. The Intuit team, offended by the lack of ethics they saw in that approach, refused to increase their initial offer.

"You told us to come in with our best offer, and that's what we did," an irate Proulx told the MECA representative. "Tell the MECA board to go ahead and take the ChipSoft offer if they think it's better. I want both MECA and ChipSoft, and the next deal I do will be to acquire ChipSoft. So I'll either get MECA now, or I'll get them as part of the ChipSoft acquisition."[4]

MECA had gotten wind of Intuit's deal with Dan Caine; when MECA management pressed for details, Proulx's insistent unwillingness to share more information angered them. So the next day the investment banker called Proulx to tell him that the MECA board had decided in favor of the ChipSoft offer. That he had successfully maneuvered with the code agreement only partially salved Proulx's disappointment that ChipSoft had prevailed.

When Intuit's deal with Caine came to light, Harris and Gaylord were livid. They tried to persuade Caine to break the deal. Then, without any prior warning, the Department of Justice (DOJ) intervened. Bill Clinton's new Democratic administration wanted to make a mark in antitrust, and the DOJ notified Chip-Soft that it would contest the deal. An attorney at the DOJ who read about the deal in the *Wall Street Journal* had recently purchased tax software and had noticed only two products, TaxCut and TurboTax, on the shelf. This lack of competition sparked his intervention in ChipSoft's acquisition of MECA.

Harris exploded when he heard the news, telling the Chip-Soft board, "We're totally hosed. We cannot purchase MECA, but Intuit can if it wants to."[5] ChipSoft offered to give either the Tur-boTax or TaxCut code to Peachtree Software of Atlanta, Intuit's business accounting software competitor, to reduce anticompeti-tiveness in the category, but still the DOJ quashed the ChipSoft-MECA deal.

Once the MECA deal died, Gaylord and Harris contemplated their next move. ChipSoft's situation was dire. If Intuit acquired MECA, the combined entity would have formidable products in both personal finance and tax software. Gaylord and Harris decided they far preferred a merger with Intuit to competing with a merged Intuit and MECA. So they bent their considerable persuasive skills toward convincing Intuit to make a 180-degree change in course.

CHECKMATE

Bill Harris flew to Menlo Park the week after the DOJ announcement to suggest again that Intuit buy ChipSoft. A series of additional discussions ensued, and Intuit weighed the benefits of purchasing MECA, with the TaxCut code they preferred, or purchasing ChipSoft for its tax market muscleman, TurboTax.

In August, discussions with both MECA and ChipSoft kicked into high gear. ChipSoft executives returned to San Francisco for a meeting at the fancy Fairmont Hotel in a windowless basement conference room. Harris showed a Visio presentation arguing for the merger, which Dunn and Cook found compelling: Harris articulated a multidimensional strategy across different products, customer groups, distribution channels, and technologies. ChipSoft demonstrated not only its ability to persuade but also its seriousness about the deal, having gathered even its East Coast directors for the meeting.

Despite Harris's persistence, the Intuit management team disagreed about which company to purchase. The DOJ made it clear that Proulx's original plan to acquire both companies would not fly. Most senior managers preferred the ChipSoft management team to MECA's. "ChipSoft has five solid senior managers covering all aspects of the business," Cook pointed out, "while MECA only has one."[6] Cook also worried about ChipSoft's reaction if Intuit acquired MECA; ChipSoft's most likely response would be to approach Microsoft about a merger, a scary prospect.

Because of Dan Caine and his team, Proulx and Dunn still favored the MECA alternative. "We've already got his engineering code locked up, and Caine's is a much better product. It's like the tax product we would have developed if we had developed a tax product," Proulx retorted. "In addition, since we have the Legal Knowledge option, no one else will want to buy MECA. We're the only bidder. We can get them for cheap."[7] But board members emphasized the superior benefits of buying the market leader ChipSoft, even though ChipSoft would cost substantially more.

Ultimately, Intuit execs went for the ChipSoft management team. Serious price negotiations between Intuit and ChipSoft began. Gaylord and Harris needed the Intuit–ChipSoft deal, but they fought for a good price. They knew their option to approach Microsoft gave them clout even though Gaylord discouraged contact with Microsoft throughout the negotiations so that the team could focus on closing the Intuit deal without distractions. Gaylord and Harris thought they had to move quickly because of the relationship between Intuit and Legal Knowledge Systems.

In late August, Dunn, returning from his annual vacation trip to Maine, received an urgent message from Cook: "Bill Harris is here and we're talking terms."

When Dunn arrived at Cook's new house in Woodside, still under construction, Harris had a new proposal: "Maybe the two companies should not merge immediately but can strike a marketing deal that will keep us aligned. Then we can merge in a year or two."[8] Cross-selling Quicken to more than five hundred thousand TurboTax customers, even via alliance, intrigued Harris, but Intuit executives refused. Proulx had finally persuaded Cook to purchase a tax software company, and he did not want to settle for just an alliance.

After Harris returned to San Diego, frustrated at his lack of progress with Intuit, he remembered that Dunn had admired his new laptop, an HP Ultra Portable. To restart negotiations, he sent the laptop to Dunn with his compliments. Dunn, surprised and affected by the gesture, realized that ChipSoft was still serious about making a deal. He persuaded Cook to revive discussion about the ChipSoft merger. By digging deeper into Intuit's treasury and revaluing ChipSoft's market share, Cook finally managed to find a price acceptable to both companies. Intuit would buy ChipSoft for $232 million.

After choosing ChipSoft, Intuit had to eliminate the Legal Knowledge Systems deal. Proulx called Caine and told him that Intuit had decided on ChipSoft. The news disappointed Caine, who had viewed an Intuit-MECA merger as his chance to finally join the Intuit team. Caine could have made Intuit's deal difficult with the DOJ by exercising his put option, forcing Intuit to acquire the rights to TaxCut's engineering code, but his professionalism and regard for Proulx made him agree to quietly allow Intuit to buy out the contract.

On September 1, 1993, Intuit rented the auditorium at a local Palo Alto high school for a meeting with its local employees. Stunning many Intuit employees who had presumed the company would acquire MECA, Cook, Proulx, and Harris jubilantly made the merger announcement. Bill Harris presented alternative names for the new company. When he suggested "ChipTuit" and "InSoft," a roaring "No!" arose from the crowd. "ChipSoft" may have paid homage to engineer Mike Chipman and his wife Evy, but Intuit's brand recognition trumped it. The company would remain Intuit. Proulx and Harris predicted the deal's closing in sixty to ninety days.

Immediately after the Palo Alto meeting, Cook, Harris, Proulx, and Gaylord hopped on a jet and flew to San Diego where they delivered the announcement in person to ChipSofts's San Diego employees. Since the merger announcement happened to coincide with ChipSoft's scheduled annual miniature golf tournament for employees, the four executives then shot a round of putt-putt golf.

Dunn next called the investment analysts. "Throw away your financial projections for Intuit," he joked. Senior management watched the stock prices of the two companies carefully, taking measure of the market's reception. The companies' stock prices fluctuated wildly while the antitrust issue was undecided, but once the DOJ relieved the companies by announcing it would not challenge the deal, prices stabilized. Intuit's stock price increased about 20 percent by the time the ChipSoft acquisition closed, even though Intuit's innovative decision to write off the goodwill from the ChipSoft deal would be costly: For the next three years, Intuit would have to show a $30 million accounting charge (noncash) in its generally accepted accounting principles (GAAP) earnings statements. To show investors Intuit's actual combined earnings, the company would also show pro forma earnings; this "virtual pooling" approach would mark the first embrace of pro forma accounting in Silicon Valley.

In the midst of this stressful closing period, a message from John Watts of the SEC startled Dunn. With great trepidation, Dunn picked up the phone, worried that the SEC objected to the merger at the eleventh hour. But Watts simply asked for help getting into a password-protected Quicken file for a case. To Dunn's great relief, he said nothing about the Intuit-ChipSoft merger.

Intuit and ChipSoft executives also took time during the closing period to get to know each other better. Leaders from both companies met in San Diego for a lighthearted team building offsite (see figure 12-2). One notable task required the executives to wear blindfolds while using a rope to form a perfect

FIGURE 12-2

Charlie Gaylord and Scott Cook prepare for their team building task.
Source: Courtesy of Charlie Gaylord.

square. Unfortunately, the team was not able to accomplish this mission within its time limit.

On December 13, 1993, Intuit and ChipSoft became Intuit North in Menlo Park and Intuit South in San Diego, respectively. Overnight, the staff mushroomed to more than one thousand employees and the annual revenues to over $200 million. Proulx finally had achieved his dream: Intuit was now in the tax business. After a yearlong effort beginning with the IPO and ending with the completed merger, Proulx decided he needed a well-deserved break, and in March 1994, he left Intuit for a sabbatical. Now could the company pull off the coordination and integration needed to truly succeed?

CHAPTER 13

COACH CAMPBELL

I n spring 1993, Intuit's head of customer service, Marsha Raulston, had invited Scott Cook to have lunch with her at the rustic Alpine Inn in Woodside, beloved by bikers and Silicon Valley execs alike. "What's wrong?" she asked him in her Texas accent as they found a seat on one of the Alpine's hard wooden benches. Cook asked her what she meant, and Raulston looked him straight in the eye. "Are you having as much fun as you should be? We seem to have some conflict on the executive team," Raulston continued. "Things could be going better, and you don't look too happy."[1]

Struck by her blunt observations, Cook looked inward. Were things going well? Was he having fun? Cook concluded that Raulston was right. A consummate entrepreneur, Cook had loved the challenges of a start-up. Visionary, hands-on, and driven, he had excelled at managing an emerging Intuit. Cook's passion for the customer and creative energy had worked best when Intuit's size allowed for a single decision-making authority. Leading a larger organization, however, required a different set of talents—day-to-day delegation, coordination, and operational rigor. Cook realized something was missing.

Considering further, Cook wasn't sure he could pull off the kind of leadership that Intuit now needed, and he realized that he didn't even want to try. As he had in the past, Cook confided in his friend, investor Peter Wendell. "I'm not the right guy," Cook told Wendell thoughtfully. "I am holding the company back." At the end of Cook's monologue, Wendell agreed with Cook's conclusion: Intuit needed a new CEO.

In the flurry of Intuit's IPO, VMOVA process, MECA auction, and ChipSoft merger, Cook bided his time, not wanting to act on this conclusion until the company stabilized. But once the ChipSoft executives came on board, Intuit's need for a new CEO became acute. At the fall 1993 Comdex convention in Las Vegas, Cook announced his intention to hire a new CEO at an unconventional location: the honeymoon suite at Caesar's palace, the only room large enough to hold the newly combined executive team. Seated uncomfortably around the circular bed and marveling at the heart-shaped bathtub en suite, the Intuit and ChipSoft executives listened intently as Cook outlined his reasons for hiring a new CEO and becoming Chairman of the Board.

The need for a new CEO became urgent as the companies tried to work together. Before combining, Cook and Charlie Gaylord had agreed that ChipSoft should continue operating in its current location, but this geographic separation accounted for only part of the escalating problems. Intuit and ChipSoft each brought a specific set of strengths to the new marriage—strengths rooted in the companies' core cultures. Intuit's superior system of gathering and using customer insight ensured that its engineering and marketing groups focused on optimizing the customer experience. Intuit's VMOVA process, its 360-degree performance reviews (which gathered information from employees' colleagues as well as managers), and its employee feedback surveys all bespoke a culture that empowered and valued workers, and the company's egalitarian offices (even Cook's was modest in size and style) reflected its nonhierarchical management.

Shaped by the imperative that the tax customer had to receive software on time, ChipSoft's culture differed sharply. ChipSoft relied on focused, operational managers in a more hierarchical

structure with top–down decision making. When Intuit's entrepreneurial senior executives clung to their inefficient, consensus-
based decision making, this strained executive meetings to the
breaking point. Intuit South executives did not attend even by
phone and the newly combined company's top leadership stopped
working together.

As management tensions escalated, Cook kicked his CEO
search into high gear. The search had initially dismayed board
members. John Doerr, in particular, had objected to Cook's argument. "Usually [venture capitalists] have to push ineffective
founders out. But you're willing to hand over the reins at this
stage?" he had asked incredulously. Cook did not intend to depart
Intuit, but he resolved to hire a CEO to focus on the things that
he could not do well.

Cook had originally hoped he might find a successor from
among the Intuit South executives, but that did not pan out. Gaylord would not relocate to northern California at that stage in his
career, and Intuit North leaders deemed Bill Harris not yet seasoned enough. The company desperately needed an experienced
CEO to lead Intuit to greater success.

In late fall of 1993, Cook hired an executive search firm and
began interviewing candidates. Driven by Cook's commitment to
people and increasing interest in process and continual improvement, Intuit searched for a strong leader who championed development of people, management discipline, careful measurement
of business outcomes, process improvement, and operations excellence. Cook tried to convey the skills he wanted in CEO candidates, but the search firm failed to turn up candidates that fit his
demanding criteria.

Then Doerr stepped in. Once he accepted Cook's idea,
Doerr honed in on a candidate with experience in high-tech
leadership, software, and innovation. Doerr's CEO candidate excelled at marketing and sales, and had run several high-tech divisions and companies. Doerr believed this candidate's skills and

personality would perfectly fit Intuit. And so, Cook began to take the measure of Bill Campbell, the former CEO of Claris Software Company and GO Corporation.

Born in Homestead, Pennsylvania, a steel town with a tough reputation, Campbell had a bio that would impress any up-from-the-bootstraps entrepreneur. "You couldn't have a better place to be brought up," says Campbell about his hometown. "You get to deal with wonderful, hardworking people."[2] Those "wonderful, hardworking people" began with his father, Bill Campbell Sr., who worked in Homestead's school system as a high school teacher, junior high school principal, and finally district superintendent. Homestead kids and colleagues dubbed the firm, fair arbiter, "Coach."

In addition to the school district job, Campbell's father worked in the steel mill. Campbell's mother would pile the kids into the family car under a blanket to drop him off for his midnight to 8 A.M. shift. When the family picked him up, he'd come out of the plant clean and dressed for school, and they would accompany him there. Campbell Sr. slept after school and went back to the steel mill at midnight, and his hard work made a deep impression on his son.

By his senior year, Campbell played as star linebacker for the Homestead High varsity football team, one of the best teams in the state. Hoping to be drafted by a big football school, Campbell chose to attend Columbia University after the football powerhouses ignored him. He found the adjustment to New York City college life difficult; college academics were much harder than high school's. Campbell did not feel comfortable nor perform well in classes until his junior year.

Campbell worked furiously to master the academics and social elements of Columbia. After finishing his undergraduate degree, Campbell decided to continue at Columbia for a graduate degree in education. During graduate school, Campbell worked from 5:30 A.M. to 8:30 A.M. in the dining halls to pay for his meals, served as a residence counselor to pay for his room, and helped out as a part-time assistant football coach, to help pay his living costs. For nearly a year he also worked at UPS from 5:30 P.M. to 2:30 A.M. When he finished the second degree, Columbia offered Campbell a job coaching football. Campbell accepted and began coaching the defensive ends full-time in fall 1962.

Coaching taught Campbell essentials that he applied throughout his later business career. Leadership, strategy and tactics, motivation, competitiveness, team building, and winning all became part of Campbell's professional lexicon. Later, he would observe that coaching college football and motivating executives presented many of the same challenges—most significantly, persuading individual talents to work together for the good of the team.

But after six years as head football coach at Columbia, Campbell tired of coaching. He said, "I left Columbia because my record wasn't good enough, and there was not enough support to make a good team. When I started, it was kind of a lark. I wanted to be Joe Paterno, leave a lifetime legacy where I could influence kids and really put a sports legacy in place. Later, I didn't see that happening. It was a hard decision, but I made it."[3]

By this time, his domestic life was also shaping his priorities. Campbell had married Roberta, a dean at Columbia and the first woman to attain such a distinguished position there. In time, the Campbells had two children.

When he left Columbia, three companies offered Campbell jobs. He chose an advertising position with the J. Walter Thompson agency because he wanted to learn about consumer marketing. After training, Campbell took over the Eastman Kodak account in New York. He became a VP at J. Walter Thompson, before Kodak hired him away to direct its film business. After running the film division, Campbell and his family moved to Europe with Kodak.

Campbell returned to the United States to join Apple Computer in 1983. John Sculley recruited Campbell as VP of marketing. Campbell excelled at the Cupertino company, leveraging his leadership and business strategy skills to become an executive VP. At Apple, Campbell lived the challenges of running an engineering- and marketing-driven company. Here Campbell learned how to work with engineers, sell new technology hardware into the home market, and deal with a visionary, strong-minded leader.

In 1987, Campbell went to Claris Corporation in Santa Clara, California, a software spinoff from Apple, as that company's president and CEO. At Claris he learned about developing and selling shrink-wrapped software to home and small business customers. When Apple's board refused to let Claris achieve independence via an IPO, Campbell began searching for innovative new technologies to bring to market.

Campbell found innovation at GO Corporation, in San Francisco. Founded by Jerry Kaplan with an investment from Mitch Kapor of Lotus 1-2-3 fame, GO focused on creating a computer tablet device that used a pen instead of a keyboard. As CEO at GO, Campbell learned to sell a brand new kind of technology, make alliances, and, ultimately, fail. GO's technology showed great promise and garnered significant investments, especially from Kleiner Perkins's Doerr, but in the end the competitive and technology problems could not be conquered and it could not find a market.

Campbell's final lesson at GO was about cutting losses. Its investors sold GO Corporation to AT&T in 1993 for a pittance, and so Campbell looked for a new company to join as Intuit searched for its new CEO.

Campbell and Cook had an amicable first meeting, but did not hit it off particularly well. "Bill Campbell and I had breakfast at the Stanford Park Hotel. It was OK—but there were no sparks from his heels. He didn't wow me, and I am not going to stop the search," Cook reported to Doerr. The athletic, fit man with the graying hair, intense stare, and raspy voice had not won over the cautious Cook.

Cook worried that Campbell was not strategic. At first blush, Campbell struck him as a "good ole boy." Eric Dunn's wife, Susan, however, had been outside counsel to GO, and she thought Campbell was a top-tier type. Tom Proulx had met Campbell in 1992, and weighed in from his sabbatical to say that Campbell impressed him, too.

When Doerr suggested that Cook "schedule some open time on a Saturday or Sunday" to talk to Campbell some more, Cook set up another meeting. Cook and Campbell met at Campbell's Palo Alto house one Sunday and talked about business. Sitting on the green plaid couch in Campbell's study, Cook showed Campbell a demo of QuickBooks. The demo stirred Campbell's enthusiasm. Campbell realized that Cook's vision for Intuit extended far beyond Quicken, and the possibilities in multiple markets and products intrigued him.

For his part, Cook focused his interview questions around specific skills such as Campbell's ability to develop people. For every question asked, Campbell convincingly demonstrated his thorough experience and abilities with multiple examples. Later, as they walked along University Avenue, Cook realized that Campbell was growing on him. "You feel, over time, what he is," Cook recalled. "He and your guts start to bond. You start feeling energized by being around him." That moment was a turning point. "I came back and said I didn't see it before but this guy is really good at the stuff that we are looking for."[4]

Campbell began interviewing in earnest, meeting with company directors as well as all VPs and the outside board members. In all, he spoke with more than fifteen people and won them over one by one. Dunn said, "We were willing to be led. Bill Campbell seemed like a nice guy, a little bit of a stranger to us, but overall we told Scott to go for it."[5] Cook, convinced he'd found the right person to lead the company, offered Campbell the job. In April 1994 Bill Campbell became the second president and CEO of Intuit, while Scott Cook remained as chairman of the board (see figure 13-1).

FIGURE 13 - 1

Bill Campbell joined Intuit as president and CEO in 1994. He became chairman of the board in 1998.
Source: Courtesy of Intuit.

THE BRADY BUNCH—MINUS THE PARENTS

When Campbell joined Intuit, he swiftly identified and priori-
tized the company's three major weaknesses. He focused first on
making the merger work and integrating the companies, since a
dysfunctional merger would threaten the company's future. Operational improvements, in areas such as manufacturing, tech support, and internal systems, required Campbell's next most urgent
attention, as inefficiencies in these areas impeded profitability and
growth, and combining with Intuit South further complicated
operations. Finally, Campbell looked for new markets for Intuit,
including acquisitions and international opportunities, to fuel the
company's growth.

Cultural differences were the biggest stumbling block in the
integration of Intuits North and South. They resembled each
other in many ways, with similar focus on financial products, size,
employees, and attitudes. But each had its own history, rituals, and
habits. Each believed strongly in its own way of doing things and
attributed its success to its characteristic values.

As Intuit South executive VP Bill Harris put it: "We're like
two groups of children now part of the same family. Like a mom

with kids already, a dad with kids already, and now they're married. We were like the Brady Bunch but from a managerial point of view, there was no mom or dad in the house. Scott Cook was still the leader from the vision and strategy point of view but was never interested in day-to-day administrative things. We had these new kids cohabiting and nobody to tell them when it was time to go to bed."[6]

Campbell formalized executive committee meetings and required regular attendance by all senior managers. First, though, he had to gain agreement on just who were the senior managers. "John Monson's view was that a lot of San Diego guys didn't contribute and were not up to the same caliber," Campbell noted, "so he fought having some of them on."[7] Moreover, executives functioning at the same level did not always have the same titles, even within Intuit South. Once he had quashed the protests and named his team, Campbell held mandatory Monday morning meetings, sometimes in San Diego, with all Intuit senior managers. These meetings became the cornerstone of Intuit's executive decision making.

Next, Campbell reorganized Intuit to increase its operating effectiveness. Having experienced various organizational structures in his career helped him. Before the merger, Intuit had been managed in large functional groups such as marketing and product development. After the merger, this structure became unwieldy. Campbell reorganized the company into business units (BUs) and gave each BU manager profit and loss responsibility.

The Personal Finance Group, with Quicken as its anchor, became one BU, with Eric Dunn as its leader. Automatic Financial Services, responsible for Intuit's online strategies, became another, with Steve Pelletier as its head. QuickBooks morphed into the Business Products Group under John Monson. Personal Tax operated as an independent group under Mark Goines, and Bill Shepard managed the Professional Tax group, with Bill Harris overseeing both as executive VP of the tax BU. Supplies continued under Jim Heeger's management. Functions that served all the units, such as marketing communications and customer research, remained centrally located, but the new structure promoted responsibility, decision making, and a measure of autonomy within the newly created business units.

Campbell next initiated a strategic planning process for the company. Intuit's VMOVA effort had set the cornerstone for strategic planning by identifying the company's values and mission. Campbell built on these to codify and energize strategic operational thinking. He instituted monthly operation reviews, in which senior managers provided updates so that Campbell could help set goals and track revenues and expenses. Cook welcomed the discipline in these monthly reviews, which harkened back to the quantitative analysis and metrics he'd introduced to marketing.

In the middle of each quarter, Campbell held an offsite at which each manager submitted a business plan with numerical goals and reviewed performance against these goals. Business leaders presented quarter-to-date results and objectives for the next quarter; at each meeting leaders had six weeks' performance data for the current quarter and six weeks to plan for the next one. Each manager could change key variables—staffing, expenses, direct-marketing spending, tech support, and so on— before the next quarter began. In addition to planning for their own units, managers also worked together to tackle corporate issues that cut across businesses. Over a period of time, Campbell's meetings generated a perpetual quarterly plan.

These management planning offsites, often held at the coast in picturesque Half Moon Bay, unified the company. Intense pool-hall battles followed the strenuous all-day meetings. Campbell valued the social as much as the strategic elements of the meetings because he knew that stronger relationships would improve teamwork and business results. After a few quarters, he had a management team working effectively together, both formally and informally. Intuit was beginning to function as a whole instead of as Intuits North and South.

Campbell believed that Intuit could grow only as much as its individual employees grew, and so he fostered feedback and development mechanisms throughout the company. He created a class about management and values and recruited senior managers to teach it throughout the company. He insisted on regular performance reviews and comprehensive training for employees. He formed a committee to support gay and lesbian employees and worked to ensure that Intuit was a good place to work for everyone. He expanded the human resources department and worked to standardize employment and compensation practices across the company. He mentored and promoted women managers across the company. Of all Intuit's operational values, "It's the people" mattered most to Campbell. This heartfelt dedication to employees resulted in a deep level of loyalty to Campbell.

During his first several months, Campbell faced several difficult decisions. First, Campbell found that Intuit's call center in Palo Alto did not operate efficiently. So Campbell made the tough and painful call that Intuit management had been putting off: He closed down the Palo Alto center and moved the customer service and tech support functions to the newly opened Tucson call center that ChipSoft had commissioned before the merger and to another new call center near Albuquerque.

Tucson's and Albuquerque's relatively low cost of labor compared to California had attracted ChipSoft. Though the company offered to move any employee that wanted to join Intuit in Tucson, only about ten employees decided to move. Other positions were found for about 140 of the employees, but 150 were let go in Intuit's first real layoff, which shook Intuit's culture.

Campbell also closed Intuit's anachronistic manufacturing facilities in Menlo Park, outsourcing both manufacturing and distribution. This change saved Intuit millions of dollars in the first full year. The company centralized purchasing negotiations and processes. Heeger streamlined the supplies acquisition process, entering into a series of strategic, long-term check vendor contracts that solidified the company's strength in this important profit center.

Campbell, working with VP of sales Alan Gleicher, made sales more disciplined and professional. When Egghead asked for a special deal, Campbell called its CEO. "Let me tell you what we're doing," he began. "You get the same deal as everybody else. If I gave you a deal you'd wonder if somebody else got a better one. As long as I am CEO there are *no* deals. We have integrity at the highest level. Nobody puts their hands out to us."[8] On this issue Campbell would not compromise.

To improve Intuit's call centers and direct-marketing operations, Campbell hired an experienced Apple operations manager, Dave Kinser, as a consultant. In the call centers, Kinser standardized operations. The direct sales and service groups interfaced with each product group and with direct marketing. As Kinser observed, "Basically there were four masters yanking the call centers all over the place. We got them to feel like they were more of an independent organization; they could stand up and impose some requirements on the rest of the company to get consistency."[9]

By making the merger work and introducing real improvements, Campbell won the trust and respect of Intuit's employees. Harris ruefully observed, "Many of us, fascinated by various questions, were quite happy debating them well into the night. We were a bunch of articulate people who believed passionately in stuff, and that's fun but not very efficient. When Campbell came he would quickly delegate decisions and everyone would go on their way. Bill Campbell is a nuts-and-bolts, operations-oriented, let's get it done kind of guy."[10] Campbell's decisive approach and warm manner ended debates and moved the company forward.

THE TEST

Campbell's reorganization couldn't anticipate certain wrinkles. One crisis occurred in its software system for managing customer orders and relationships. Merging the information systems from the two companies had strained the organizations. In late summer 1994, a call center manager had authorized the installation of a beta version of the MACS software, ordering system software from Manufacturers' Agents Computer Systems, to support all order taking for Intuit. This decision, made without sufficient oversight, proved disastrous. The beta version, not fully tested or documented, ground to a halt during the busy holiday season. Customer service representatives had to take orders by hand; reps had stacks of paperwork and no system for communicating orders to the distributors or manufacturer.

One customer in California ordered a copy of TurboTax and ended up with an entire, sealed pallet full of product. When he called in to customer service to report the problem, a *second* pallet was delivered to his home. Fortunately the customer had a sense of humor; when he called in to report delivery of the second pallet, he said, "Look, this time can I just take one copy off so I can start my taxes?" Clearly, the ordering system was ineffective, and Campbell commanded a rapid migration to an alternative system to fix the problems. Such operational crises, though, underscored the difficulties in achieving scale for future growth.

The company also experienced a significant software bug in 1994, this time in the TurboTax program. A customer using Turbo-Tax in late fall discovered that the program did not correctly calculate depreciation and its tax effect. Intuit knew nothing of the bug until the customer called technical support about it. Because of the type of calculation involved, the bug would affect only a few customers, causing them to underpay their taxes. The customer who called was a "cheap professional"—Intuit slang for a professional tax preparer who violated the company's licensing agreement by purchasing the consumer version of TurboTax and reusing it instead of buying the more expensive ProTax version. When the customer called again, technical support unwisely ignored him.

The displeased customer next called the *San Francisco Chronicle*. "Tax Bug in TurboTax" screamed the headline that Cook read the next day on his way out of town on a business trip. Cook continued on his trip, leaving damage control to Campbell. Even though Campbell and his team reacted with amazing swiftness, they couldn't prevent the story from spreading to the *Wall Street Journal,* CNN, the *New York Times,* and local television stations and newspapers.

Some of the pre-Campbell animosity resurfaced, as certain managers from Intuit North blamed the culture of Intuit South for failing to honor the customer. But this initial dissension disappeared with Intuit South's "do what it takes" efforts to fix the problem. Mark Goines, head of the personal tax business, went without sleep for four nights in a row. Brainstorming solutions with the management team, he used a private plane to fly to Tucson and obtain the customer's data to fix his tax return. Within three days, Intuit had installed new high-capacity phone lines to handle the call surge resulting from the negative publicity.

Customers everywhere wanted to know how the bug would impact their tax returns. Goines and Bill Strauss, head of the Tucson call center, joked about their offensive odor after days without showering or sleeping. With memories of the Quick-Books bug fiasco in mind, Intuit issued a series of press releases the same day the story broke that straightforwardly addressed the issue, revealed five additional problems, and outlined Intuit's solution. Intuit shipped anyone a fixed version of TurboTax upon request, no questions asked. It set up automated phone ordering for concerned customers and spent about $300,000 shipping product and hiring temps to handle phone calls.

In the end, managers pulled together and weathered the storm. Managers at Intuit North agreed Intuit South had handled the crisis well. Intuit South was pleased with the response from customers and colleagues up North. Three weeks after the bug, Intuit's tax software revenues increased, as even the negative publicity turned out to be good publicity. Customer satisfaction declined at first because customers couldn't trust the product, but that ultimately rebounded as well.

With operations streamlined and the latest crises conquered, Campbell turned to the next big challenge facing Intuit: finding new opportunities for growth. Years ago, Cook had been determined to transform Intuit into more than just a one-product wonder. How could Campbell now help Intuit achieve an even broader strategy?

CHAPTER 14

EXIT FOCUS.
ENTER MICROSOFT.
AGAIN.

B ill Campbell's arrival at Intuit coincided with the end of an era. Despite occasional offers to return to Intuit, cofounder Tom Proulx had never returned after the sabbatical he'd arranged after the ChipSoft merger; to freely trade his stock while on leave, he had severed most ties with the company to avoid insider information. Proulx eventually decided to resign altogether to focus on a new challenge, a California ballot initiative to make frivolous shareholder lawsuits more difficult to file in state courts. Proulx's sister-in-law, Virginia Boyd, had earlier left Intuit for business school, and Tom LeFevre also resigned to invest in real estate. Intuit hosted a sentimental slide show for Proulx at a nearby movie theater to say farewell. For many, especially the old-time engineers, Proulx's departure was bittersweet. By mid-1994, Scott Cook and Eric Dunn were the only senior employees left from Intuit's earliest days.

Intuit's culture had evolved under Campbell's leadership. Campbell's innate people skills, honest approach, and natural charisma effectively motivated and led the troops. His enthusiasm and passion for the company were infectious, and his ubiquitous bear hugs, disarming. Campbell brought a new level of management and leadership to Intuit. His focus on operations and his skill at developing people made him the ideal managerial complement to Cook.

With Campbell, Cook, Dunn, John Monson, Steve Pelletier, Bill Harris, Charlie Gaylord, Alan Gleicher, and Jim Heeger now on the executive team, Intuit made steady progress in its core business areas. The tax group's ground-breaking cross-platform code base rolled out successfully across the full line of TurboTax and ProTax products, providing a much more efficient, reliable, and flexible way for engineers to update tax products each season. Requiring three years to develop, the tax code base provided a single unified architecture so tax forms only needed to be built once every season for all platforms. Intuit recognized its tax code base as an important competitive advantage.

The QuickBooks group steadily improved its product, tech support, and marketing, finding new and profitable ways to acquire customers through print, radio, and television ads. Vertically-oriented QuickBooks ads geared toward specific industries like farming and construction paid out handsomely. The supplies group, selling checks, invoices, and envelopes, improved its product catalog and its service levels in areas such as error rates and order turnaround, resulting in higher customer satisfaction and lower costs.

Quicken continued to improve its product and market leadership position, successfully competing against Microsoft Money's annual upgrade enhancements. The Quicken group boosted profit margins by introducing a higher-priced, more fully featured Deluxe edition in addition to its lower-end Basic edition. This high-end line extension strategy was another marketing innovation in the software industry and later became common practice.

Quicken also successfully fended off a new competitor, Simply Money by Computer Associates of Islandia, New York. This personal finance program shipped more than a million copies quickly because the price was right: Computer Associates gave out their first version free. Intuit nervously scrutinized market research data to determine how to respond to Simply Money's pioneering giveaway technique but because Simply Money did not gain significant usage or upgrade rates, the company did not take further action.

Despite these successes, Intuit struggled to find a sense of identity and purpose during 1994. As the company's core businesses thrived, the "what's next" question hung over everyone's head. Intuit employees knew that Wall Street and senior management alike expected constant growth from the company, especially given the overall growth in high tech. Despite the company's success at fending them off thus far, the fear of formidable Microsoft entering other businesses or launching newer, more successful products loomed. By mid-1994 the company furiously embraced a dizzying array of new business opportunities to drive growth and trump competition, but success at these new efforts proved elusive.

FUMBLES

As part of his impetus toward growth, Campbell put Intuit's acquisition and business development efforts into high gear. In early summer 1994, Campbell and Harris led Intuit to its first major acquisition post-ChipSoft: Parsons Technology of Cedar Rapids, Iowa, bought for $31.5 million and $36 million of Intuit stock. Intuit chose Parsons because it made the third best-selling tax preparation software product of the time, Personal Tax Edge, as well as a personal finance product, MoneyCounts, and several other consumer software products.

Acquiring Parsons kept competitors, particularly Microsoft, from purchasing it and threatening Intuit. Parsons was the one company other than Intuit that could provide Microsoft an instant foothold in tax. If Microsoft bought Parsons, improved its products, and used the behemoth's marketing clout to sell them, it could theoretically pose a big threat to Intuit.

Moreover, Parsons, with its many different types of consumer software, had a huge direct-marketing proficiency with nearly two million customers. More than 90 percent of its $50 million in 1994 revenues resulted from its direct-mail, catalog, and telemarketing efforts. Campbell believed that Intuit could learn from Parsons' well-developed direct marketing practices. Parsons' operating profits—approximately 10 percent—slightly exceeded Intuit's, which were in the 8 or 9 percent range, and Campbell hoped that Parsons' focus on operating profit also would instruct Intuit managers.

Initially, Parsons seemed to be a successful acquisition. Intuit locked up Parsons' products, and Parsons used its direct-mail programs to cross-sell Intuit products. Over time, however, integrating Parsons' remote operations and divergent culture posed problems. Culturally, Intuit and Parsons were poles apart: Intuit focused like a laser on customers and innovation in financial software, while Parsons produced diverse products, from financial and medical to Bible verse software, and emphasized refining their direct marketing rather than developing breakthrough products.

Intuit tried to assign Parsons' functional groups to their corresponding Intuit groups to transfer learning between the two companies, but turf battles sprang up. Eventually, Campbell agreed to a standoff in which Parsons operated as a separate entity from Intuit. Unlike the situation with ChipSoft, Parsons' minor contributions to Intuit did not warrant the effort needed for full integration.

Intuit also found mixed success growing internationally, even though Microsoft succeeded in its international markets. Dunn had overseen the creation of Intuit offices in the United Kingdom, France, and Germany in 1993 and 1994, and the international group now tried to establish viable businesses in Japan, Mexico, South America, and other European countries.

The company's method for opening new markets involved recreating a miniature version of itself in each location, but this approach sometimes lacked an effective local element. Not only did business practices in the other countries vary widely, but so did currency, banking, and credit systems. Intuit's technique did not always reflect these divergences. In general, Intuit underestimated the local investment that the international businesses required to succeed.

Dunn believed that Intuit also faced bad timing. The company rolled out additional international software products just as interest in home banking intensified. To respond to this interest and prove its technical aptitude, Intuit had to spend a lot of money in Europe to connect its products to banks. Trying to work with foreign banks and making international connectivity alliances competed for attention with both the international software businesses and U.S. bank alliance efforts. Although Intuit's efforts in Canada succeeded, creating profitable businesses in other countries remained a daunting task.

Intuit also considered myriad other alliances. The *Wall Street Journal* and Reuters each approached Intuit trying to tie business news content into the company's software, but those deals came to nothing. Intuit struggled to decide on relevant criteria for alliances, but none of the alliances offered enough for Intuit to risk the distraction.

On the product and platform front, as though to prove that growth could come as much from internal innovation as from external acquisition, Intuit developed a huge—if not exactly sizzling—array of new financial products. Many of these utilized the CD-ROM technology that Intuit executives embraced as "the next big thing." In 1994, helping consumers manage their finances by providing reams of data via CD-ROM seemed a natural addition to the company's software efforts.

The company's 1994 development projects included the following:

- *Pocket Quicken* for personal digital assistants such as the Tandy Zoomer, HP 200LX, and General Magic

- *Quicken Companion* to do home inventory and tax estimation

- *ExpensAble* expense account tracking software

- *Your Mutual Fund Selector* mutual fund analysis software

- *Parents' Guide to Money* to help parents understand the costs of raising children

- *Quicken Family Lawyer,* a rebranded version of Parsons' It's Legal software product

- *Quicken Financial Planner* retirement planning software

The Quicken Financial Planner story typified these efforts. Data affirmed that most people living in the United States didn't have a retirement plan, but needed one. Developing an easy-to-use software product to help the large baby boomer market plan for retirement seemed like a no-brainer. The product idea fit in the financial arena and could provide a real benefit to consumers.

The Quicken Financial Planner product team began with the "right" customer research approach, the method that Intuit had found successful in the past to develop its new products. The product team conducted numerous focus groups, usability tests, and phone surveys to fine-tune the product and marketing. They created software using an interview format that made entering the needed data straightforward. The product gave users an evaluation of where they stood with their retirement planning and suggested steps to meet their goals. Even with the rigorous research, an easy-to-use software design, the Quicken brand name, the marketing directly to Intuit's installed customer base, an attractive price point, and rigorous retail support, Quicken Financial Planner, a CD-ROM release, did not sell nearly as many units as planned. The product dominated a market that remained stubbornly tiny.

Quicken Financial Planner, like the other products Intuit introduced in 1994, fit strategically but was not profitable. Campbell said, "Intuit can't afford to have $5 million revenue products; we know that the fixed marketing and engineering expenses preclude it. We have to have products that scale to make at least $10 million to make them worthwhile."[1] Intuit continued to experiment, hoping that its projects would reach the $10 million milestone.

WAVE OF THE FUTURE?

Though its many other efforts drew time and resources, Intuit's major strategic impetus revolved around the banking industry. Intuit's focus on banking issues increased after Microsoft released an advertisement for its new version of Money in early 1994. The two-page ad, violating then-current software advertising norms, showed no people but rather a lone desk and chair with PC at nighttime and ad copy touting the benefits of banking at night. Although Intuit internally mocked Microsoft for highlighting what was then a minor software feature, the ad nonetheless increased Intuit's interest in signing up banking partners. Pelletier, head of Automated Financial Services, worked furiously to enroll banks in the online services Intuit offered before Microsoft locked them all up.

Intuit's executive team thought that home banking would become popular, and enabling customers to pay bills online (i.e., electronic "billpay") seemed a good first step to help customers manage their finances electronically. Dunn and Pelletier predicted that electronic billpay and home banking would grow quickly, even using conservative assumptions about rates of adoption. Home PC penetration had increased to about 28 percent of U.S. households in 1994, and most PCs shipped with built-in modems.[2] The company's decision to bet on e-finance entailed the same calculated risk taking used for previous development bets on new operating systems.

But Intuit didn't take every bet. Ten years after Intuit had come up dry when it sought financial investors, many companies wanted to partner with the most successful financial software company in the country. E*Trade, then a dial-up brokerage service offered through CompuServe, offered to let Intuit purchase it for less than $100 million. E*Trade believed that Quicken could be used to drive more customers to E*Trade's brokerage services. Pelletier and Cook worried that owning a branded brokerage service would alienate the popular brokers and banks used by Quicken's customers, so they persuaded Intuit to pass up its opportunity to acquire the electronic brokerage, later worth more than $2.5 billion.

Wells Fargo also proposed an alliance. The banking giant told Intuit it would pay the company to handle all Wells Fargo's dial-up financial transactions. While the offer included the possibility of a joint venture into e-banking, Wells Fargo required that Intuit discontinue business with every other financial institution. Cook and Campbell decided that an exclusive arrangement with Wells did not suit Intuit.

Intuit did decide to invest in electronic bill payment. Dunn had added billpay to the Quicken program in 1990. For a short time, Intuit had contemplated creating its own billpay fulfillment service in the early 1990s, but after investigation Dunn and Cook had conceded that electronic bill payment was too operations-intensive for Intuit to handle.

In April 1990, Dunn chose CheckFree Corporation of Columbus, Ohio, the leading provider of bill payment fulfillment services, as Intuit's electronic billpay provider. For every Quicken customer signed up with CheckFree, CheckFree paid Intuit $20, and if the customer was still using the service a year later Intuit got another $20. After a slow start in Quicken 3.0 for DOS, Intuit made electronic bill payment central to Quicken 4.0 for DOS, and signed up about one hundred thousand billpay customers over several years for CheckFree. In return, CheckFree paid Intuit nearly $4 million during the early 1990s.

When Dunn had renegotiated Intuit's deal with CheckFree in 1991, his concern about Microsoft entering the personal finance software market prompted him to propose an exclusive deal with CheckFree if Intuit met certain sign-up levels. CheckFree agreed: so long as Intuit signed up at least 6,500 customers per quarter, CheckFree would not provide its bill payment services to any other financial software company.

In the early years, both Intuit and CheckFree ignored this exclusivity, but when Microsoft entered the personal finance software market in 1991 the importance of Dunn's clever exclusivity clause became clear. Microsoft added electronic bill payment to its version 3.0 of Money in early 1994, and after Intuit enforced the exclusivity clause in its multiyear CheckFree distribution contract, Microsoft was forced to offer its billpay services through a secondary bill payment provider, National Payments Clearinghouse, Inc., located outside Chicago.

Intuit continued to work with CheckFree for electronic bill payment fulfillment, but CheckFree's customer service concerned Intuit. A significant number of customers complained to Intuit about missed payments and poor customer service at CheckFree. Intuit and CheckFree also argued about who ultimately "owned" the joint Quicken-CheckFree customers. So, Intuit began searching for an alternative solution to its CheckFree alliance and identified another possible billpay provider, US Order. That alternative was abandoned when Dunn and Pelletier learned that Visa was in the process of purchasing that company.

"This Really Is from Bill Gates . . ."

With the US Order avenue closed, the search for alternatives to CheckFree continued. Charlie Gaylord, Intuit's executive VP at large, and Pelletier came up with the idea of purchasing a billpay provider outright, to ensure that Quicken billpay would meet Intuit's standards for customer service and to extend Intuit's customer relationships. After Visa bought US Order, only CheckFree and National Payments Clearinghouse remained. Given its market valuation, CheckFree would cost Intuit about $200 million to purchase, while the privately held National Payments Clearinghouse was available for under $7 million.

Even though CheckFree was the market leader, Intuit executives had always had a strained alliance with the company and were not eager to acquire it. Intuit looked down on CheckFree's poor customer service, and many senior Intuit managers were uneasy with CheckFree's CEO, Pete Kight. Moreover, they knew that National Payments Clearinghouse was Microsoft's billpay provider and thought that having Microsoft depending on them for a key service would be an audacious competitive coup. So, Intuit purchased National Payments Clearinghouse in late summer 1994.

After the acquisition, Campbell discovered to his dismay that National Payments Clearinghouse had fairly primitive capabilities in the fulfillment area of its service. The company used a low-end Tandem computer to process payments and low-tech HP laser printers to print checks. The company saved on postage by manually collating all checks to the same vendors. When Intuit acquired it, National Payments Clearinghouse had limited transaction volume from Microsoft Money and its telephone billpay service, so scale challenges had neither arisen nor been addressed. Intuit executives were flabbergasted at National Payments Clearinghouse's primitive service and their own due diligence failure. In their zeal to acquire Microsoft's provider, Intuit had seriously erred in not pursuing a thorough investigation of the company.

But there were compensations. In September 1994, *Business-Week* ran an article about Scott Cook that mentioned Microsoft repeatedly. The reporter discussed electronic banking and billpay as central to the Microsoft Money team's strategy—and also disclosed that Intuit had just purchased Microsoft's electronic bill payment provider.[3] This revelation caused great, if petty, satisfaction among Intuit executives and probably affected what happened next.

As head of Intuit's Automated Financial Services group, Pelletier needed to form relationships with National Payments Clearinghouse's clients after the purchase. In that vein, he sent an e-mail to the head of the Microsoft Money team to kick off discussions between the two companies, which were now partners as well as competitors. Pelletier did not receive a reply directly. Instead, in late September, an e-mail with the sender name of Bill Gates startled Scott Cook. The brief e-mail included a copy of Pelletier's e-mail to Microsoft. "This really is from Bill Gates," the e-mail began. "Let's talk about something bigger."[4]

CHAPTER 15

ONE MORE BILL

Cook called his executive committee together to read them Gates's brief but tantalizing e-mail. Though Gates spelled nothing out, his interest in a bigger deal could only mean one thing: Microsoft wanted to purchase Intuit. John Monson spoke first. "You have got to be kidding." Bill Campbell, who had led Intuit for only five months, chimed in, "Never in a million years!"

Through acquisition and development, Microsoft had become the market-leading provider of word-processing software, spreadsheets, databases, presentation software, and other application programs to complement its operating system dominance. Its 1994 revenues were $4.65 billion, up from $1.84 billion just three years earlier. Its stature and market share increased with nearly every market it entered—except personal and small business financial management.

In late summer 1994, Microsoft agreed to a Department of Justice consent decree that prohibited the company from requiring computer manufacturers who licensed Windows to also license other Microsoft software products. The consent decree ended several years of antitrust litigation; critics claimed that the decree barely checked the company's monopolistic practices.[1] Though the Internet boom was on the horizon, Netscape Communications, of Mountain View, California, had not yet seriously threatened Microsoft.

In his initial response to Gates, Cook aimed to smoke out whether Gates had launched one of Microsoft's infamous fishing expeditions. Cook remembered all too well Microsoft's licensing offer for Quicken on the Windows platform that had fallen through three years earlier. Two phone calls later, Gates convinced Cook of his genuine interest.

Gates had decided that if he couldn't beat Intuit, he would buy it. As Microsoft executive VP Mike Maples noted, "Intuit never turned its market share advantage into profitability. It was in the 7 to 10 percent profit range, which was pretty dismal. Good software companies should have profitability in the 20 to 30 percent range."[2] Microsoft thought it could improve that bottom line.

Microsoft's interest galvanized a ferocious, polarizing debate among Intuit's senior managers. Those in favor of the merger cited several major benefits. Becoming part of Microsoft would speed up Intuit's drive to provide the technical interface between consumers and financial institutions. For many years, Intuit, driven by a vision of universal home banking, had envisioned serving banks and brokers by providing Quicken as their consumer interface. But the company was struggling to get financial institutions to support statement downloads into Quicken. As part of Microsoft, Intuit's Automated Financial Services unit, led by merger proponent Steve Pelletier, would immediately gain the credibility and stature to convince banks and brokerages to choose Quicken as their computer interface with consumers.

Merger supporters also cited Microsoft's international success and global presence. Intuit had fought to create a global business; the Microsoft name would instantly improve Intuit's credibility, and distribution, around the world. Further, becoming part of Microsoft would reduce some of the overall business risk still facing Intuit. Microsoft's robust financials and enormous resources would enable Intuit to achieve its business goals while buffering the company against problems.

Finally, merging with Microsoft would eliminate the continued threat of Microsoft's operating system dominance. Most Intuit executives worried about Microsoft including competitive software directly in its Windows operating system, thereby destroying Intuit's businesses. The experience of several software companies that had seen their products' functions subsumed into Windows confirmed these fears. Quarterdeck Software expired when its memory management features were built into Windows and DOS 5.0. Stacker, leader of the stand-alone $100 million disk compression software category in 1992–1993, disappeared when similar technology was built into Windows. The Microsoft Outlook e-mail program offered free with Microsoft Office started to chip away at cc:Mail's e-mail software dominance in the mid-1990s.

Despite these fears, not everyone favored being swallowed by the giant. Intuit managers opposed to the merger believed the company could achieve its goals without becoming part of Microsoft. They feared that Microsoft would impose its own decisions on Intuit, redirect the company away from its objectives, and jeopardize Intuit's zeal for achieving its "big, hairy, audacious goals." These managers worried that Intuit's unique culture, with its fierce focus on customers, would disappear if the companies combined. And Intuit's productive and close retailer relationships—a significant competitive advantage—would also vanish.

Board member John Doerr and still-new CEO Campbell, who was hardly ready to relinquish his role as leader of an independent company, both opposed Intuit's "surrendering to the enemy." Both vigorously argued that Intuit would simply become a "burr under Microsoft's saddle."

All of the Intuit executives, familiar with the "buy and burn" concept in which a company would acquire another company and then absorb and eliminate it, worried about how Intuit would fare post acquisition. Many thought that Intuit would eventually be dismembered and its employees either laid off or forced to move to Redmond. Even for the pro-merger managers, this concern loomed large. Managers also naturally worried that competitor Microsoft might use merger discussions to gain unfair knowledge about Intuit's business and plans.

Cook listened, and he formulated his negotiation points with Gates to address these worries. In his first in-person meeting with Gates, held at the United Red Carpet Club at the San Francisco Airport, Cook told Gates that Intuit could not provide Microsoft with any confidential information, strategy, or product plans until (and if) the two companies had physically merged. Gates had to agree to conduct all due diligence using only public information on Intuit. He instantly agreed. Gates spent the rest of that meeting detailing his overall vision for the high-tech industry and Microsoft's role in it. Since Gates had initiated discussions, Cook felt comfortable questioning him about a wide range of Microsoft's strategies and initiatives. Cook left this meeting, his first intense discussion with Gates, thoroughly impressed with Gates's vision and leadership.

Despite these good feelings, Gates was not able to change Cook's lingering bias toward Intuit's independence. After meditating on the meeting and on the possible merger benefits, Cook structured a memo for a board of directors meeting in which he detailed a "devil's advocate" position on every positive aspect of the merger, including the possible market power the combined company might possess. After each hypothetical assertion about how the merger was necessary for Intuit, Cook presented a rebuttal showing why it was not and why Intuit would succeed by itself. After the board reviewed this document, most agreed that Intuit should continue independently. Cook then told his executive staff that he did not favor pursuing the merger with Microsoft.

Pelletier and Business Products Group general manager John Monson, never natural allies at Intuit, both received this news with dismay. Over the next two weeks, they worked to convince Cook that while Intuit could succeed alone, the increased resources and market power afforded by a Microsoft merger would accelerate the accomplishment of Intuit's key objectives. That Monson and Pelletier agreed vehemently swayed Cook. They convinced Cook that the merger, while not necessary for Intuit, would help the company better achieve its mission. Despite his presentation to the board, he decided to set up another meeting with Gates.

ONE MORE BILL . . . .

At the next meeting, Cook exacted an important concession: Gates agreed that if Microsoft purchased Intuit, Microsoft would keep Intuit intact and in California. Intuit managers would run Intuit's business and all related pieces in their current locations, and all Microsoft efforts related to finance and electronic commerce would be transferred to Intuit's control. Gates told Cook that he wanted to purchase Intuit not for the software code the company had created but for the team that had created it. As Microsoft had done with its PowerPoint division, Gates planned to keep Intuit alive and independent in California.

Gates also agreed that Microsoft would remove the likely antitrust concerns from the merger by selling its Microsoft Money software to another credible software company. At the end of this meeting, conducted in the United Red Carpet club meeting room at the Sea-Tac Airport, Cook jeopardized their cloak-and-dagger approach by exclaiming loudly just as he and Gates walked into the crowded airport club lobby, "This could be the biggest merger in software history!"[3] Both men worriedly surveyed the room and relaxed only when they saw that no one had overheard Cook's impulsive remark.

When he returned from Seattle, an optimistic Cook reported on Gates's response to his executive team and the company's board. Both groups appreciated that Gates intended to keep Intuit separate and relatively autonomous. This, they believed, would allow Intuit to continue to "Wow" its customers. Selling Microsoft Money was another huge compromise. With the leading objections addressed, the next logical question arose: How much would Microsoft be willing to pay? This debate spawned discussions of appropriate share prices; managers and directors peppered Cook with estimates of appropriate valuations.

Cook had planned a vacation for the following week in August, and he refused to let business exigencies stall his family plans. As a result, the final top-level negotiations between Gates and Cook, concerning price, were conducted over the phone, with Cook telephoning Gates from the only convenient phone near his Lake Tahoe rental: the pay telephone at the nearby 7-Eleven convenience store. The negotiation, with Cook speaking furtively as shoppers bustled past, spanned several days and broke off three times over impasses. But finally, as Cook shivered in the unseasonably cold thirty-degree Fahrenheit morning chill outside the store, he secured an offer from Gates for a price that would satisfy Intuit shareholders. The total deal would amount to approximately $1.5 billion in Microsoft stock, a 40 percent premium over Intuit's current value. Remarkably, Gates, intent on acquiring Intuit, agreed to a downside deal price limit but no upside cap on the deal's value. So, if Microsoft's stock price increased before the merger was finalized, Intuit's actual purchase price would grow over the initial $1.5 billion offer.

After the general agreement, Cook worked to make Campbell comfortable with the deal. If the merger went through, Campbell would lead the former Intuit, Microsoft's new financial software division, while Cook was to report directly to Gates to formulate Microsoft's overall electronic commerce strategy. Campbell had to be comfortable with Microsoft management in order to make the deal work. As Campbell learned more about Microsoft and his likely new boss, Mike Maples, he warmed to the arrangement, even though it meant sacrificing Intuit's complete independence and his own new CEO title.

Yet ambivalence lingered as board members debated the merger's pros and cons. Campbell had become a convert. In September, as Campbell and Doerr flew to Tucson for a meeting, Campbell told Doerr that Cook's enthusiasm and arguments had convinced him to support the deal. "Scott started Intuit," Campbell told Doerr, "and Scott really wants this deal. So let's just do it."[4] After additional vigorous, thoughtful discussions about the cultures, strategies, technologies, and roles of the two companies, Intuit's board decided to proceed.

Campbell and Bill Harris led the transaction negotiations for Intuit. Campbell focused on securing appropriate salaries and titles for Intuit employees. Wanting to maintain Intuit's retail edge, he insisted to Microsoft's executive VP Steve Ballmer that Intuit maintain a separate retail sales force, and Ballmer eventually capitulated. Campbell and Harris also ensured that any Intuit staff laid off with the merger would receive generous financial packages.

In October, Campbell, Harris, and Gordy Davidson, Intuit's outside counsel, flew to Seattle for the final one-day negotiations. That one day turned into a three-day marathon, and no one had packed for an overnight. The first day's meeting ran so late that the Intuit team had to rush to buy clothes before the stores closed. They ran to Sears and grabbed underwear off the shelves, throwing packages of clothes to each other across the aisles while talking on cell phones. Harris recalled, "I'm sure these guys at Sears thought they'd just been invaded by aliens. We all wore polyester shirts for the next few days."[5]

Intuit and Microsoft planned to announce the merger on October 13, 1994. On October 12, the Intuit team remained in Redmond finalizing the merger agreement. By late that evening, they neared completion; only a few minor points remained. As the night wore on, the exhausted senior Microsoft staff gradually departed, in reverse seniority order.

Finally, at 3:00 A.M., the group reached its last issue. Only one Microsoft representative, the most junior attorney of the whole group, remained in front of his PC with three Intuit representatives hanging over him. Everyone had been awake for hours, and the Intuit team began dictating words to the Microsoft attorney, who was mindlessly typing whatever he was told. Finally Harris dictated something to this attorney that had been hotly contested but unresolved. Harris told him to type the terms that Intuit wanted. The junior attorney was awake enough to realize this and paused for a moment, before conceding. "Tell Bill Neukom [Microsoft's chief legal officer] I fought like hell," he said.[6] He typed Intuit's language and then fell asleep on his office floor.

On October 13, 1994, the Intuit negotiating team returned to the Bay Area with the final agreement in hand. Both the Intuit and the Microsoft boards reviewed the final copies and gave their approval, though some at Microsoft, including Paul Allen, disliked the deal's high price and thought Microsoft should go it alone in the financial arena. News of the proposed merger leaked, and Intuit issued a press release confirming the two companies' discussion. Intuit's stock price increased 34 percent during the next day's trading.

ONE MORE BILLION

Intuit employees speculated about the potential acquisition. Cook realized that the news would surprise employees no matter how he announced it. He sent an e-mail to the company that said, "The rumors are true. Stay tuned." Very little work was done that day as Intuit employees indulged in endless hallway speculation. The raising of a large white tent in the Intuit parking lot traditionally used for company meetings further fueled speculation. By mid-afternoon, managers announced group meetings and confirmed the news to their teams: "We're going to merge with Microsoft." Right after the group meetings, employees walked out to the white tent for a historic all-hands discussion.

Once all the employees had filed in and the San Diego and Tucson offices were connected via videoconference, Scott Cook addressed the company that everyone present had worked so hard to build. First, Cook talked about the great new version of Quicken 4.0 for Windows, its features and large initial orders, drawing a defiant cheer from the crowd. He continued, "But now onto the big news of the day . . . in Beirut . . ." drawing a nervous laugh from the on-edge audience.

Then Cook got serious. "We've never been a company of tiny, small, wimpy ambitions," he began. Intuit's mission, he went on, was to dream of doing more than other companies ever dream of, of truly revolutionizing people's financial lives. And these financial lives were incredibly important, allowing people to have money when they need it—for college, for insurance, for their lives' needs. Flanked by Campbell on one side and Gates on the other, he confirmed the truth: "When we're done we will have led the revolution in digital financial services. We're in the big leagues now. In order to hold our own, to serve customer needs well, to make sure our ideas, our ideals, and our people triumph, we're teaming up with somebody today."[7] The crowd was hushed.

In the rhythmic phrases of a polished orator, Cook continued:

I have studied the Microsoft Corporation for four years. I've gotten to know them from afar, and up close over the past four months. There is no company in software and technology that has anything close to the leadership and track record that we have except one, and that's Microsoft. Only one that has the focus on the long-term, not short-term earnings, that has the phenomenal energy to recruit and have people as good as ours, and that's Microsoft. There's only one company so huge and yet so entrepreneurial in its divisions. There's only one company whose focus on continuous improvement is as good as ours, and that's Microsoft. There's only one company that I'd be proud to join, and that's Microsoft. Now there's no stopping us. . . . We'd rather make a bigger impact on the world.[8]

After Cook had concluded with a humorous "Top Ten Reasons to Get Psyched About the Microsoft Merger" (see figure 15-1), which had been e-mailed to all employees by its two marketing employee coauthors, Gates rose to address the crowd and affirm the reason for his interest in Intuit: "No matter how wonderful

193

FIGURE 15 - 1

Top Ten Reasons to Get Psyched About the Microsoft Merger

10. Close-up view of what a state-of-the-art pocket protector looks like.

 9. Easier to call in sick when the boss is in another state.

 8. Good excuse to move into the grunge scene.

 7. Free finger food on Thursday night and leftovers on Friday.

 6. New business cards for everyone.

 5. Intuit T-shirts now valuable collector's items.

 4. Makes spying on Microsoft much easier.

 3. Free Excel tech support.

 2. Employee meetings now to be held in the San Jose Arena.

 1. Access to exclusive Hawaiian wedding pictures.

Written by Christine Garofoli and Laurel Lee.

your market share is—and your market share is pretty wonderful (here he was interrupted by big applause)—that's not your enduring asset. The enduring asset is the quality of the people and their commitment to evolve things forward. Obsoleting your own products is the mark of a great company."[9] Gates continued in a positive and humorous vein, disclosing that TurboTax could not handle the number of digits involved in his personal tax return and closing his brief talk with an overhead slide of his picture with a conversation bubble drawn in exclaiming, "I switched to Quicken!"

When Gates finished, Campbell rose to speak. Unlike the two previous speakers, Campbell made clear his empathy for employees' ambivalence. "This," he said more than once, "is scary as hell."[10] Campbell affirmed Intuit's commitment to keeping Intuit an independent, thriving part of Microsoft. He echoed Cook's statement that, combined with Microsoft, Intuit's reach would be tremendous, empowering the company to leap forward in its core businesses. Even with the conciliatory words, however, Campbell had infuriated Gates with his frank acknowledgment of the potential worries about the deal for Intuit employees.

Cook's wife, Signe Ostby, drove to Sacramento that afternoon. She told her husband later that she listened to the meeting via her cell phone with tears running down her face. Ostby knew intellectually that the merger was good news, but emotionally, it saddened her. Intuit employees reacted similarly; some cried, and others were simply stunned. Senior management had already absorbed the news, but rank-and-file Intuit employees, who had fought Microsoft from the trenches for several years, bitterly lamented the loss of independence and struggled to accept the change.

After the meeting, Cook invited employees to a reception outside the tent, and handed out T-shirts to all. On the front, the shirt said "One More Bill" (Intuit had four VPs named Bill in addition to CEO Campbell) and on the back: "One More Billion." Quicken product manager Roy Rosin boldly asked Gates for his autograph, which Gates obligingly agreed to write along with the phrase, "Quicken is great!" Intuit issued a second press release to announce the acquisition, and the die was cast.

Although Cook believed in the Microsoft merger, he and Campbell worried about its impact on employees. To ensure they could properly address concerns, they commissioned employee focus groups in several company locations. Campbell and Cook found employees very worried that Intuit might not retain its company culture and roots and that people might lose their jobs. Employees feared Microsoft's culture and values. "Intuit values people and understands that employees have families," one commented. "With Microsoft, that's not the case. They're very driven; Microsoft is your life."[11] Another employee fretted: "Why wouldn't Microsoft try to decrease redundancies in the future? Why would Gates want to keep us autonomous?"[12]

Other Intuit employees resented the focus on Quicken in the company announcements about the merger: "All we hear about is Quicken, but we're not Quicken. How do we fit into a company that has mostly a personal (home computer user) product line? What's going to happen to us after the merger takes place?"[13] And some employees just hated the idea of the sale. "I'm quite disappointed that Scott could even consider this. Betrayed.

Beating Microsoft has been our focus. We're being sold to the devil, despite our hard work and effort. His excuse regarding international market access is a cop-out."[14]

A Gates misquote that appeared in *Fortune* magazine in February 1995 further alienated employees in the QuickBooks group. "You won't see us doing applications like small-business accounting," Gates was quoted as saying. *Fortune* published Gates's letter to its editor, in which he asserted: "You quote me as saying, 'You won't see us doing applications like small-business accounting.' What I actually said was, 'You won't see us doing accounting and finance applications beyond this QuickBooks small-business accounting thing. That is a very exciting part of Intuit.'"[15]

The retraction failed to quell the fury in the small business group, whose employees felt homeless and bereft in the face of the consumer orientation of the Microsoft merger announcement. Cook and Campbell struggled to address these broad-ranging concerns in the days following the announcement.

Further evidence of the companies' differing cultures lay in the stark contrast between Intuit's white tent meeting, with its T-shirts and hoopla, versus Microsoft's announcement to its Money team. Managers phoned Money team members at home on October 13 at 6:00 A.M. and asked them to report to work by eight o'clock that morning with no further explanation. Buses immediately whisked the team to a nearby hotel where, to their shock, security guards accompanied them inside. Microsoft managers informed the assembled team that Microsoft had agreed to acquire Intuit and sell Money to Novell. Since Microsoft was communicating this insider information while markets were open, they confined the entire Money team to the hotel conference room until the markets closed, with no access to phone or fax. Security guards even escorted workers to the bathroom.

Before he left for Menlo Park, Gates stopped in to discuss the change. Gates told the shocked team that his decision to acquire Intuit did not reflect problems with the Money product; rather, it showed that personal finance interested Gates. Gates said that the Money team, with its limited resources, had increased industry and public fascination with the category. Despite these placatory words, a Microsoft manager recalled that the team was, "definitely a stunned group at first. None of us had foreseen any of this coming. It threw us for a loop."[16]

But since the deal was not yet approved by the government, the Money team snapped back quickly, "We're going to show them; we'll build a better product," said one. Team morale returned with a vengeance as the group developed Money version 4.0 as a back-up strategy. A month of brainstorming had already gone into the new version, and Gates's news strengthened the team's resolve: "We can beat these guys. Microsoft doesn't need to pay outrageous amounts of money for personal finance software; we can do a better job. Let's show Bill Gates that he's wrong!"[17]

The acquisition announcement caused strong reactions in the financial industry. Gates had been widely quoted as saying bankers were "dinosaurs" in an interview earlier in 1994, and the dinosaurs saw the potential of Microsoft plus Intuit as very threatening indeed.

Microsoft's acquisition of Intuit "will reshape the home-banking landscape just as surely as it will change the structure of the personal-finance software market," wrote a columnist in *American Banker* magazine. "Joining forces, they pose an even bigger threat to the bankers who had been wary of each company's power to muscle in on customer financial relationships."[18]

Gates's blatant power mongering angered Microsoft competitors already disappointed by the weakness of the Justice Department's 1994 consent decree. Purchasing the market leader—a company with a market share higher than 75 percent in key areas of financial software—seemed an egregious extension of Microsoft's market dominance. *BusinessWeek* lamented that the recently announced, tepid decree did not slow "the juggernaut approach" of Gates one bit: "Some rival executives contend that the limited nature of the consent decree had emboldened—rather than chastened—Gates."[19]

CHAPTER 16

GOODBYE, GODZILLA

F or a short time, the Department of Justice (DOJ) issued no ruling or comment about Microsoft's proposed purchase of Intuit. In November 1994, however, the DOJ requested more information from both companies about the proposed acquisition, indicating that the deal might face intense antitrust scrutiny. Intuit and Microsoft management had expected this "second request," although avoiding it would have been a big win. Intuit executives believed that a big, high-visibility deal like the Microsoft one, with some obvious competitive issues, would draw the DOJ's infamous second request for more information about competitive issues.

According to the *LA Times,* the DOJ was trying to weigh the merger's implications for something that had not yet started but was expected to explode: the market for online electronic transactions. Gary Reback, an antitrust specialist at the Wilson Sonsini Goodrich & Rosati law firm in Palo Alto, prepared a white paper for the DOJ that argued Microsoft's clout and strategic purchase of Intuit would enable the company to become an even more dominant force in controlling networks Americans would use to make purchases and do banking. "Intuit controls most of this market," said Reback. "Microsoft is the only potential competitor. . . . [This deal] lets Microsoft seize another gateway that would otherwise take them five or six years to get."[1]

To determine whether the merger would harm consumers, the DOJ examined Intuit's prices on the Windows platform after Microsoft had entered that market. Intuit conceded that its software prices were lower in the Windows market, which obviously benefited consumers. Trying to finesse this potentially damaging data, the Intuit team provided information about the difficulty of persuading customers to migrate platforms along with the requested information on share and pricing.

Share and pricing information made up only part of the DOJ's daunting information requests. Intuit, and Microsoft to a lesser degree, had to provide market share and marketing plans for the previous ten years, as well as data on OEM activity, new product releases, market research, company acquisitions, and revenue by channel by month for the entire lifetime of the company. The company also had to recount significant meetings with other companies in the industry. Several people worked full-time to pull this voluminous information together. In addition, lawyers searched employee office files and scrutinized hard drives.

With its ChipSoft and Parsons deals, Intuit had had some success in winning government agreement to acquisitions. But when Intuit tried to collaborate with Microsoft's lawyers on responding to the DOJ, Microsoft rebuffed Intuit's people and its conciliatory approach. Increasingly, as Cook watched Microsoft interact with the government, he began to find Microsoft's attitudes disrespectful and entrenched. Instead of trying to work with the DOJ, Cook thought that Microsoft's attorneys defied the government. Cook characterized their response to the DOJ as "Get out of my face."[2]

At the same time, Microsoft publicly reiterated its commitment to the merger. As the holidays came and went, the two companies began discussing how to integrate and jointly meet with financial institutions. Even though Cook found Microsoft antagonistic toward the DOJ, Microsoft had made a major concession in selling Money. Given that special consideration, the companies still believed that the merger would go through.

REVERSAL OF FORTUNE

On Valentine's Day, 1995, U.S. District Court Judge Stanley Sporkin issued a ruling that stunned observers: He overturned the DOJ's 1994 Microsoft consent decree. Sporkin's unprecedented ruling found that the DOJ's consent decree had not gone far enough to protect the public and that the DOJ had not considered a broad enough range of charges before issuing its decree.

Sporkin's ruling ushered in a newly critical federal environment for Microsoft. Even though Janet Reno, then attorney general, fumed at Sporkin as she filed suit to appeal his ruling (and as Microsoft, ironically, joined her suit against the federal judge), the ruling deeply embarrassed Anne Bingaman, assistant attorney general in charge of the DOJ's Antitrust Division. The chorus of criticism increased, and Microsoft competitors bayed that the assistant attorney general had been "too lenient" with Microsoft. For her part, Bingaman remarked, "We get complaints about Microsoft all the time. We have become a kind of Microsoft complaints center. And we take them very seriously."[3]

Press response to the federal ruling focused on its effect on the potential Intuit deal. "Justice officials refused to say how the appeal of the consent decree might affect the agency's review of Microsoft's pending $1.5-billion purchase of Intuit Inc., the largest personal finance software company and a potential gateway for Microsoft to enter the huge home banking industry," reported the *LA Times*. Quoting Anne Bingaman: "The Microsoft's the same, but Intuit had nothing to do with this previous case. So we take these things a case at a time, a fact at a time, an allegation at a time, and that's a different case."[4]

When Bill Harris got the news about the Sporkin ruling, he immediately grasped the new risk for the Microsoft-Intuit deal. "It was a big red flag. And it was a rallying cry for criticism of Microsoft from many quarters."[5] Scrutiny of the Intuit deal mushroomed, Harris added. "All of a sudden the deal seemed more questionable."[6] Intuit executives fretted that Novell was a weak buyer of the Money product, given the company's lackluster performance in home productivity software that helped home PC users complete tasks. (Besides Intuit's financial products, home productivity software included products such as PrintShop and Microsoft Works.) Even though Intuit's stock price increased steadily, resulting in a much higher acquisition cost of $2.4 billion to Microsoft due to Cook's cannily negotiated terms, Intuit knew that hedge funds were betting that the deal might not go through, based on the 10 percent discount of the stock's trading price to the deal price.

Over the next three months, signs that Microsoft might withdraw from the deal started to mount. As the DOJ continued to question the companies, Microsoft refused to offer any further concessions. At a meeting in Redmond in April, Intuit was stunned to realize that Microsoft had not filed key papers with the DOJ by the specified deadline. This oversight jeopardized the entire negotiation with the DOJ.

When the DOJ went public about finding a copy of Cook's "devil's advocate" memo in the file of a senior Intuit executive, the publicity caused a serious turn for the worse. Rather than acknowledging the memo's unmistakable conclusion (that Intuit could succeed independently), the DOJ quoted Cook's assertions about increased market power due to the merger out of context and omitted the memo's lengthy rebuttal that disproved those assertions.

The *LA Times* also quoted from the September 1994 memo, which referred to Microsoft by the code name Godzilla, "an image whose significance wasn't lost on the antitrust department." Just as damaging, according to the lawsuit, was Cook's devil's advocate view on how the merger would affect business: "Elimination of competition will enhance that success, perhaps greatly."[7]

In May, the DOJ announced that it would file suit to prevent Microsoft's purchase of Intuit. Cook immediately vowed publicly to fight the DOJ, but when reporters asked Microsoft representatives about the ruling, Microsoft responded in vague terms. Cook then requested a meeting in Redmond to coordinate the upcoming legal battle.

Cook, Campbell, and Intuit legal counsel Gordy Davidson flew to Redmond, where about half a dozen Microsoft people met them in a conference room. Gates drew a decision tree on a whiteboard, illustrating various possible outcomes. Gates concluded that sitting in limbo for the long period of a trial would harm Microsoft. Money would continue to flounder. Quicken would continue to overshadow it. Ultimately, if the DOJ said no on the deal, Microsoft would suffer strategically.

Campbell recalled: "He was telling us that this was over. I know Scott, in his earnest way, was engaging on the tree. I sat there, listened, and finally said, 'You're telling us you want to bag the deal.' And Gates said, 'Yeah.'"[8] Cook had not expected this response. He had come to Redmond to explore ways to accommodate the DOJ and make the deal work. Attorney Davidson had formulated a list of actions that Microsoft could take to make the DOJ happier.

But when he heard Gates' answer to Campbell, Cook realized the deal had ended. Gates thought an appeal against the DOJ ruling could take as long as three years to win, not a worthwhile commitment in such a dynamic market. The time value of each company's assets was too high for such a delay. The DOJ had successfully prevented the possible merger.

Campbell and Davidson negotiated the end of the agreement. Cook knew they needed to make an announcement quickly, so they called Harris from the airport, got executives ready, and waited for Microsoft's final sign-off. Intuit wanted to announce the breakup the next morning, May 19, 1995, but Microsoft, in a pattern now familiar to Intuit executives, delayed.

Intuit announced the stunning dissolution of its merger with Microsoft late in the afternoon May 19. When Cook announced the news in an e-mail, the spontaneous cheers in the company's headquarters startled him. For some Intuit employees, he realized, a nightmare had ended.

"THANK HEAVENS FOR UNANSWERED PRAYERS"

Over the weekend following the announcement of Microsoft's withdrawal from the Intuit deal, Intuit employees fluctuated between elation at the return of their independence and anxiety about the future. Everyone at Intuit had taken note of the increasing stock price. When Microsoft canceled the deal, they worried that their own potential financial gains would reverse themselves.

Although the stock fell about 20 percent from its high of $77 (in 1995 unadjusted pricing), it held steady in the low sixties, a much higher level than the $44 it had been trading before the merger. Intuit also got a $46.5 million breakup fee from Microsoft that contributed to its positive financials. Intuit, courtesy of Microsoft's attention, gained significant financial value.

Steve Pelletier later found the missing puzzle piece that helped explain the deal's breakdown: "I learned subsequently that Gates had had one of his 'think weeks' in May of 1995. At that time, Gates had awakened to Netscape as an operating system threat to Microsoft. Before then, Microsoft had been incredibly complacent about the Internet. In that think week, Gates recognized the Internet tidal wave: 'This is the first competitive threat we've ever really faced, so we have to cut back everything else.'"[9] While some at Microsoft, like executive Mike Maples, had enjoyed working with Intuit and wished the deal had worked out, many there had begun to worry about the impact of the Internet.

In the weeks following the merger's end, Cook came to believe that almost merging with Microsoft created a better set of opportunities for Intuit than merging or never announcing a merger. "Announcement of the merger put us on the radar screen of board rooms at financial institutions all over the country. And it increased our valuation tremendously. But what we did not realize at the time was the taint of Microsoft. After the merger ended, Intuit had managed to both establish its credibility and lose the toxic association with Microsoft."[10]

In later meetings, "Thank Heavens for Unanswered Prayers," a Garth Brooks song that Cook enjoyed, became the hindsight-view theme of the almost–merger. Though not all employees shared the relief of many at Intuit's headquarters, most still believed that Intuit would succeed solo. Management trumpeted the idea that not only could Intuit go it alone, it must thrive to keep Microsoft at bay. The enemy turned suitor was the enemy once again.

Some Intuit employees suspected that Microsoft had known that the merger wasn't going to happen but had requested confidential information from Intuit anyway. The management team, however, had not shared confidential, forward-looking data. Already once burned, they were more than twice conscious. Campbell recalled: "During the time we were under the umbrella, we fought like hell to make sure that we did not reveal anything that would help us move forward as a separate company. We were very careful to make sure we could go on. We made sure that as we danced with them we compromised nothing."[11]

The Microsoft merger had not slowed Intuit's core Quicken, QuickBooks, and TurboTax product development, but other areas suffered. "We hurt ourselves by not hiring enough functional support during the deal," Campbell said. "When I came to Intuit we had no treasurer, and when the deal happened we did not hire one."[12] In fact, Intuit had even lost one key employee, having agreed to send a senior Intuit sales manager, Steve Schiro, up to Redmond to fill a vacant position there as part of the "cross-fertilization" efforts the companies were planning for after the acquisition. The company had also hesitated to make alliances during the waiting period.

Given these partnership delays, Cook was intrigued by the exuberant bundle of red, white, and blue balloons he received in his office the day after the merger was called off. Attached to the colorful balloons was the message: "Happy Independence Day! Can we talk?" The signature was that of Steve Case, CEO of America Online. After Cook responded affirmatively, Case flew in to discuss possibilities with Cook.

Intuit and AOL had been discussing a potential partnership before the Microsoft merger deal was announced. Case had been livid when he heard about the Microsoft deal, feeling blindsided by the news. Now just seventy-two hours after the Microsoft merger fell through, Case handed out bullish Morgan Stanley analysis reports about AOL to Intuit executives in an Intuit conference room. The charismatic Case, clad in casual khakis and a button-down shirt, deliberately built his case that the two companies were natural partners. Intuit, an expert in software, was moving into online financial services. AOL, an expert in online services, had developed some lightweight financial software tools such as an investment return calculator. Didn't it make sense to work together?

"The AOL partnership was a dream for us in Automated Financial Services," said product manager Andy Cohen. "We knew how hard it was to build the back-end infrastructure needed for online services. But unfortunately, Intuit's software teams only evaluated AOL's Mickey Mouse financial applications, not the robust systems behind their service."[13]

Case proposed a 20 percent stock swap between AOL and Intuit, and Harris was a loud proponent. Cook, however, ultimately vetoed it. However much the AOL offer boosted Intuit's psyche, "We didn't think AOL's business fit our needs. We didn't think that we needed the services of a general-purpose network to make our vision happen. We thought they were not important to automating people's financial lives. So why would we trade stock for something that was not crucial?"[14]

In addition to AOL, several other companies began discussions with Intuit for various alliances and acquisitions. "Microsoft's interest educated others that Intuit was doing interesting stuff," noted Cook.[15]

Harris agreed: "Regarding deal making, we were in the cat-bird's seat. We had resources and money. We were appealing to work with and/or work for. Despite the internal anguish and the 'we're not sure what we're going to be,' it was a pretty exciting place to work and we had a fabulous reputation in the market."[16]

Then came the Internet.

CHAPTER 17

CATCHING THE WAVE

C ook and Campbell dove back in to leading an independent Intuit. At the June 1995 board meeting, Cook asked board members to participate in a "thought experiment" and bring up anything that the company might have overlooked while dealing with the distraction from the Microsoft merger. The list generated helped Campbell and Cook, but the real meat of that board meeting turned out to be a handwritten presentation by John Doerr.

The powerful, passionate Doerr had a newly found obsession: the Internet. Catching the spark at Netscape, where he also sat on the board, Doerr quickly saw the potential for Intuit in the exploding new medium. At the Intuit board meeting, he gave an enthusiastic overview of the Internet to Intuit's executive team. The Web, he claimed, would quickly surpass proprietary, closed networks like AOL, and it offered immense opportunity to Intuit including joint ventures, Web-ready products, and Web sites.

The year 1994 had seen the Internet's first banner advertisement, first online malls, and first Web-based radio broadcast. By 1995 Seattle's RealAudio, providing technology for transmitting sound through the net; Sun Microsystem's Java, a programming language ideal for the Web; and the eBay auction Web site (then named AuctionWeb) had all appeared.[1] On August 15, 1995, Netscape would hold its record-breaking initial public offering. By the time of Doerr's presentation, the Internet had riveted Silicon Valley's attention.

Doerr evangelized: Intuit could soon become the premiere provider of personal finance on the Internet. The company had the brands and could build the technology to dominate. To realize its potential, however, Intuit would need to adopt the knowledge, savvy, and impudence that characterized upstart Web-focused companies. Cook and Campbell, galvanized by this presentation, set out to foster such an approach at Intuit.

Cook and Campbell began courting Internet visionaries and seeking out Web pioneers. "If we don't move now," Cook told his executive team, "we'll be shut out forever." In the disruptive era facing Intuit, the company feared becoming a fossil. Cook knew the Internet boom represented a shift of giant proportions. Those who didn't change would get left behind. Intuit had to act fast to learn how to thrive in it, even though nobody knew exactly what the shift would bring.

Throughout Intuit, Cook and Campbell encouraged managers to experiment and learn. Cook and Campbell realized that Intuit's successes had naturally bred a conservatism and incrementalism that would prevent Intuit from leading on the Internet. So they preached the virtues of change and modeled techniques to spawn a burst of new agility. They insisted their managers seek novel outside thought and learn swiftly. They fostered guerrilla efforts so that Intuit could release new products into the swiftly evolving market and gain even more learning.

Doerr's message fell on particularly fertile ground with Bill Harris. A former magazine executive enamored of subscription revenue, Harris began to advocate a move away from the software company's traditional view of itself: "Why should somebody buy Quicken for $29.95 and use it for five years? Why shouldn't it be a service instead where a user pays $19 a year to subscribe?"[2] In the view of Intuit's Internet proponents, the faster the company could get online and stake out territory, the more their efforts, expertise, and Web presence might eventually pay out.

DIVING ONLINE

Harris and Steve Pelletier began a skunk works project to create a "community network for online users," to give Intuit users the opportunity to do research and interact with each other on the Web. A small team handpicked by Harris decided to create a Web site and launch it when Quicken 5.0 for Windows shipped. Within ninety days, the team brainstormed, researched, and created the site. Harris closed a partnership deal with Concentric Network Corporation to provide Internet connections to Quicken users. Agreeing to pay $1 million for the extra floppy disks containing Internet software, Dunn and Pelletier integrated the Netscape browser into Quicken to drive traffic directly to Intuit's site.

The team worked frantically to complete its Web development. They rushed through customer research, made a hasty survey of the few financial Web sites then available, and designed the site to perform the tasks they knew customers wanted. The Quicken software had a firm launch date; since the browser was included in the product, the team had to launch its Web site simultaneously. Some of the Quicken group complained that the last-minute addition of the browser jeopardized Quicken's launch date. But the Internet team's business argument was simple: If users downloaded business forms for a fee, the investment would break even; meanwhile, the Web site and browser gave Intuit traction on the Web and a platform for doing more there.

Intuit trumpeted its arrival online. The company's press release for the October 1995 launch proclaimed, "Quicken 5.0 for Windows will include three bonuses when it goes on sale October 26: first, a tightly integrated version of Netscape Navigator, the leading Internet client software from Netscape Communications Corp.; second, free access to the Quicken Financial Network, Intuit's new World Wide Web site; and third, low-cost full Internet access through service provider Concentric Network

Corp."[3] The company had officially entered the Internet age just four months after Doerr's catalyzing presentation.

Intuit's Internet accomplishments broke new ground. The company was the first to ship a free browser with its software and the first to give free access to its Web site (through Internet service provider [ISP] Concentric), even for those without an ISP, the majority of users at that time. But the innovation ended there: Intuit's Web site did not provide anything that wasn't already available at other financial Web sites such as Yahoo! Finance.

TurboTax's new version, launched soon after Quicken, also included the Netscape browser and Concentric Internet service, providing TurboTax users with access to the TurboTax home page on the Quicken Financial Network. The TurboTax Web site advertised three benefits for its users: advice provided by a tax expert, technical support, and downloadable software.

But the QuickBooks group, skeptical about the longevity of the consumer Internet frenzy, declined to include a browser in its release for 1996. John Monson, head of the small business group, observed, "The personal finance group is a bunch of maverick cowboys out to conquer the Wild West, while we in the business products group are more mature, seasoned, and rational business managers. We rely on research and analytics and so are not rushing to the Internet."[4] Monson continued, "We just can't see why small businesses would want to do their accounting on the Web instead of their desktop."[5]

As Internet activities increased at Intuit, some veteran managers decried the lack of systematic customer research and careful execution. What was "mission critical" to some were careless missions to others. Monson told Cook, "We're not as rigorous as we once were. Remember when we analyzed every possible action as quantitatively as possible? We're not doing that any more." Cook realized that Monson was right, but tolerated the lack of discipline in the environment of the rapid experimentation that he and Campbell wanted to foster.

Many at Intuit decried the company's embrace of the Web. Quicken Financial Network product manager Andy Cohen remembered receiving an e-mail from marketing services director Tanya Roberts that read, "The Internet just isn't ready for prime time. Customers are not ready for the Internet."[6] Despite such warnings, the Internet race continued.

In quick succession, Harris used his considerable deal-making skills to spearhead the acquisition of two companies to add content to Intuit's new Web site: Personal News Inc., a California investment research and analysis software company, which would lend content to the new site, and GALT, of Pittsburgh, Pennsylvania, a mutual fund and portfolio Web site. Intuit planned to link the Quicken Financial Network to GALT's NETWorth Web site, which offered mutual fund information.

Harris next increased the suite of financial services available to Quicken and TurboTax users on the Web via alliances with other companies, the standard transaction of the Internet age. In late 1995, Harris invited Steven Aldrich, CEO and founder of the online insurance marketplace Insurance Internet Services, to California. Insurance Internet Services had a Web site that allowed consumers to easily shop for life insurance and compare options after answering a few straightforward questions.

Harris teed up an alliance whereby Intuit's Web site could link to Aldrich's site and provide Intuit customers with the insurance service. He completed the deal swiftly. Aldrich recalled, "Harris conveyed a clear vision of Intuit's future—providing a broad set of financial transaction capabilities. Intuit had the financial portal Web site, GALT as the mutual fund part, electronic billpay, and now, insurance—a suite of products to make money from the Quicken customer base."[7]

Intuit announced a different kind of deal in late 1995 to extend the company's Internet reach. Although Intuit had passed on the opportunity for an AOL stock swap, the company wanted access to the rapidly growing ISP's traffic. In November, Intuit and AOL announced BankNOW, a simple downloadable online banking product, as well as an alliance in which Intuit and AOL would jointly provide electronic banking to AOL members. Intuit created an area on AOL that included links to the Quicken Financial Network, while AOL made Intuit software products available for sale on its site. Both companies sponsored joint promotions to introduce their products to each other's customer base.

In the Intuit-AOL BankNOW press release, Cook said, "Intuit is building electronic channels for banks to reach millions of existing and new customers. These types of electronic banking services are already available to Quicken users; making them available to the fast-growing millions of America Online subscribers will help us to expand our services to customers who are not currently users of personal finance software."[8]

SHOW ME THE MONEY

Old-school Intuit managers resisted the impetus to revolutionize the company's core businesses. Unhappy with the changing culture and speed of approach, they preferred to devote resources to Intuit's proven product-based culture. Employees wondered why Intuit would invest in the unproven, unprofitable Internet when they knew that people would buy software and that the company would make money selling it.

And Intuit's core products continued to evolve. QuickBooks releases included new features such as industry-specific customization, time tracking and estimating, and job costing. On the tax front, TurboTax and MacInTax for Business introduced new versions specially designed for sole proprietorships, S-corporations, corporations, and partnerships.

The Quicken team still strived to do right by customers, even with its most unhappy ones. One day Eric Dunn was surprised to receive a smashed PowerBook from an irate customer along with a letter: "Please find enclosed two installation disks for your Quicken for Macintosh software. I would like to get my money back for the software as I found it quite unfriendly, as indicated by the condition of my home computer, which was in good working condition until I tried to use Quicken to simplify my bill-paying chores. Unfortunately, one of the disks is stuck in my Macintosh PowerBook."[9]

After describing his difficulties, the customer continued, "Nothing worked. In a momentary—and for me, quite unusual—fit of frustration, I hit my keyboard. The screen went blank and the computer started making funny noises. I then tossed the computer and it broke in half."[10] Quicken product manager Steve Grey conferred with Dunn and sent the angry customer a new PowerBook.

Campbell's original drive for growth in 1994 meant that Intuit had been developing offline products before it created its new online ones. In January 1995, the company launched the Intuit Professional Partner network for professional tax preparers, which aimed to sell products directly to influential accountants and, via recommendation, to their clients. Intuit's various CD-ROM product launches got off to a slow start, failing to meet volume projections. Like many companies at that time, Intuit had seen CD-ROM technology as a wave of the future and had rushed to produce several financial "content" products on that platform. But since the Web could offer such financial content and tools for free, Intuit now saw that the Internet would quickly and mercilessly eliminate CD-ROM products' business rationale.

Intuit also ramped up its international efforts in 1995. Campbell sent longtime Intuit leader Mari Baker to launch Intuit products in France and began development of a Spanish version of Quicken for Mexico and Latin America. In both markets, Intuit worked to put together consortiums of banks and provided bank downloads enabled in their product as a key feature. Despite its Internet focus, the company continued its rapid pace of development in the other areas it valued: core products, new offline products, international businesses, and electronic banking.

FINALLY, E-FINANCE

The dissolution of the Microsoft merger enhanced Intuit's long-standing efforts to enable electronic finance. Intuit had worked to link users with financial institutions since the Accuret automatic bank statement reconciliation project was introduced in the late 1980s. Accuret's successor, the Quicken Credit Card with Intel-liCharge service, gave users the convenience of downloading credit card statements directly into Quicken. The card's profits and high user satisfaction told Intuit that downloads worked. Customers also liked the electronic billpay feature in Quicken, even though electronic bill payment had not yet taken off as quickly as executives had predicted. Pelletier, as the head of the Automated Financial Services group, fought for years to get banks to download bank statement data into Quicken to make banking faster and easier for customers.

Finally, and suddenly, in summer 1995 banks reciprocated Pelletier's interest in connecting via Quicken. Once Intuit no longer intended to merge with Microsoft, banks agreed to download statements into Quicken at a record pace. Their accelerated interest resulted partly from Intuit's higher post-Microsoft profile and partly from a desire to avoid being coerced into working with Microsoft. In just over three months, Intuit signed thirty-five medium and large banks to download statements into Quicken and included its bill payment service as part of every deal.

But Intuit billpay was a bitter pill for banks to swallow. Banks feared Intuit's potential hijacking of their customers and hated Intuit Services Corporation's customer service (this was the reborn National Payments Clearinghouse, Inc., which Intuit had acquired in 1994). Bankers worried that electronic bill payment could be useful independent of banking, and Intuit's prominent brand in its billpay service alienated bankers. Pelletier told Cook, "Banks resent us and fear anyone interfering in their online relationship with their customers." Because banks controlled access to their customers' statements, Intuit needed the banks for downloads, and so Intuit management walked a precarious tightrope between building the online billpay business and placating banks.

To compound the problem, Intuit Services Corporation's primitive fulfillment capabilities, a problem inherited from National Payments Clearinghouse, broke down under the increasing volume. "We were getting into a service business for the first time, and it was a pretty substantial business," Pelletier observed. "We had fifty thousand transactions the first day and had to provide 24/7 support. Wells Fargo and others complained about our service levels, justifiably. But the banks all worked with us. Quicken had strong brand loyalty so they didn't dare not work with us."[11] Intuit struggled to make its risky billpay purchase pay out within its larger bank strategy.

Intuit's online forays, its multiple new products, and its success at signing so many banks all fueled the company's continued stock price increase. The company moved into several office buildings previously occupied by Sun Microsystems at a new "campus" in Mountain View to accommodate its growth. In early fall, industry analysts responded positively to the company's banking strategy announcement. Intuit had successfully positioned itself as the leader in electronic financial services, as *the* hub customers would go to first. Intuit's stock climbed throughout fall 1995 based on these expectations.

CHAPTER 18

NO SACRED COWS

E ven though Intuit now offered myriad products and services, the company's core culture still centered on its inaugural product, Quicken. Quicken myths dominated company lore, and Intuit's roots lay deep within its personal finance category (figure 18-1). Then, in 1996, Intuit's stock price began to fall, concerning all three thousand plus employees.

The stock price degradation started with Quicken. The fall 1995 Quicken launch marked Intuit's worst sales performance ever against plan. Sales came in 20 percent lower than forecast, and managers weren't sure why. Were prior year forecasts inflated unsustainably by all the hoopla surrounding the Microsoft merger? Or was the bet on e-banking and billpay a bad bet? Those services had consumed all Quicken's product development resources, yet consumers didn't seem to be buying. The sales shortfall and the questions surrounding it demoralized employees and depressed Intuit's earnings.

A second serious bug in TurboTax in February 1996 also called the tax group into question. A *New York Times* article condemned Intuit: "For the second consecutive year, Intuit Inc. is warning customers of errors in its popular tax preparation software that could lead to miscalculations on returns. The company said yesterday that fewer than one percent of users of TurboTax

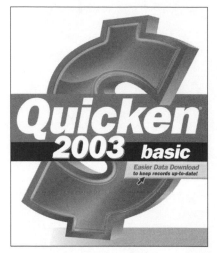

FIGURE 18-1

Quicken's packaging evolved from its earliest design (see figure 3-1) to one using a bold dollar sign graphic. Over 15 million customers worldwide use Quicken to manage their finances.

Source: Courtesy of Intuit.

and MacInTax should be affected by the bugs, which have led to wrong entries involving the depreciation of cars and real estate, self-employed taxpayers and contributions to individual retirement accounts. . . . Different flaws were found in the same programs last year."[1]

A lack of focus also plagued the company. Steve Pelletier's success in signing so many banks to download statements into Quicken distracted the Quicken development team. The Personal Finance Group juggled proliferating product development and launch efforts. If product groups had trouble maintaining focus, so did customer service representatives who struggled to keep up with all the new products and announcements.

Managing workload wasn't the end of the trouble. Many of Intuit's new products failed to meet revenue goals. Quicken Financial Planner captured a 90 percent share of the category, but its tiny unit volume earned little for the company. Unlike Quicken and TurboTax, where Intuit's innovative products had caused the product category to blossom, the financial planning software category did not expand much with Intuit's entry. Pocket Quicken failed because none of the handheld platforms had sufficient volume at that time. ExpensAble, Intuit's expense tracking software, never caught on. And the Internet quickly made all CD-ROM based products obsolete: Parents' Guide to Money, Quicken Companion, and Your Mutual Fund Selector all disappointed. This string of consistently lackluster new product introductions frustrated employees. Many groused that all Intuit's new products were flops.

The threat of the Internet notwithstanding, Cook believed that Intuit's product collapses resulted mostly from the company's misreading of true consumer needs. Cook reembraced a P&G fundamental—that new products should be based on actual customer behaviors, not on what customers *said* they wanted to do. Many customers said that they should do a better job of retirement planning and told the company that they would purchase Intuit's product to do so. However, since customers by and large did no financial planning before Intuit's planning product came to the market, Intuit's product could not persuade them to start. Most simply did not purchase Intuit's Quicken Financial Planner; the few who did turned it into "shelfware." Cook resolved that for future new product development, Intuit should rely on customer actions, not words.

Unprecedented internal conflicts, the result of growing and competing business units, also increased tension throughout 1996. The Quicken Financial Network Web site caused clashes between the Automated Financial Services and Personal Finance groups. Quicken linked directly to Quicken Financial Network, but who owned the user interface? Who had final decision-making power over link placement and Web site layout? "It was a civil war," Quicken Financial Network product manager Andy Cohen recalled. "There was bad blood around the hallways."[2]

Automated Financial Services also fought with the Business Products Group about who should own the payroll business, QuickPay. In John Monson's Business Products view, Intuit product families included all of their Web businesses, but Pelletier of Automated Financial Services thought all online activity belonged to his team.

For Pelletier, these struggles took on unusual intensity because they threatened his group's very existence: If payroll was part of QuickBooks then by the same logic, electronic billpay should be part of Quicken—and there should be no Automated Financial Services group. The struggle also reflected the traditional software versus new Internet thinking at Intuit. Team-oriented Bill Campbell eventually brokered a compromise, and Pelletier agreed to jointly manage his projects with the product groups. But the scathing conflict corroded morale in management and among the rank and file.

Energy spent on these conflicts affected Intuit's continued investment in the Internet. Although Intuit broke new ground for the financial services industry in 1995 with its Quicken Financial Network Web site, the Web businesses earned few revenues for Intuit, and by late 1996 the company had not significantly increased its Web innovations. Internal political battles for resources impeded additional investments in the Web. Intuit did purchase its insurance ally Interactive Insurance Services in 1996, which reflected Cook's enthusiasm about the potential for Internet marketspaces (i.e., Web sites that aggregated services from multiple providers). But Cook began asking the Internet managers questions like, "What is the value of Quicken.com for us?" Cook insisted that Intuit's mission was not to become a media company. No matter how hot the Internet frenzy became, without a clear business model Cook was disinclined to fund additional Web experimentation.

Intuit did not give up on Internet investments entirely. Bill Harris believed that, to support an advertising business model and to increase transaction revenues, Intuit needed a source of steady traffic for Quicken Financial Network. To achieve this, Harris began negotiations with Yahoo! and Excite, at the time the two Web sites with the most heavily visited financial areas. Harris talked with both companies simultaneously about providing their financial content. Ultimately, Yahoo! decided that it wanted to build its own finance functions and that Intuit would not contribute enough to its effort. So Yahoo! passed. On August 26, 1996, Intuit and Excite announced a groundbreaking distribution alliance in which Intuit would provide Excite's finance channel functionality, and Excite would host Intuit's Web site.

But most of the news continued to be bad. In another troubling turn, Parsons Technology exacerbated Intuit's financial downslide. Throughout its affiliation with Intuit, Parsons had been a sinkhole of management time. In 1995, fueled by the brief industry success of CD-ROM–based products and the onetime Quicken cross-sell boom, Parsons had done well, but by 1996 the Iowa-based software division headed toward financial losses. Intuit had tried unsuccessfully to integrate Parsons' operations into Intuit's, but company management hardly relished the idea of continuing to work with a difficult company whose products were beginning to fail and whose technologies the Internet made even less relevant. And so, Campbell asked sales VP Alan Gleicher to take on the project of cutting Intuit's losses by selling Parsons.

Intuit's international efforts also floundered during this trying period. "Intuit did nothing in the core U.S. product to make life easier for international," said Roger Bass, an Intuit product manager from the United Kingdom. "Doing one-off localizations was a tricky task, as the product was not structured in a modular way to make it easier to convert internationally."[3] The company suffered from very poor distribution management in Germany, where Intuit overspent, miscalculated sales, and absorbed $12 million of returned product. In France, the banks that had originally joined together to support Quicken downloads soon worried that Intuit could interfere with their customer relationships. Those "partners" started to clamor for Intuit to leave the market, infuriating company management.

Despite these international difficulties, Intuit purchased the Japanese Milky Way Software Company in early 1996, enticed by the country's lucrative market potential. Acquiring the DOS-based accounting software producer, Intuit continued to try to grow in countries where it had found early success: Canada, the

United Kingdom, and Germany. Yet the future for international businesses was far from certain, and Intuit's earlier confidence in tackling these new markets vanished.

The company's reputation took a further hit with the public revelation of insider trading on Intuit stock by Cathy Lane, the wife of former CFO, Bill Lane. Lane had taken over the CFO role from Eric Dunn when the ChipSoft merger closed, and the affable Lane had trusted his wife with details about the potential Microsoft merger, both as it began and as it ended. Without his knowledge, she passed this insider information on to her grown children from a prior marriage, who profited handsomely until the SEC caught them. When Intuit discovered the impropriety, Lane announced his already-planned retirement. By the time the story became public, the blunder tainted no current Intuit employees, but the company's self-esteem suffered a blow from the negative publicity when the SEC fined Ms. Lane and her children.

For years Intuit's growth and its attention to employees had engendered loyalty and longevity. But now, the company's operational difficulties flared just as the promise of the Internet fueled hundreds of start-ups in Silicon Valley. For the first time, Intuit employees began leaving in droves for lucrative and exciting opportunities. Compared to the glamorous dot-com companies luring workers with stock options and start-up dreams, Intuit's culture seemed stodgy and slow. These unprecedented defections further demoralized remaining employees.

Quicken Financial Network's product manager was a case in point. "Intuit had all these incredible people, a great brand—the company could have owned the Web but didn't," reflected Andy Cohen, who left to join an Internet company. "Intuit tripped over its own software company culture; it's hard to invest in a different kind of business. Lots of companies externally wanted to work with us but internally we were being suffocated. The Web is totally different, it demands new business models. We lost a year in infighting and let E*Trade, Yahoo! Finance, and six other companies take Intuit's space. We lost that ground irrevocably."[4]

But others disagreed. Campbell believed strongly that Intuit had properly invested in the Internet business that could most directly benefit Intuit—specifically, embedding a browser to drive traffic to its sites. And Cook knew that firms like E*Trade and Yahoo! already surpassed Intuit in operationally intensive areas where the company had traditionally failed. Following them would require a massive investment that might never deliver success. Would those different business models prove worthy of that investment? The internal debate boiled.

Cook noted increasing employee departures with some dismay, warning his board, "We have a crisis of confidence among employees and management. This is not a midlife crisis; it is not related to our age, but to the tremendous effect of the Internet tidal wave."[5]

DOUBLE-DOWN OR FOLD

None of the Internet's challenges to software products compared to its fundamental impact on Intuit's banking strategy. The Internet made the company's persistent efforts to be the technology connecting banks to consumers obsolete almost overnight. For consumers who dealt primarily with one bank for their daily finances, widespread access to the Internet ensured that they could easily reach their bank online. Previously, customers had needed Quicken to connect; after the Internet, banks and brokerages became direct competitors to Quicken's online services. And large financial institutions had an advantage over Intuit: They had customers' financial data and Intuit didn't. Why would banks give Intuit the data as well as the page views and customer attention that the data attracted? Since Intuit needed banks' permission to access customer data, the company suffered a disadvantage. An entire class of customers Intuit had been counting on began to dry up.

In mid-1996, Dunn came to Campbell with bad news: Intuit's banking strategy wasn't working, and as the Internet grew its losses might increase. Intuit's billpay service—the fulfillment service that Intuit had created by purchasing the anemic National Payments Clearinghouse—was losing money. With the rise of Internet technology, banks no longer had to cooperate with Intuit and offer the service. In a last-ditch effort to save Intuit's electronic banking strategy, Campbell called his friend Dave Kinser out of retirement to try to deal with the operational and cost issues. Despite Kinser's expertise the Intuit Services Corporation could not be made competitive without a massive additional investment in technology.

Intuit execs, facing internal disagreements, revenue shortfalls, and shrinking profits, agonized about what to do. On the one hand, the electronic banking initiative had been the cornerstone of Intuit's strategy after Microsoft had disappeared. Abandoning Intuit Services Corp., a central part of that approach, meant abandoning the strategy that had initially propelled Intuit's stock to new highs in 1995. On the other hand, operational difficulties and the coming pervasiveness of the Internet cast serious doubt on Intuit's success.

Large numbers of systems and merchant billers made providing electronic bill payment services a daunting struggle. Intuit's main competitor for bill-payment solutions, CheckFree, still dominated the market. Intuit was so far behind CheckFree in market share and technology that Harris made a compelling argument to the executive committee: "Intuit has only two choices. Either we acquire CheckFree or we sell them Intuit Services Corporation. It's time to double-down—or fold."[6]

The raging arguments about banking strategy divided the company. Campbell believed that "automating the back end of banking" would require unsustainable losses. Dunn advocated purchasing CheckFree, arguing the future of Quicken was in electronic banking and billpay; so did Pelletier. Other managers felt that banking and billpay drained precious resources.

Campbell called a special 10:00 A.M. meeting at the Palo Alto Holiday Inn to end the debate. Nearly fifty managers attended; Campbell wanted to involve a large number of people in making such an important strategic decision—both so every angle could be examined and so most employees would buy into the outcome. Passionate voices echoed off the slightly grubby white walls of the old conference room; aging chairs squeaked as people shifted uncomfortably. Dunn, regretting the absence of ally Pelletier, spoke emotionally: "Electronic billpay is what Intuit has been trying to do from day one. Buying CheckFree is the critical next step that will help us cement the market for such transactions."[7] Other managers dissented with equal verve. The group split evenly on either side of the argument. Finally, at 6:00 P.M., Campbell made the call: Intuit would sell Intuit Services Corp.

Although he did not say much at the meeting, Cook sanctioned the sale. He had come to believe that the Internet would eventually make the billpay fulfillment business less important. Once consumers could pay bills via the Web, they would no longer need such services.

And so, Intuit sold Intuit Services Corp. to former rival and now ally CheckFree in September 1996. Even though Intuit profited handsomely from the sale, Cook hardly saw the episode as Intuit's finest hour. "We'd put in about $40 million and sold it for over $250 million, but it *was* a failure. It was a failure of acquisition process, a failure versus our own criteria for service, and a failed strategy."[8]

BusinessWeek was less judgmental, lauding Cook for his readiness to move on:

> *Scott Cook knew when to let go. On Sept. 16, Intuit's chairman announced that the No. 1 personal-finance software maker will sell its money-losing ISC electronic bill-payment subsidiary so it can refocus on the Internet. CheckFree will pay $268 million in stock for the unit, which Intuit bought two years ago for $8 million. The bill-paying business clearly was problematic. ISC provided a private network for users of Intuit's Quicken software to*

*pay bills and bank electronically. Banks balked at Intuit as
middleman, however, and analysts guess it lost more than
$20 million on the business in two years. Such transactions
now are better suited to the Net, anyway."*[9]

REINVENTING INTUIT

The intense arguments about Intuit's future during the electronic
banking discussions troubled Campbell. What was Intuit's best
strategy? Cook worried that he did not know how to address such
intense organizational conflicts. How could he help reunite and
reenergize the company? To address both these serious needs,
Cook and Campbell decided to review Intuit's strategy carefully,
objectively—and quite openly.

Beginning in September 1996, Campbell devoted five
months to a focused re-strategy effort that revisited all of the
company's products and business plans in a highly networked
world. His objective was to radically rethink Intuit's strategy in
light of the Internet. In a departure for the company, Campbell
hired a large consulting firm, McKinsey & Co., to facilitate the
effort. McKinsey provided analysis of other financial and technical institutions, so Intuit could compare its own strategies with
others. The project involved as many as eighty managers with
widely varying perspectives throughout Intuit.

The strategic group assessed the potential of dozens of possible actions. What were the company's potential business opportunities, and how did particular opportunities fit with core compe-
tencies? Besides looking at new ideas, the group critically
examined existing businesses. The team held three big retreats with
all eighty members and in between smaller subgroups worked on
specific subtasks. To set the tone, at the first large team meeting at a
Palo Alto Hyatt Rickeys conference room, Campbell announced
to the group, "There are no sacred cows." He made clear that the
group should consider every aspect of Intuit's business.

"Bill Campbell and Bill Harris drove the restrategy meetings," recalled engineer Carl Reese. "Employees worried because we were unclear about which direction to go. We were excited by the possibilities but anxious about what to do and eager to start executing. Those meetings brought people together, and we came out of them with a solid strategy. It took a long time, though. It was pretty trying for everyone."[10]

Group members debated the extent to which the Quicken business would drive growth. Although some team members from the Quicken group argued the product still had potential, the group as a whole decided that Intuit needed to invest in growth engines other than Quicken.

Accordingly, the restrategy effort resulted in a four-pronged plan of action for Intuit:

1. Alter investment allocations to shift away from international and core Quicken software and toward small business and the Internet. Investment in tax product development would remain unchanged.

2. Embed the Internet in all desktop software products to extend software products to the Internet.

3. Relaunch the Quicken Financial Network site as Quicken.com and make it the leading online financial destination by allying with large portals if possible. Create a community of online users.

4. Create a series of Web-based transactional businesses, such as insurance, mortgage, and tax solutions, and look for other online businesses that were marketspaces or that reinvented products for the Web.

The Internet lay at the heart of Intuit's new strategy. McKinsey principal John Hagel III released his book *Net Gain* in spring 1997, and he sold Intuit leaders in 1996 on the theories the book espoused: The Internet would help companies build communities, which would result in stronger customer loyalty and higher profits. These virtual communities built on common interests (Hagel's favorite example was travel) and a free flow of information would shift power from companies to customers. The best Internet models would monetize these powerful communities through advertising and transactions.

Intuit's marketspace initiatives made sense under this new paradigm: Intuit could help customers make apples-to-apples comparisons across different financial services vendors, resulting in easier and better decisions. And Quicken.com could leverage its online traffic into an ad revenue business. Intuit managers embraced this philosophy as a unifying theory underlying the company's strategy. But would these business initiatives succeed in practice?

Once Intuit identified its new strategy, the company needed to organize itself to achieve it and to quickly respond to ever-tumbling morale. But the new strategy required some painful steps on the personnel front. In early 1997, Intuit examined number of employees per revenue dollar for each of its groups to try to reallocate its resources appropriately. Its Quicken group fell outside the company norm for employees per revenue, and by late spring Intuit had identified several other areas where revenues did not support staffing levels. In June 1997, the company turned its back on Cook's long-ago resolve and laid off a broad cross-section of employees, shutting down its Albuquerque call center. In total, Intuit let go about 10 percent of employees in a move some feared would alter the company's fundamental character forever.

ON THE FIRING LINE

With exquisite mistiming, an ongoing effort by Harris to expand Intuit's alliance with Excite came to fruition twenty-four hours after the company announced it would lay off 420 workers. The seven-year deal involved a $40 million investment by Intuit and gave the software company a 20 percent stake in the Internet search engine company. The *San Francisco Chronicle* commented unfavorably on the juxtaposition of the company's layoffs and its large investment; in a critical article, it said that Intuit officials blamed "the whirlwind courtship between Intuit and Excite for the unfortunate timing of the back-to-back announcements."[11]

This trend of negative Intuit press continued into December: "When Intuit bought a $40 million stake in Excite, an Internet search operator, large banks likely gasped at the potential threat to their collective customer base," wrote *American Banker* magazine. Even though Intuit had dropped its electronic banking initiative, the banking industry still regarded the company with suspicion. The *American Banker* article quoted investment bank Piper Jaffray's Bill Burnham: "The Intuit-Excite alliance is bad for large banks because it competes for customer attention and makes product selection more competitive. For smaller financial institutions and product specialists, it will level the playing field by providing an additional avenue for them to sell products."[12]

Despite the pervasive turmoil, one person, with his total team orientation and intense regard for people, held the company together during this difficult period. In a dramatic display, Bill Campbell proved his devotion to employees when Mari Baker needed his help in the spring of 1997. Baker suffered a gallbladder attack on a plane flying from a Software Publishers Association meeting in Washington, DC. When the plane landed in Newark, New Jersey, she was rushed to the local hospital emergency room, where a mother of another ER patient looked through Baker's purse and found her business card. The woman called Intuit and told Campbell about Baker's condition. Campbell found a pilot and private jet to fly Baker's husband out to New Jersey to pick her up. Recovering enough the next day to fly back to the Bay Area, Baker felt extremely grateful for, and awed by, this tangible proof of Campbell's caring.

But Campbell's devotion could not completely compensate for the continued press barrage. In June 1997, the *Washington Post* fired its salvo, "What Intuit Didn't Bank On: Counting Its Click Fees Before They Hatched, the Online Financial Service Leader Laid an Egg," in which it broadly condemned the company's efforts to own the online market.[13]

The most scathing article, headlined "Is Intuit Headed for a Meltdown?" ran in the August 1997 issue of *Fortune* and was widely read by Intuit employees and businesspeople across the country. "'Quicken is over!' says David Farina, an analyst at William Blair in Chicago. 'It's done. It's almost a non-factor.' Farina, strangely, is talking about a program that remains undisputed king of the personal finance software hill. The software's pretty good—it's the hill that's eroding. Intuit, the company that built its reputation on Quicken, is learning the hard way that owning a market niche doesn't mean much when new technology comes along and washes it all away."[14]

This kind of devastating coverage was a harsh blow for a company used to being a darling of the press. Intuit employees wondered if things could get any worse.

CHAPTER 19

NEW ECONOMY INSANITY

W ith a new, Internet-focused strategy inform-
ing its choices, Intuit labored to pull itself out
of the doldrums. Savvy CEO Bill Campbell
had confidence in the company and knew the
creativity, determination, and grit of its employees would reverse
the declining fortunes. Campbell's conviction infused the executive team; despite the barrage of bad press and continual Internet frenzy surrounding Intuit, morale began slowly to improve.
Though some employees continued to leave in search of greener
pastures, few of Campbell's key direct reports departed, a direct
testament to his charisma and leadership. Campbell ensured that
these loyalists led the company toward new achievement.

From his broad experience, Campbell recognized that Intuit's
slide could be turned around, and he genuinely believed in Intuit's
future. To achieve the company's new strategy, Campbell relied on
several key employees to lead the charge toward the Internet and
increasing profits. One of these was Bill Harris, and Campbell's
respect for Harris's business development aptitude led Campbell
to an important decision.

In March 1997, Pointcast of Santa Clara, California, a company pioneering "push" technology (technology that transmits data
to people's computers periodically, without a specific user request), offered Harris a position as its president with a significant

equity share. Harris could not decide whether to leave Intuit for the new Internet company. He informed Campbell of the attractive offer, and the CEO pondered his dilemma: Should he let Harris depart, or make him an offer to stay at Intuit? After consulting with management and the board, Campbell believed that Intuit could not afford, particularly in this period of Internet transformation, to lose Harris's energy and deal-making talents (figure 19-1).

Although Harris had no experience leading the kind of large, multiple-product company Intuit had become, Campbell decided to name Harris as his successor to persuade him to stay at Intuit. When Intuit senior managers got wind of this choice at the December 1997 offsite, a few privately protested the decision. Harris's management style attracted some and worried others; some found him frustratingly inconstant despite the vision that many recognized. Many also worried about his operational skills.

But Campbell, Scott Cook, and Eric Dunn believed that Intuit could not afford to lose Harris's Internet savvy just as the company most needed such expertise. The decision stood, and Campbell agreed to surrender the CEO position to Harris at the

FIGURE 19 - 1

Bill Harris became CEO of Intuit in 1998.
Source: Courtesy of Intuit.

end of fiscal year 1998. The additional clout afforded Harris by this recognition fueled his efforts at further acquisitions—a strategy that Harris had always championed.

SPEED WITHOUT RIGOR

Quicken 1998 marked Intuit's first vigorous push toward its new Internet strategy (the company had switched from naming new versions by number to using calendar years). The ever-popular software found a new purpose: to link customers in myriad ways to Intuit's new Web site, Quicken.com. Launched on Halloween day 1997, Quicken.com became the nexus of Intuit's previously decentralized personal finance Internet initiatives.

If the company had experimented rapidly with its earlier Internet efforts, the Quicken.com team, under Harris's oversight, created its Web site at breakneck speed. "Get it up and change it later" became the team's mantra. The company had announced its stake in Excite in June 1997; by October it had moved the crack GALT engineering team to Mountain View (from Pittsburgh), rehosted the Web site at Excite, and overhauled what had once been the Quicken Financial Network. Since Quicken 1998 had a firm launch date, the Quicken.com team *had* to release on time because of the numerous links to Quicken.com in the software. The team also wanted to prove to Excite that Intuit could be a nimble—even dangerous—ally.

To provide a key section on the Quicken.com site, another skunk works Intuit team pulled off an innovative online mortgage site that would shake up the mortgage industry. Beginning with the premise that mortgage lending could not only be more efficient and profitable if conducted online, but could also help customers obtain lower rates from multiple lenders, this group had worked feverishly to test the concept, design the system, engineer the Web site, and sign up lenders. Product manager Alison Wagonfeld found six lenders initially interested in participating; the

$50,000 per lender charge for enrolling in the service helped defray some initial costs.

The first version of QuickenMortgage.com enabled qualified users to get a loan prequalification letter on Chase Manhattan's letterhead from the site. The company received about twenty-five dollars from Chase for each prequalification and a couple hundred dollars for each full application. This revenue structure did not make QuickenMortgage.com profitable at the beginning, but the site received many interested consumer visits. Using advertising and links, the mortgage site drove as much traffic from Quicken.com as possible. That it competed with other, paying customers for Quicken.com advertising space caused no shortage of battles between the Quicken.com and QuickenMortgage.com teams.

The renamed Interactive Insurance Services Web site, Quicken InsureMarket, became another section on the Quicken.com Web site that also competed for advertising space as it added new insurers and a streamlined customer questionnaire. Although the InsureMarket staff wanted to broaden insurance offerings to automobile and small business insurance, they could not sign up large insurance companies who would agree to offer their services through a third-party Web site that enabled them to be comparison shopped. Still, the Web site offered users competitive bids on life insurance from several carriers.

To create an online selling channel that harnessed Web site traffic, Intuit introduced the Quicken Store in 1998. For the first time, the company offered online downloads of its software as an alternative to CDs or floppy disks. Most of the volume online came from customers who had previously purchased over the telephone or through the mail, so selling customers products through the lower-cost online channel increased company profits. By 1998 the Quicken Store was putting about $120 million annually into the company's coffers, stoking the company's growing Internet revenue.

To make its launch date, the Quicken.com group sought other content with ruthless—and perhaps even reckless—speed. They persuaded Standard & Poor's to provide Intuit with business data that no one else offered online, and added free SEC filings from eLogic of Los Angeles, an Internet start-up discovered by chance. The question was: Would this slapdash content site click?

When, just before launch, Harris came to review the new Web site, Quicken.com product manager, Tapan Bhat, sat on the edge of his seat. Bhat had designed the Web site with tabs leading to separate topic Web pages and a stock quote detail page as the centerpiece. Clicking through the Web pages for Harris, Bhat rejoiced: "It worked! Everyone started clapping and then we knew that we were going to have a launch."[1] Until that moment, the team had not been sure they would make it. Harris uncorked champagne to celebrate.

Once the new site launched, Intuit focused intently on driving traffic to Quicken.com. First, in October 1997, Harris closed a deal to make Intuit the exclusive provider of the personal finance channel on CNNfn.com. Under the agreement, Intuit would host and maintain a cobranded version of its Quicken.com Web site for the New York media giant. The CNNfn Web site, which launched in December of that year, offered news, stock quotes, and other financial functionality. Intuit's $1 million per year deal with this site further broadened its reach; in the frenetic late 1990s, any alliance that increased a company's page views and online traffic appeared a winner.

To get even more traffic, Intuit next went after the big guns. In early 1998, Intuit announced a five-year deal with AOL, which owned the most trafficked group of sites on the Web. Harris arranged a complicated pay-for-position alliance that gave Intuit prominent site listings in several areas on AOL and its subsidiary CompuServe. The bold deal cost Intuit more than $30 million; unlike earlier years when Intuit tested its way into profitable marketing programs, its deal with AOL was a jump based on blind faith.

On the heels of the $40 million Excite deal, the AOL deal positioned Intuit as one of the most aggressive players in the on-line financial services industry. The only major online presence not allied with Intuit was Yahoo! Old economy banks, broker-ages, and credit card companies scrambled to figure out how to tackle the new online landscape and work with or against high-tech newcomers like Intuit.

FOLLOWING SUIT

As the Quicken.com group led the charge to the Internet, other groups followed close behind. In a notable technical achievement, the product extension of TurboTax to the Web functioned smoothly; visitors to Intuit's TurboTax site could prepare and file their personal tax returns directly on the Internet as easily as they could use the desktop software. The tax group had to carefully address matters of Internet privacy and security; once it did, the site gained traffic, aided by the Internal Revenue Service's (IRS) drive to increase its proportion of online tax filing. More traffic came from Intuit's alliances: In February 1998, Intuit and Excite announced the launch of TurboTax Online, heralding it as "the most complete Internet-based personal tax preparation program for consumers."[2]

On the small business front, Intuit decided to expand payroll services for businesses via a partnership. After its billpay difficul-ties, Intuit did not want to run an operations-intensive payroll business. Yet offering payroll services made sense strategically be-cause customers preferred having their payroll integrated with their accounting software. Since acquiring new customers and tediously reporting hours by phone drove traditional payroll service expenses, Intuit's QuickBooks customer base and its electronic interaction capability offered a significant cost advan-tage. Computing Resources in Reno, Nevada, offered what Intuit needed with its payroll experience and centralized operations, and Intuit struck up a partnership.

The jointly developed QuickBooks Payroll Service launched in September 1998. QuickPay had always generated profits; the newly expanded payroll and direct deposit services quickly won customers though high costs made it not immediately profitable. Campbell supported the partnership: "Payroll is important for growth and recurring revenue," he said. "It's high value added for the purchaser, and for us it's annual recurring revenues as long as we do a good job. And customers like it."[3] With QuickBooks payroll, along with its newly launched online store at Quick-Books.com, the small business group had an Internet play.

For the supplies group, the Internet provided new opportunities for efficiency and customer service. By 1998, Intuit's unglamorous but consistent supplies business had grown to a $94 million business used by consumers and small businesses everywhere. Businesses could order paper checks, invoices, envelopes, and even letterhead from Intuit. The forms worked with their Quicken and QuickBooks programs, and customers could request custom logos on them. The group designed its Web site to record order information exactly as customers entered it. The quality and speed of supplies fulfillment rocketed. So did profitability.

Dunn led another Internet effort. Under his enthusiastic leadership, a small team began to develop WebQuicken, a version of Quicken that would work entirely on the Internet. The costly R&D took place off Intuit's income statement; Dunn created a partially owned subsidiary named Venture Finance Software Corporation to fund the project. Several historic Intuit financial backers, including Kleiner Perkins, put money into this new venture.

And Intuit's competitors, particularly Microsoft, also awakened to embrace the Web. In addition to Yahoo!, Quicken.com faced off against Microsoft's robust MoneyCentral Web site, a part of the invigorated Microsoft Network portal. Formerly the Microsoft Investor site, MoneyCentral moved quickly to offer services and compete with Quicken.com. In response to Quick-enMortgage.com, Microsoft introduced its similar Home Advisor service. Working with vendor SecureTax, the Redmond company launched an online tax channel. And other financial portals such as Schwab.com, with services including online brokerage, increased in popularity.

Microsoft also ramped up its online small business efforts. The company bought small business company LinkExchange and used it to anchor its new bCentral site for small business. Quick-Books faced other challenges from Peachtree's efforts to become a business portal powerhouse and from new online small business company NetLedger, funded by Oracle's leader Larry Ellison. On the tax front, in addition to SecureTax and TurboTax, TaxCut, which had been purchased by H&R Block in the mid-1990s after the failed MECA-ChipSoft merger, launched an aggressive online customer acquisition effort.

SCALING BACK, AND FACING THE SKEPTICS

To increase company focus on its numerous Internet activities, Intuit discontinued many businesses that had struggled in 1995 and 1996. Intuit's CD-ROM content publishing products ceased. The company abandoned its Pocket Quicken for personal digital assistant (PDA) versions and canceled development of stand-alone Quicken Financial Planner, Quicken Companion, and other ancillary products. Intuit also consolidated its flailing international offices into a single European office in Germany, laying off nearly one hundred international employees. Intuit maintained offices in Japan and Canada—the company purchased a second Japanese business software accounting firm in 1997, bucking the divestiture trend to acquire Japanese Windows expertise—but significantly reduced its other overseas investments. Discontinuing these businesses, along with the earlier sales of Parsons and Intuit Services Corp., freed resources for additional Internet investments.

Further concerns about profitability drove a major cultural and financial change for QuickBooks: The company began to charge for QuickBooks technical support. Technical support for the now feature-rich QuickBooks product had consumed about 22 percent of its revenue, versus 13 percent for Quicken, and as Intuit scrambled to put every dollar against Internet opportunities, QuickBooks had to fix this problem.

Introducing fees for support without alienating customers tested the QuickBooks team. QuickBooks' complexities forced the change, however; QuickBooks tech support staff spent significant time answering accounting questions in addition to technical questions. Accounting software competitors already charged for technical support, so the change wasn't out of the ordinary for the category. However, charging customers for tech support marked a big cultural shift for Intuit, which had provided free, unlimited, lifetime technical support since the 1980s.

The company's focus on its Internet investments alienated some of its managers. The executive team argued heatedly about the best allocation of development and marketing resources between software and the Web. Many old-timers still did not believe in the newfangled Internet business model. Skepticism about the Internet pervaded the software groups, and some employees working on Internet businesses felt blocked and frustrated by these battles. "We had huge internal debates," Wagonfeld noted. "[For example,] would calling our site QuickenMortgage dilute the Quicken brand?"[4]

As Intuit's Web operations lost more and more money, long-time Intuit managers fulminated at the big dollars being spent on Internet deals. Some employees rejected Intuit's Internet age. After running the Business Products Group for two years, ten-year Intuit veteran John Monson departed in 1997 citing the divergence of the culture in the Business Products Group from the rest of the company. "My group was the last bastion of the 'old' Intuit," Monson said later. "The merger with ChipSoft and other factors were driving the rest of the company toward more conventional management techniques. Bill Harris, in particular, did not embody traditional Intuit principles."[5]

Monson thought that profitability problems in other areas of Intuit meant that his group had to forgo growth to provide profits that covered "misses" in the other units—and this need to compensate for unproven yet substantial Internet investments infuriated him. Campbell found Monson's overt lack of team playing unconscionable, and Monson soon left Intuit.

Monson was not alone. The bad feelings that had surfaced in June 1997, when executives had announced layoffs just before the huge Excite investment, increased as Web business losses grew. Employees struggled to understand core business spending reductions as Intuit simultaneously planned risky expansion efforts. And Harris's efforts to make Intuit a data consolidator, which few understood or embraced, fueled the fire.

Internet product development differed markedly from software practices. Releasing new versions of Web sites every few months on unstable technology caused enormous stress. Engineers and marketing managers, accustomed to the regularity of annual software product releases, struggled to keep up with the frantic, self-imposed release schedules for the Internet. The teams cut corners and focused on speed of execution; on the Internet, they reasoned, things could always be revised in the next version.

The internal combustion at Intuit was matched outside the company. In the late 1990s, tech companies experienced dizzying increases in valuations. Business rhetoricians were trumpeting the notion that he who had the eyeballs—that is, the most Web site page views—would win. Industry pundits preached that in any Web-based service provision, economies of scale would dominate. Whoever got big the soonest, the prevailing logic claimed, would establish the valuable franchise for the long run. Service providers, including Intuit, paid whatever it took to partners who could provide lots of eyeballs to make sure a company's Internet presence mushroomed, with the hopes that profits would follow. Harris admitted, "I, certainly, and the company in general, adopted this point of view and engaged in this economic behavior. We paid a lot to buy Internet traffic. It made sense in concept."[6]

Intuit formally announced in May 1998 that Harris would take the helm at Intuit as of the first of August. As Harris became CEO, Campbell moved into position as chairman of the board, and Cook created a new title for himself: chairman of the executive committee. To congratulate Campbell on his promotion to chairman, Cook threw a dinner party in the backyard of his Woodside home.

At the memorable dinner, Intuit's leaders stood up one by one to talk about Campbell and all he meant to them. Echoing an ad that Cook and the team placed in the *San Jose Mercury News* (figure 19-2), employees feted their embarrassed leader: "the perfect manager," "helps people reach their potential," "completely selfless," and "I have perfect faith in him."[7] They called Campbell cheerleader, critic, coach, confessor, sounding board, father,

---

FIGURE 19 - 2

San Jose Mercury News Bill Campbell Ad, August 1998

Congratulations to the most revered CEO in the valley.

Bill Campbell, President and CEO of Intuit, is moving to the position of Chairman. And those of us who have worked with him for years want to tell the world what he means to us:

Bill, you made all the difference in getting us where we are today.

Under your leadership, we have quintupled our market value and significantly improved our management practices. You led us through the big challenges, whether successfully combining over 20 merged companies, or steering us to leadership on the Internet.

Who would have thought that someone with two fake hips could move so fast?

You instinctively knew what each of us did well and could coach us to solid improvement. You told us straight out when we were off base, but never let us doubt that you were rooting for each of us all the way.

Your wonderfully personal style made us want to work for you and want to achieve more than we ever thought we could. And through it all, you made us laugh, you made us dream and you made us see the possibilities.

And the good news is, we don't have to say goodbye to any of that. Thanks, Bill, for all you've given us as CEO, including your choice of Bill Harris as our new CEO. And welcome to your new role as Chairman.

From your colleagues at Intuit.

Source: Mari Baker.

mentor, trusted advisor, hugger, team builder, communicator, and friend. With typical modesty and graciousness, Campbell downplayed the accolades and joked about the compliments.

"I don't think you could ever say enough about Bill Campbell's impact on the company," Mari Baker said. "He saved it. He was the right person at the right time."[8] Worried employees regretted the changing of the guard.

DAZED AND CONFUSED

New CEO Harris was raring to go. In his first months, he expanded Intuit's relationship with Excite to include a small business channel and struck a multifaceted deal with Charles Schwab.

Under his influence, Intuit invested in a rash of California companies—VeriSign of Mountain View, Concentric Networks of San Jose, Homestore.com of Westlake Village, and 724 Solutions of Santa Barbara—and bought stakes in Security First, an Atlanta firm that made Internet applications for financial institutions, and in Chicago's Quotesmith.com, an online stock quote company. All these Web investments positioned the company's portfolio for the Internet boom. And as their individual values grew along with the Internet bubble, so did Intuit's, reaching over $4.3 billion by the end of 1998.

Intuit also made a spate of acquisitions. The company announced its biggest to date, a whopping $400 million acquisition of Lacerte professional tax preparation software of Plano, Texas. Lacerte expanded Intuit's network of professional tax preparers. Harris, in an interview in *Investor's Business Daily* magazine, waxed enthusiastic about how the acquisition would serve the important professional segment of the tax business. "We're attempting to link users and their financial professionals—such as accountants, tax preparers and advisers."[9]

Lacerte was only the beginning. In quick succession, Intuit bought seven additional companies, including two professional tax companies, two small business services companies, a streaming investment quotes provider, and two other notables: Microsoft's online tax supplier SecureTax.com of Rome, Georgia, and Intuit's erstwhile partner Computing Resources of Reno, its Quick-Books payroll service provider.

Intuit's history of managing partnerships did not auger well for these many new deals. The company's longest standing partner was CheckFree, its longtime billpay fulfillment service. In early 1998, Dunn had signed a contract extension with CheckFree that prohibited Intuit from working with CheckFree's competitors; in return, Intuit exclusively distributed CheckFree's services in non-financial institution Web channels like the then-popular portals and search engines. Within six months CheckFree started to negotiate with Yahoo! in direct violation of this agreement. Intuit protested vigorously via letter and phone call, and finally sued CheckFree, winning an injunction. Clearly, signing a partnership deal and getting a partnership to work required different skills.

Administering the many partnership deals and acquisitions stretched Intuit employees already stressed by the proliferating Internet projects. Each time Intuit acquired a company, managers worked to integrate the new firm operationally, financially, strategically, managerially, and culturally. Most new acquisitions continued to operate in their remote locations, and integrating the distant operations required Intuit to develop new transition strategies. Exploiting new strengths, avoiding previous mistakes, and orienting the new company to Intuit's operating values required resources and commitment. And so Intuit struggled to make its acquisitions work.

Meanwhile, Intuit grappled with its other deals. Its five-year AOL alliance particularly vexed managers. Under the AOL deal, Intuit provided financial services on aol.com and through its ISP subscription service. But AOL's deals were structured to be more immediately rewarding to the portal and less rewarding to the service partner. Intuit depended on transaction volumes from AOL to make the deal economically viable, but AOL lagged in helping the company maximize revenue. Intuit invested countless hours trying to work with its AOL representatives to increase volume, with little improvement.

Although layoffs, discontinuing some businesses, and core business growth improved Intuit's financial performance, its Internet businesses—with the exceptions of the Quicken Store and TurboTax Online—struggled. The spate of acquisitions and complex partnerships and the lure of exciting new start-ups dizzied Intuit employees. Even though Intuit's approximately 20 percent turnover rate during the Internet frenzy of the late 1990s was lower than turnover at other Silicon Valley firms, it still marked the greatest employee exodus Intuit had experienced in its fifteen-year history. The company's unfocused speed dazed and confused its workers; even though revenues increased, no one could aver that the company's frantic pace moved it forward overall.

Internet time took Intuit from its rigorous, nearly religious reliance on customer research and data-based analysis into a more ad hoc, rapid pattern of decision making. While employees acknowledged the importance of moving quickly, the wholesale shift away from the discipline that had made the company successful in the past discomfited many. The Internet suddenly enabled Intuit to gather reams of page views and click-streams, but teams weren't analyzing the customer data so that it could be made actionable.

Founder Cook, who still held powerful sway on the Intuit board, lamented that the company was drifting away from some of the core strengths that had fueled growth in earlier years. Even the leadership seemed erratic. When Cook pushed managers to articulate business strategies for some of Intuit's Internet efforts, the managers sometimes could not respond convincingly. "If you can't even tell me your plan for leadership or profitability in this area, how can you hope to achieve it?" Cook asked.[10]

When he viewed an off-strategy television ad for Quicken InsureMarket that featured a man squirming in a dentist's chair on a busy city sidewalk, he knew immediately that the ad would fail.

Despite Cook's warnings, the InsureMarket team went ahead with the television ad placement and, as predicted, the ad performed miserably. Cook found his vision and attention to rigor all too often ignored.

Cook also had difficulty ensuring the company's overall strategic direction. "Though we realized after the restrategy session that our company was half consumer and half small business, Harris's attention and passion was the consumer side. Our small business sales already outpaced our consumer sales. Payroll, Quick-Books, Quicken used for business, ProTax, TurboTax used for business, business supplies—all added together—made up 50 percent of our total sales and well over 50 percent of profits. But this realization hadn't penetrated into the company."[11] How to correct the company's orientation stumped Cook.

More discord began in December 1998, when Harris took the witness stand against Microsoft in the government's historic antitrust trial against the giant software company. Outside of Sun Microsystems and a few others, not many companies had wanted to confront the giant, and so Harris's testimony created waves. Some Intuit managers questioned whether participation would benefit Intuit, but Harris wanted to make his case against Microsoft. Later, reflecting on the decision, he admitted, "There was a lot to be risked, not much to be gained, and it's unclear how much has been gained."[12]

Some employees considered Harris's testimony and the resulting public controversy a serious error. As internal angst increased, they began to question his performance as CEO. From the start, operations manager Dave Kinser had opposed Harris in the CEO role. "Harris never should have been CEO; he didn't have the capability. Cook and Campbell saw him as the guy who did the deals. They thought if he was so smart there, he must be good in the CEO role. But as CEO he wanted to write books, not lead Intuit. He took the job around August 1 and within a week he was floating around book ideas. He was supposed to be the CEO!"[13]

Back in 1994, when Campbell had become Intuit's CEO, he had focused on building a quality organization. Warm and caring, Campbell had built Intuit's organizational structure, worked to develop employees, and increased training. From his earliest days as a football coach, Campbell had earned his reputation as a people person—he put teams together and ensured they worked in harmony. Campbell had believed that Intuit would grow if it had the right people in the right spots with the right training.

The enthusiastic Harris, on the other hand, focused on growth through acquisition and the next big idea. At ChipSoft, Harris had cemented market leadership by acquiring key players. Through acquisitions he had also acquired key leaders—albeit leaders who had not necessarily shared ChipSoft's values. Under Harris, Intuit's spate of acquisitions and partnerships produced big returns. But, for all of his energy, Intuit employees felt a huge shock to the system going from caring Campbell's internal planning to intellectual Harris's disparate passions.

As Harris's focus drifted, Campbell and Cook inserted themselves to stop decisions that lacked strategic fit and rigor; for example, they discouraged Harris's attempts to write a book and buy a data consolidation company and a mortgage company—not at all in line with Intuit's agreed strategy. As 1999 arrived, many employees came to question Harris's style and thought him too easily distracted. "The day-to-day operating issues were really not his focus," Campbell conceded. "He regularly left or missed management team meetings to deal with potential major strategic partners or ideas. This, of course, angered his staff."[14]

The effects of Harris's leadership on the company deeply worried Campbell. Although he appreciated Harris's skills and contributions, Campbell recalled, "When Harris took over, he was immediately driven by big strategic ideas. He really wanted to put his strategic mark on the company, not concentrate on operations. When this became evident, the board acted quickly. They asked me to take an office and work with him on a day-to-day basis."[15]

So Campbell returned to Intuit to help manage the company. Beginning in early 1999, he worked daily with Harris to help him become a better operational leader. Campbell also stepped in as leader when other activities and deals consumed Harris.

After some months, Harris wearied of the hands-on coaching and of the demands of the CEO position. Finally, in a quarterly management meeting in San Diego in September 1999, Harris shocked Intuit employees: "I have an announcement. I am going to resign today to pursue my own entrepreneurial interests."

"Let me tell you why," Harris continued. "You know me. I'm an entrepreneur. You know that. I like being hands on with our business, you know this. I'm in your pants all the time. The job I want is your job." Everyone laughed because they knew it was true. "But," he continued, "that's not the job that Intuit needs. There are already lots of entrepreneurs here. They need a manager of entrepreneurs. I'm not it. I'm going to go and be an entrepreneur and Intuit's going to go and get a great manager for its many far-flung businesses."[16]

POSTMORTEMS

Even though Harris proudly pointed out during his resignation speech that 20 percent of Intuit's previous six months' revenue had come from the Internet, the company still faced doubts about its new strategy from without and within.

"The maker of wildly successful software programs like Quicken, TurboTax, and QuickBooks should've had no trouble duplicating that success online," began a fall 1999 article in *IDG*. "But the company is learning that the Internet is a different beast altogether." After recapping the phenomenal success of Quicken, which it said appealed to "the inner accountant in millions of Americans," the article drilled in on what it called "Intuit's identity crisis":

*In the beginning, there was Quicken. The personal-finance
software program appealed to the inner accountant in millions
of Americans when it was introduced by Mountain View,
Calif.–based Intuit in 1985. No other personal-finance application, including Microsoft's Money, has come close to edging
Quicken out of the top spot in the market.*

*Today, Quicken is to the desktop what everyone, including
Quicken, wants to be to the Internet. But as a host of competitors are already providing the tools consumers need to handle
their finances online, Intuit's finding itself in an awkward position—behind.* [17]

As *IDG* described Intuit's Internet shortfall, Cook mused:
"Bill Harris is the best deal maker I have ever met. Intuit benefited hugely from some of the investments Harris led—we've
made $900 million plus by selling our stakes in two of them at the
height of the bubble. But nobody wants a CEO who only stays
for a year. This is not our finest hour."[18]

And yet, Cook realized that when Harris had considered
leaving in 1997 for Pointcast, Intuit had had few alternative internal
choices for CEO successor. Not only did Intuit need a new CEO,
it needed more outstanding senior executives to groom as future
CEOs. Cook resolved to make executive-level hiring a priority.

As Cook thought further about what Intuit had learned during its past several years, he blamed himself for many of the missteps.
He had encouraged new thinking and fast action—which were
good—but he'd failed to reinforce the intellectual rigor and crisp
response to results that should accompany such speed. All too often,
Cook thought, Intuit had turned its "Think fast, move fast" operating value into "Think sloppy, move fast, and don't look back."

Cook feared that he had failed to demand that Intuit practice the "rigor with urgency" that had made the company successful. Cook told Campbell, "It's not the failures themselves I
rue. Failures are expected and normal as a part of leading and
innovating. It's the 'how.' The lack of dealing with data. The lack

of recognizing reality as it was happening and moving swiftly to readjust thinking, respond, and correct. The lack of analysis of in-market learning. We were glacially slow to realize and react even to businesses way off any expectation we had."[19]

As the company sought new leadership, Intuit had to return to its roots, attend to its core culture and businesses, and reconnect with its values. To be certain that Intuit found critical traits in a new CEO, Cook developed a list of criteria to shape the headhunters' approach (figure 19-3). Could Intuit find a new president who could help the company refocus, solve problems, execute well, and leverage its assets into greater success?

FIGURE 19 - 3

CEO Criteria

Memo from Scott Cook
Subject: CEO Criteria
Date: 9/26/99

Here is the compilation of CEO criteria to give specific guidance to the headhunter and our board on what's essential.

Must Have

- Must be a real people and organization leader
  - Develops, retains, and attracts the best people, then delegates and inspires them to action
  - Works through others—inspires their creativity, energy, and ownership—and can bring diverse groups together
  - Manages by guiding people, sometimes firmly, to great outcomes and top performance. "I love working for this guy."
  - A builder: builds great teams and strong durable organizations
  - Good communication skills

- Fast-acting results
  - Must be energetic, fast-paced, decisive, and impatient for action and results . . . to keep Intuit speeding up to Internet speed
  - Results-oriented, decisive, tough when needed. Gets organizations to perform beyond their own expectations
  - Drives to win . . . as our businesses are often winner-take-all

- Must have succeeded as a General Manager leading a complex organization through change
  - Complex means many interconnected organizations; e.g., business units and functional units. Not simply a functional organization around a product line
  - Succeeded leading the business through rapid change

(continued)

FIGURE 19 - 3 *(continued)*

- Technology and strategy confident
  - While need not be a technologist, must have technology comfort, not aversion
  - Most likely will have succeeded managing businesses where R&D was important to success
  - Must be comfortable thinking, deciding, and leading complex strategic issues
  - Develops a point of view on our future and drives us there
  - Flawless integrity, straight, values-driven
- Smart
  - Loves smart people
  - A learner—a sponge for learning, information, and data
  - Gets up to speed quickly
  - While not required, understanding of service businesses and infrastructure they require would be a plus

Not Required

- Need not have been CEO/president of a public company; e.g., the GM of a complex business inside a large enterprise can be OK
- Need not have high-tech or Internet background; e.g., Joe Galli from Black & Decker or Meg Whitman from Hasbro/FTD/Disney
- Not important to be "known"
- Need not be from financial services

FYI, here is a list of other criteria that while important I didn't see as quite as essential as those on the Must Have list.

- From background where the customers were consumers or small businesses (<50 employees)
- Installs the common processes and technologies that help the BUs [business units] win
- Knows the Internet . . . branding . . . financial services . . . service businesses
- Entrepreneurial
- Global experience
- Presence, represent us well to partners, the government
- Basic belief in and affection for what we do
- Curb appeal, impressive resume
- People warmth
- Strategically brilliant
- Data-driven, but comfortable making intuitive decisions
- Good at developing personal networks
- Experienced w/alliances, partner deals
- M&A deal experience
- Strong public speaker
- Strong negotiator
- Not afraid to take risks
- Quality-oriented
- Not a self-promoter

Source: Scott Cook.

CHAPTER 20

WHY PLAY IF YOU CAN'T WIN?

A s Intuit searched for a new leader, Bill Campbell returned as interim CEO. As always during difficult times, Chairman Campbell held the company together during the difficult transitional period. Management morale improved and the company began to feel more confident.

Good financial results increased the optimism. The late fall of 1999 saw Intuit's best-ever fiscal year: fiscal year 1999 revenues were up 43 percent to $847 million, with a net income of $376 million. Intuit's stock price continued to swell. Quicken had twelve million customers (approximately triple Microsoft Money's), 20 percent of U.S. tax returns were prepared using TurboTax, and 20 percent of the company's revenues came from the Internet.

But some bad news remained. The Quicken.com Web site, already well behind the leading financial Web site, Yahoo! Finance, in traffic, fell to fourth place in overall traffic. The company had mounted an enormous effort to launch WebQuicken, employing seventy-five people to create its service, but had failed to meet its milestones or volume targets. InsureMarket never hit its financial targets. QuickBooks rode the Y2K boom into a record-breaking 1999 (many customers who feared data loss had purchased QuickBooks 1999 for its data fail-safes), but its sales slumped for its 2000 edition. And Microsoft had announced it was entering the tax software category.

Despite Harris's departure, the pace of change at Intuit did not immediately slow. In October 1999 alone, Intuit announced its latest round of Internet-partnership initiatives: a new Quicken.com shopping channel and alliances with WebEx, Signio, Autoweb.com, First Sierra, UpShot.com, and E-Stamp.[1] In November, Eric Dunn led Intuit into a second five-year deal with AOL to exclusively provide its online billpay software and to create new online tools for its customers. Joining up with AOL's Personal Finance channel enabled Intuit to compete more effectively against Microsoft's Money-Central channel and Yahoo! Finance on the Web. December saw the launch of TurboTax Online through both the Fidelity and Vanguard brokerage Web sites.[2] Intuit's multifaceted development and distribution strategies continued at a quick pace, but Intuit management struggled to figure out how to win in all its markets.

One market that was posing new problems was the online mortgage area. QuickenMortgage's success in attracting applicants did not translate into either financial success for the group or satisfaction for its customers. Functioning as an online marketspace had a huge downside: Intuit couldn't control all the transactions with its QuickenMortgage customers.

Anecdotal and survey evidence suggested that several of the financial institutions affiliated with QuickenMortgage had not treated customers from Intuit's site well. Lenders had ignored applications and demanded unreasonable additional documentation; customer service agents had been rude and condescending. These relationships were forged on an Intuit Web site, so customers believed Intuit bore responsibility for their bad experiences. Intuit's reputation depended on the behavior of its partners—behavior it could not control.

And so, in late 1999 Intuit purchased Rock Financial to help control fulfillment of its Internet marketspace activities. Located in Livonia, Michigan, Rock Financial, renamed QuickenLoans, allowed the company to own the end-to-end customer lending experience. Buying Rock gave Intuit the high margins associated with actually closing mortgages as well as a small group of bricks-and-mortar offices in Michigan.

EAST COAST INCOMING

In addition to overseeing day-to-day operations as acting CEO, Campbell led the critical search for a new CEO. The key to the search was targeting the best candidate to fit Cook's criteria regardless of industry. Cook and Campbell found the first candidates they interviewed, who had technology industry backgrounds, unimpressive, confirming Cook's industry-neutral perspective. Eventually, a more attractive candidate emerged from outside the Silicon Valley.

Crisp and self-confident, Steve Bennett was a multitalented manager who had made an unprecedented rise from an entry-level position in a General Electric (GE) warehouse to executive VP at GE Capital Corporation in Stamford, Connecticut. The tall, athletic Bennett, in his mid-forties, had spent his entire career at GE; despite his success there, he was interested in the challenge Intuit offered. And Intuit executives, in turn, became very interested in him.

Steve Bennett was born in Madison, Wisconsin, but the Bennett family moved frequently as Bennett's father moved up the career ladder as a sales manager. Bennett hadn't dreamed of a life in big business. He'd dreamed of success in the big leagues. Bennett recalled: "I have been a very competitive, athletic success-driven person my whole life. I played football, baseball, and basketball in Madison and was All-City in all three sports. When I was nine or ten years old, I was playing on my cousins' age twelve to fourteen league team in baseball. I wasn't the best but I always wanted to play in the biggest game."[3]

Bennett applied a characteristic pragmatism to his decision not to pursue professional baseball, despite his talent and passion for the sport. "I played baseball in college and had friends in the big leagues but I decided that by thirty I'd be better off in business than in baseball. I had a good friend who played for the Yankees, and at thirty I was making more money than he was—and had better long-term potential."[4]

After college, Bennett began his career at GE. He worked hard and applied his laserlike focus to advancement and learning, eventually working his way up from an eight-dollar-an-hour warehouse job to executive VP. Before leaving GE for Intuit, Bennett had run a division of GE Capital with more than twenty thousand employees and $15 billion in volume. Just prior to that, as the first CEO of GE Capital's e-business unit, Bennett had integrated the Internet throughout GE Capital's worldwide suite of businesses while launching that company's small business credit Web site.

Bennett credited his success at GE to his "passion for excellence in everything that I do—business, my relationship with my wife, golf, tennis. Success early on in life breeds success. If you have success you do anything you can do to keep it—except break the rules. Why play if you can't win?"[5]

Intuit executives believed, after an additional round of interviews, that Bennett was operational, strategic, and insightful. "He seemed to have a strong feeling for Intuit's operating values," Campbell observed. "In terms of people, he valued growth and development for managers. He had used the GE and Intuit model, business units with functional groups to support them, for years. He seemed like a man of integrity, had operational soundness, and showed clear strategic thinking."[6] Among the Intuit executives, Campbell first asserted that Bennett was the right person for the job.

Dunn agreed. "He seemed like a nice, sharp guy with a decent sense of humor. He struck all of us as a good candidate early on, although the GE part [its large and rigid company culture] was a little scary for me."[7] Like others, the pragmatic Dunn appreciated Bennett's forceful confidence and goal orientation.

Cook told Intuit's board, "This is the man for the job. He's got a perfect combination of operational and process excellence. He meets our criteria." After meeting with Bennett, the board agreed, and so despite the potential culture shock of introducing an East Coast, large company, non–high-tech manager into the very

FIGURE 20 - 1

Steve Bennett joined Intuit as president and CEO from GE in 2000.
Source: Courtesy of Intuit.

West Coast entrepreneurial Intuit culture, Campbell, Cook, and the board chose Steve Bennett as Intuit's new CEO (figure 20-1).

Bennett began as CEO on January 24, 2000. "I decided quickly," he said. "I'd made it at GE, but I wanted to prove I wasn't a one-trick pony. How many people were successful just because they were at GE the whole time? I had already done well financially, so getting out of my comfort zone was good. Also, I thought I'd learn more from Scott Cook, Bill Campbell, and John Doerr than I'd learn spending another ten or fifteen years at GE."[8] Intuit's culture and the recession–proof nature of its businesses attracted Bennett. No matter how tough the economy, Bennett knew that people still had to pay their bills, prepare their taxes, and manage their business accounting.

Bennett's response to Intuit's offer quashed any latent fears among the executive team that someone from a large company might move too slowly for Intuit. With startling decisiveness, Bennett accepted Intuit's offer on a Friday morning, quit GE and sold all his GE stock that afternoon, flew out to northern California on Saturday, and bought a house in Woodside on Monday after the press conference announcing his appointment.

Wall Street analysts reacted favorably to his appointment. Morgan Stanley's Internet analyst Mary Meeker said, "Stephen Bennett appears to be a great add to the Intuit team."[9] A Bear Stearns investment analyst agreed: "We believe Mr. Bennett's experience managing a complex, fast-growing, world-class financial enterprise with more than twenty thousand employees and $15 billion in annual volume should serve Intuit well as the company continues its push into e-finance and accelerates its revenue growth."[10] Intuit's stock remained largely unaffected by Bennett's new presidency, closing January at roughly the same price it had opened the month.

THE IDES OF MARCH

Bennett was uncharacteristically quiet during his first weeks on the job. "You come into a job like a sponge; you have ideas but you don't do anything but listen. For the first five or six weeks I traveled and listened."[11] Employees listened to Bennett, too, concerned about how a GE executive would fit into Intuit's traditionally consensus-oriented culture.

Bennett soon proved more decisive than consensual. His listening period ended decidedly in March, when Bennett reorganized the company. Previously, Intuit had been divided into tax, consumer finance, and business units. Bennett reorganized to remove the layer of senior VPs who had run Intuit's consumer, tax, and small business divisions. Now, Bennett's sixteen direct reports, many of whom were VPs, ran Intuit's business units and functional groups.

On March 15 Bennett fired his second salvo during his first Wall Street financial analyst day, at which he publicly assessed Intuit's accomplishments and performance. The night previously, Cook and Bennett had met in Bennett's new office. After discussing the presentations that would be given by others, Bennett had run his evaluation of the company by Cook.

Bennett spoke diplomatically. He gave Cook an overview of his judgment of the company that didn't call a spade a spade. Recognizing this delicacy, Cook said, "Steve, hold on. I think you should tell them what you really mean here. You think Intuit is underperforming. Though you haven't used those words, you believe it and they believe it, too. That's what you should say."[12] Bennett immediately agreed. He was new enough that he hadn't wanted to lead with that kind of criticism, but after Cook's encouragement, Bennett relaxed. He had thought that Intuit could perform better and had not wanted to dance around.

At the meeting the next day, Bennett shot straight. Though he could hardly complain about Intuit's results, he told Wall Street that, given its brands and employees, Intuit was underperforming. "We're just scratching the surface of what this company can become. We're innovative with great strengths, but we still have to learn how to become a big company. We have great customer innovation but high costs and inefficiencies."[13] With this open assessment, Bennett set the bar higher for Intuit's employees.

In addition to the analyst meeting, March brought Intuit mixed news. The company continued its new product offensive, introducing an innovative Web-based database product, Quick-Base, targeted mostly at small businesses. This well-received service extended Intuit's small business offerings for the Web.

But Intuit also went on the defensive in a New York courtroom, where a consumer filed suit alleging that the company fraudulently collected and sold online user data, including sensitive financial information like personal incomes, to advertisers. Intuit investigated and discovered that its advertising server, run by a New York–based firm called DoubleClick, gathered unauthorized personal information. "Intuit never saw it coming. In March the company discovered that its customers' personal data, including their incomes, was leaking out to advertising firm DoubleClick through Intuit's popular Quicken Web site," reported the *Industry Standard*.[14]

Intuit settled out of court, but the negative publicity and the discovery that DoubleClick had obtained personal data, even though Intuit believed the data was never viewed or used, hit the company hard. Consumer concern over privacy of sensitive information grew rapidly along with the Internet, and caused many to shun financial services sites.

March's biggest surprise was Microsoft's announcement withdrawing the TaxSaver tax preparation software it had introduced only six months before. Microsoft had uncharacteristically made a halfhearted attempt to enter the tax preparation software category, developing a federal tax product while neglecting to introduce the state software programs vital for customer usage and satisfaction. Microsoft TaxSaver's strategy to compete primarily on price also failed in the face of high customer satisfaction with market leaders TurboTax and TaxCut. Further, tax software enjoyed a natural "stickiness" factor because the programs automatically read in the previous year's tax data for customers who had used the programs before.

Said *BusinessWeek:* "Intuit (INTU) shareholders who understand such things should have been thrilled by Microsoft's announcement on Mar. 23 that it is exiting the tax software market. Microsoft characterized the move as a 'repositioning' rather than a retreat, but don't believe it."[15]

After Microsoft's announcement, all of Intuit's tax employees gathered to ceremoniously bury a Microsoft TaxSaver box in their San Diego courtyard. A designer in the creative services group made a cardboard headstone to temporarily mark the burial site. After tax business leader Larry Wolfe gave the eulogy, the group erupted in a loud cheer. Employees imbibed drinks and snacks as TaxSaver was officially laid to rest.

Tax was only the latest arena in which the tenacious Intuit emerged victorious against the mighty Microsoft. With a share of retail sales somewhere higher than 70 percent, Quicken continued to defeat Microsoft Money, and QuickBooks had chased Microsoft's Profit out of the small business area altogether. And Microsoft's Home Advisor site, introduced nearly a year after

QuickenMortgage had debuted, never quite caught up with the number of loans issued by Intuit's site and eventually closed.

Microsoft remained Intuit's most persistent and threatening challenger, but the company faced competition from others as well. In the small business arena, Peachtree's business accounting software nipped at the heels of QuickBooks. In tax, Intuit's acquisition of Lacerte had solidified its offerings in the professional tax software arena, although Intuit continued to face vigorous competition in this market and had only about 40 percent market share by revenue. H&R Block's TaxCut software contended with TurboTax for individuals using accountants to do their tax preparation and for the many millions who continued to use pencil or pen. New challenges from online competitors heated up as well, and Yahoo! Finance's continued traffic supremacy was annoying.

But online competitors were about to become a lot less threatening. In mid-April 2000, three months after Bennett joined Intuit, the NASDAQ stock index, fueled by the extravagant dreams of the dot-com generation, abruptly ran out of gas, falling 355 points in a single catastrophic session. The Dow fell with it, losing 617 points on the same day. Intuit lost more than $10 per share; 20 percent of the company's stock value evaporated in a single day. *Barron's* magazine had published an article three weeks earlier revealing the burn rates of a large and popular group of dot-com companies, and the realities behind the "Pay anything for eyeballs and market share, we can think about profits later" mindset caused the crash that still reverberated years later. The "new" economy had ended with a bang.

CHAPTER 21

THE BENNETT BASICS

After the analyst meeting, Bennett reflected, "When I came in and said the company was underperforming, employees thought I was on drugs, everybody in that room—you could tell from the faces. But I knew people could perform. After that, we set very aggressive goals."[1] His listening period over, Bennett moved to combine the best of what he had learned at GE with the values that defined Intuit.

During Bennett's twenty-three years at GE, he had embraced many of Jack Welch's imperatives. Those that he had internalized included *set a tone* (leader's personal intensity determines organization's intensity), *maximize an organization's intellect* (take everyone's best ideas and transfer them to others), *put people first and strategy second* (getting the right people in the right jobs is crucial to the success of any strategy), *foster passion* (all winners share this characteristic; they care more than anyone else. No detail is too small to sweat or too large to dream), and *reach for more than what seems possible* (when the leader stretches, the whole organization does).[2] Over the next months, Bennett exemplified these values to Intuit.

The continued presence and support of Scott Cook and Bill Campbell made Bennett's job easier. Together, Cook, Campbell, and Bennett fell into a complementary work style that enabled each man to contribute his best to Intuit. Meeting, at a minimum, every two weeks in the hours before Bennett's Monday morning staff meeting, Cook, Campbell, and Bennett worked together to ensure Intuit's best direction. Both Cook and Campbell kept onsite offices at Intuit. Cook contributed vision, and worked with specific product groups on product innovation and strategy, while Campbell added operational experience, exceptional people skills, and his broad perspectives to the company's function. As CEO, Bennett led, but all three worked together to help facilitate change.

Bennett had reviewed the company's Operating Values (see appendix). After pondering each value's relevance, he suggested only one change: Instead of "Think fast, move fast," Bennett preferred "Think smart, move fast." Cook and Campbell agreed to the change, and announced it to employees. Thereafter, Bennett embraced Intuit's values and worked to ensure the company walked its talk.

Bennett met with Intuit customers and the company's frontline customer representatives as well as with his sixteen direct reports and other senior managers. He took the company's temperature while communicating his increased performance expectations. "I learned from Jack [Welch] to manage top-down and go to the customer at the same time. He'd drive top-down via expectations, process, and strategy and he'd also find out what customers want."[3] His method allowed him to avoid the woolliness that can pervade a large organization. "The layers in an organization are like sweaters," he explained. "If you have seven sweaters on you don't know the real temperature."[4]

Believing the company lacked functional depth, Bennett also worked with Cook and Campbell to recruit senior executives to Intuit. Bennett hired Dennis Adsit, a process excellence expert, from Rath & Strong Management Consultants in Boston to instill operational rigor, and he added Sherry Whiteley from Silicon Graphics in Mountain View to improve the company's human resources. He hired Bill Ihrie as chief technical officer from ADP of Roseland, New Jersey, and Tom Allanson from GE as VP of tax strategy. Bennett also added Dan Manack, who ran the professional accountants group. Later, in 2001, he recruited Lorrie Norrington from GE as senior VP of small business. These new recruits delighted Cook, who had wanted to improve Intuit's senior-level staffing.

Bennett also created a plan to develop and train Intuit's management staff. He authored a course on leadership that outlined the expectations of leaders at Intuit. "Leaders are paid to make decisions. Everybody gets a voice, but leaders make the decisions. That's what they're evaluated on."[5] Bennett trained senior managers to deliver the class to employees in their groups, instilling a greater sense of responsibility in the company's managers. The training swept away the slow collaborative decision-making process that had both characterized and paralyzed Intuit. Developing new and stronger leaders across the company also enabled Intuit to tackle and achieve more of its initiatives.

Next Bennett began to reapply rigor to processes and innovation at Intuit. He told employees, "At Intuit we need to put process and culture together to deliver results. As ι get bigger and more complex, process and scalability become ιιore important. Bringing some of the big company process to small company customer innovation is our biggest challenge. Innovation isn't just ideas, because ideas without operational rigor just fall apart."[6] This language delighted Cook. He knew that deep, one-on-one listening drove insight into customers' needs. This insight, coupled with consistent business rigor—data-driven decision making, appropriate metrics, and process improvement—had laid the foundation for the company.

Following this rhetoric, Bennett began applying rigor throughout the budgeting and performance evaluation process. In April 2000, as he met with every functional leader in the company to hear their budget projections, he made his increased expectations known by asking carefully targeted questions. "Asking good questions is a part of strategic rigor," he said. "One of the most powerful tools leaders have is the questions they ask."[7]

As functional leaders presented their budgets to him, some managers were not able to answer these queries, including questions about exactly what they had spent money on the previous year. So Bennett made everyone restart the budgeting process from an initial budget of zero. "You can't," he told them, "increment off bad foundations."[8] He knew the managers could not improve performance without a fundamental understanding of how they had previously fared—and why.

One of those who faced Bennett's grilling was Steve Grey, general manager for online services. Grey recalled:

> *When Steve [Bennett] came he started an annual fiscal year planning process with three year planning and financials. At one meeting, some managers presented a forecast for increasing page views. He said, "Let me understand something: If you get more page views do you get more revenues?" Not exactly. "So what drives revenues?" Page views times advertising cost per thousand views times pages sold. "So if page views go down you can still get more revenues." Yes. "So, what are the key drivers? What are the things that will make you better or worse, the few things that make the most difference?"*
>
> *Steve taught us you can have hundreds of measures but if you're not measuring the right things or if they're too hard to measure you can really mess up. His approach is methodical, straightforward—but revolutionary.[9]*

Coupled with this new accountability in budgeting, Bennett worked to overhaul Intuit's performance evaluation system. Instead of a fairly egalitarian rating system, where most people received the same rating and similar salary increases, Bennett asked managers to create clear and measurable objectives with their direct reports and then evaluate systematically against these measurements. More employees began to receive lesser ratings, and salary adjustments for the highest-rated employees far outstripped those for average performers. This more critical evaluation system shocked Intuit's camaraderie-driven groups but rewarded the measurable achievements Bennett thought critical. Employee surveys later revealed that the camaraderie had masked hunger for individual recognition.

By now, employees could identify a key element of Bennett's managerial approach: focusing on the critical few. Throughout Intuit, Bennett exhorted managers to ruthlessly prioritize their time and attention around the critical few issues that most affected their areas of responsibility. Bennett strongly encouraged the Intuit leaders to identify their critical few drivers and set up consistent, accurate measurements to track them. This relentless narrowing in on those business levers that could most shape success for each manager helped to eliminate the "management by committee" approach that had dogged Intuit decision making.

Focusing on the key drivers, measuring the critical few, asking the right questions, and rewarding top performers were some of the new mantras that Bennett brought to Intuit. New senior VP Dennis Adsit recalled: "Steve brought a new focus to Intuit on accountability of performance. We've seen a big change in the managers. Some didn't like the focus—it was too intense and they couldn't answer the questions. On the other hand, some said, 'Oh my God, I'm finally getting a chance to answer these questions with upper management in the room!' The real leaders are stepping up, getting a chance to show us how good they are. When we create this kind of forum for talking about results and improvements, things get better."[10]

THE EXODUS

Not everyone was an instant fan of Bennett's leadership. Forty-eight-year-old Alan Gleicher, Intuit's eleven-year sales manager, retired from Intuit in September 2001. "I had a knock-down drag out with Steve over Japan," Gleicher recalled. "We went at it in a big way. He likes to test people and shake things up. He's not looking for "yes" people. He wants to stretch people so they will be the best they can be. After that our relationship changed. We have mutual respect and a good friendship. I think he'll do great things. Before Steve, not many people got fired or left the company. Steve's someone making the tough decisions quickly and turning up the volume. It's hard for some people to accept."[11]

By the time Gleicher departed, several other managers had left Intuit as well. Bennett announced longtime manager Mark Goines' spring 2000 departure with an e-mail so brief it shocked many Intuit employees. Other departures followed: Jim Heeger, the supplies and small business leader was next, and then in 2001 operations head Dave Kinser, consumer tax leader Larry Wolfe, small business VP Dan Nye, and, finally, in 2002, CFO Greg Santora.

Eric Dunn also left Intuit in mid-2000. Dunn, the man who had worked tirelessly as CFO and programmer since 1985, had long been Intuit's maverick leader—and its conscience. After contributing to almost every area of the company's growth and development for fifteen years, Dunn had wearied of Intuit's perpetual struggle. Bennett's big-company style did not appeal to him. Dunn decided it was time to move on and stepped aside from his "virtual founder" role to run his own VC company.

Cook believed that Intuit benefited greatly from organizational discipline. The increasingly clear layers of authority under Bennett's leadership allowed him to demand answers to questions of strategy and operations that he'd had difficulty getting answered in the late 1990s. This return to Intuit's roots, to valuing its people and demanding the best from them, thrilled Cook.

But Cook and Campbell regretted the exodus, and particularly Dunn's departure. At the same time, they believed that Bennett's systematic design for excellence delivered what Intuit needed. Bennett was returning Intuit to its early days of rigorous decision making, and he was adding top-quality performers to achieve the company's goals. Cook had listened with great concern to old-timers' laments about the quality of some employees hired by Intuit in the late 1990s, so the return to hiring outstanding talent excited him. "*A* level people hire *A* level people; smart people want to work with others who are really smart," Cook observed. "*B* level people hire *C* and *D* level people so they aren't threatened. Intuit hires only *A* level people now, and that's wonderful for the company."[12]

In 2000, small business engineering manager Craig Carlson came to Cook to discuss QuickBooks technical support. The costly tech support group did not satisfy customers, Carlson said, and he asked Cook for his thoughts. Cook responded, "I've watched this happen and it's been awful. We can't mess around here; I think we need to change so much."

"I knew it was bad but I didn't think you knew. I thought you'd just given up," said Carlson quietly

Without denying Carlson's statement, Cook said, "We need to make things different. Steve will help us get them better."

"I can do it," Carlson proposed enthusiastically. "I want to set up a tiny tech support team here. We can use onsite tech support as a test bed for new ideas and a better feedback loop."[13] As Carlson left, Cook realized they had both been disheartened about the state of Intuit's customer support. They'd both had a whole set of ideas that they hadn't even bothered to share before Bennett had arrived. Now they could reinforce each other's dedication to improvement. Cook needed to help spread this renewed dedication across the company.

STANDARDS OF EXCELLENCE

To encourage an even more systematic application of performance measurements throughout Intuit, Bennett introduced Six Sigma, a method of statistical analysis that was gaining credibility among *Fortune* 500 firms. Production lines originally used the Six Sigma system to aim for zero defect production. But it had become far more: GE had modified the process to apply it throughout its company.

Bennett began carefully introducing the analytical process, which Cook christened "Process Excellence," to Intuit. He started with the company's high-transaction areas, customer contact centers and the QuickenLoans business, because Process Excellence measurements tended to work best in operations-intensive areas. To ensure buy-in, he told affected managers, "I'll fund it from the CEO's office the first year so there's no risk to you. You'll get all the benefits and none of the costs."[14] Bennett wanted to see how Intuit would take to the process. Would people accept Process Excellence or reject it as a GE initiative?

The initial success of the initiative pleased Bennett and Cook. In a customer support area, Process Excellence methods fostered a smart rerouting of phone calls that caused a 40 percent improvement in customer wait times and lowered costs accordingly. When Intuit executives heard this news, they clamored for Process Excellence training in their groups. Tom Allanson, hired from GE and promoted to oversee Intuit's tax division, marveled: "It's interesting how this business is willing to accept change. Change is not easy and making it stick is often very tough. This organization has a huge willingness to make changes. Good ideas are really embraced."[15]

Pankaj Shukla, VP of product development for the Quick-Books group, took immediately to Process Excellence and saw the bug rate in QuickBooks decline 70 percent with its use. Like most software, QuickBooks' development life cycle had standard phases. Using Process Excellence techniques, the group defined specific tasks for each phase. Then the group tried to cut down on rework by producing high-quality work not just at the end of the project, but at each phase. This meant measuring the results in each stage of development to create metrics.

Shukla enthused, "With the phased approach we had flexibility when new requirements came in. Process Excellence means understanding your metrics at each phase and then improving them."[16] By improving its development process, Intuit's

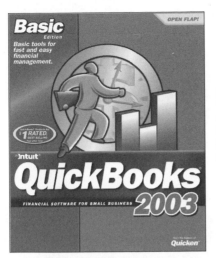

FIGURE 21-1

About 3 million small business customers use QuickBooks accounting software worldwide.

Source: Courtesy of Intuit.

new QuickBooks version had markedly fewer bugs and fewer customer complaints for technical support, increasing customer satisfaction and reducing development and tech support costs (figure 21-1).

As Intuit workers more broadly accepted Process Excellence, Bennett began training some employees to become "black belts" who could promulgate the Process Excellence process throughout the organization. As he watched Process Excellence take hold at Intuit, Adsit marveled, "Steve Bennett believes in Process Excellence to the bottom of his feet. I've never seen anything like it. Of all the senior execs I've worked with, I've never seen anyone support it as Steve Bennett does."[17] Adsit estimated that process improvements saved Intuit $10 million in its first year.

Process Excellence improved operations, but Bennett also worked to improve the company's strategic decision making. Bennett believed that if the company was not winning in a space, they should make the hard call to fix or exit it quickly. He told Intuit managers, "Deal with reality. See things how they really are, not as you want them to be. The smartest people I know try to convince themselves they are wrong, not right. Sometimes dealing with reality is not fun, but it's essential. Here, it's looking at all the businesses we're in—can we win there? What is the reality?"[18]

One reality quickly became clear. Despite Intuit's hopeful pursuit of the strategy espoused by McKinsey & Co. in 1997, Intuit's marketspace business model, which had sounded so attractive in theory, failed to succeed in practice. Intuit's attempt to develop objective aggregator sites that would allow consumers to comparison-shop financial vendors didn't make money. For large and important financial decisions, most consumers resisted relying on a Web site. Changing consumer behaviors and habits in financial arenas like insurance and mortgage proved much more difficult than convincing customers to switch from paper checkbook and pen to Quicken.

This realization, and Bennett's discipline, doomed Quicken InsureMarket. When Bennett joined Intuit, the InsureMarket team—acquired by Harris early in Intuit's Internet era—still believed they could get a critical mass of both sellers and buyers. Bennett gave InsureMarket leader Steven Aldrich, now in his mid-thirties, six months to meet this goal. But the InsureMarket team could not turn things around, so by the end of November 2000, Intuit announced the sale of InsureMarket to online competitor Insweb in Gold River, California. Intuit's once enthusiastic embrace of the Internet marketspace business concept died with this retreat, although former InsureMarket founder Aldrich remained with the company.

Another business that did not meet Intuit's new standards was WebQuicken. At the height of the Internet frenzy, many saw WebQuicken as a possible replacement for Quicken desktop software. Dunn had led Intuit's Venture Finance Software Corporation subsidiary to create WebQuicken. But the group's financial aggregation technology ultimately failed because financial institutions would not support it. Venture Finance Software Corporation also created a new infrastructure for investment tracking, and a billpay and bill presentment service that the company ran for a year as the WebPay product group. In 2001, Intuit sold these assets to Princeton eCom of Princeton, New Jersey.

Despite its contribution to company revenues of more than $113 million in fiscal year 2001, mortgage lending, with its heavy, uncontrollable influence from interest rate fluctuations, didn't meet the company's criteria of being in businesses with steady demand. "It was an earnings miss waiting to happen," said Cook. "The best time to get out of a business is when it's doing great."[19] In summer 2002, despite the group's substantial contributions to fiscal year 2002 earnings, Intuit announced the sale of Quicken-Loans back to an investor group comprised largely of its management team. According to the company's press release, "Intuit estimates that it will book a pre-tax gain of approximately $25 million to $30 million on the sale, consisting of a $23.3 million note and a 12.5 percent stake in the new company."[20]

STEVE-ISMS

Throughout his campaign for change at Intuit, Bennett stressed that Intuit must optimize all operations for three distinct stakeholders: shareholders, customers, and employees. "We have to remember all three groups."

Aldrich recalled the impact of this philosophy: "Steve told me, 'We're going to be innovative and create good things for customers but we're also going to create value for shareholders.' Intuit always did an awesome job of being a great place to work and doing everything possible for customers, but we didn't think enough about how to make money. It's amazing to see what a difference a simple statement like balancing three stakeholders and following up on it can make. For me it's been a great breath of fresh air. We can innovate faster, get people working better as teams, and get rid of what was in our way before. We were definitely not shooting for the stars before. We didn't have the same ability to make the impact we can today."[21]

Bennett's methodical approach to identifying opportunities for Intuit and shedding what wasn't working grew on most employees, who had initially had a wait-and-see attitude about their new CEO. Some groups, including many talented engineers, still resisted Bennett's more evaluative and performance-oriented approach. They worried that relentless focus on measuring tangibles might lead to Intuit's missing the next big intangible. But many other employees relished the clear lines of decision making and increased pace of improvement as the company topped $1 billion in sales.

Intuit had come full circle and rededicated itself to its traditional values. "Steve's building on what the company has been but running us on a larger scale," said Cook, summing up the Bennett effect. "We're still entrepreneurial—but now we have metrics, measures. What do you have to do to win? If we can't show that we can win, then we get out. And that frees up resources, financial and talent, and deploys them in new stuff, not the old stuff that was not winning. Now we have discipline on the strategic level."[22]

Rather than praising discipline, most employees preferred to affectionately quote some of Bennett's favorite phrases, dubbed "Steve-isms": "If you don't involve me in the takeoff, don't involve me in the crash." "Centralized—does not mean standardized." "You need a shared vision. We're not leaving here until you've got one." "Managers do things right; leaders do the right things." "Did the job run me or did I run the job?" And the tongue-in-cheek, "I'd love being a manager if I didn't have to deal with people."[23]

CHAPTER 22

A QUART OF MILK,
A LOAF OF BREAD,
AND A BOX OF TURBOTAX

Whoa... hen Steve Bennett examined Intuit's portfolio of businesses with an eye toward the bottom line, he quickly identified areas where Intuit lost money. After selling WebQuicken and Quicken InsureMarket, Bennett worked to focus the company on opportunities that he believed had received too little investment.

The company's core software markets—its real crown jewels—no longer provided the growth engine Intuit needed. In fiscal year 2001, Quicken held its 73 percent market share, but sales were down by 27 percent. QuickBooks had an 85 percent market share but flat sales. These disappointing results and the implosion of the Internet convinced Bennett that Intuit should exploit the high profitability and untapped opportunities in tax and small business.

ONLY DEATH IS SURER

Intuit's tax division, always a major driver of profits for the company, had recorded major growth in 2000 under then–senior VP

Larry Wolfe. More than 350 financial institutions offered access to TurboTax Online, and thousands of retail stores delivered more than five million desktop copies. Most of TurboTax Online's customers were new to electronic tax preparation and thus cannibalized few retail sales. Some of the million-plus customers filing their tax returns online through TurboTax every year received free tax preparation from Intuit's new award-winning TurboTax Freedom Project for low-income filers.

To create TurboTax Online, Wolfe had charged a group of creative, out-of-the-box thinkers to challenge preexisting beliefs and get something up on the Web quickly. But the rushed Web team hadn't just copied the desktop tax product; they had used Web technology to rethink tax preparation. One new feature they developed for the Web was placing frequently asked questions (FAQs) directly on the pages customers used when preparing their taxes, instead of requiring customers to search in a separate section. This idea worked so well in helping customers get answers quickly and in reducing tech support costs that it was deployed to the desktop TurboTax and QuickBooks products.

The new millennium brought TurboTax a record tax season. Nearly eight hundred Web sites, including Schwab, Fidelity, Vanguard, and the *New York Times,* offered the online version of Turbo-Tax in 2001. Excite and AOL both featured prominent links to TurboTax Online. TurboTax desktop software had a retail market share of nearly 70 percent, and nearly thirteen million citizens relied on it to file taxes.

By 2002, TurboTax strengthened its market leadership, capturing a 71.2 percent share and more than fourteen million citizens, an increase of 8.6 percent. Online, more than 2.1 million customers paid Intuit to use TurboTax, up from 1.2 million the previous year. Desktop unit sales rose to 5.5 million from 5.2 million. These record numbers came from thousands of offline sales outlets and hundreds of Web links, including a new, exclusive Yahoo! deal in which TurboTax became the sole provider of online tax preparation at Yahoo!'s tax center. The company also

FIGURE 22-1

In an innovative effort to make buying tax software as easy as buying milk or bread, Intuit sold TurboTax at Safeway grocery stores, 2003.

tested distribution at Safeway and Vons grocery stores, trumpeting that users could get "a quart of milk, a loaf of bread, and a box of TurboTax" at the same time (figure 22-1).

But Cook, Campbell, and Bennett believed that Intuit's tax business could improve further. Visionary Cook articulated a "Ten-Minute Tax Return" concept, in which he described an almost automatic way for consumers to prepare their tax forms. Using TurboTax technology, completed tax returns would be delivered to employees by e-mail from their employers or brokers. Employers, brokers, and banks would work together to preload tax-related data into the tax forms, making tax preparation automated and easy for consumers. The more users embracing TurboTax today, Cook reasoned, the more attractive such a strategy to employers and financial institutions later. Intuit's tax group worked to continue its explosive growth.

On the professional tax front, Intuit's acquisition of Lacerte software in 1998 had solidified its grasp on the professional tax accountant software market. Intuit catered to these high-margin customers by developing a professional tax Web site and a version of QuickBooks designed specifically for accountants. As a result, revenues from this profitable and influential group climbed 20 percent between 2001 and 2002.

Despite these sales successes, the world of tax in 2002 gave Intuit a few headaches. As far back as 1998, Intuit had worried about the government's ambivalence toward tax programs despite Congress's lofty goal for online tax filing: Online activity should comprise at least 80 percent of all tax filing by the year 2007. Intuit knew that TurboTax usage promoted online filing because once a user prepared taxes electronically, e-filing became a short, easy step. TurboTax generated the bulk of consumer IRS e-filings, and its online version helped the IRS get closer to its goal. Intuit's Tax Freedom Project even generated e-filings for the IRS from taxpayers who otherwise would not file electronically.

Despite TurboTax's advantage for the government, the IRS rarely cooperated with Intuit to try to enhance online volume. Instead of working with the company, the IRS flirted with the idea of building its own online, free tax filing engine, to compete with Intuit. However, by July 2002, in return for an industry agreement to offer free e-filing to at least 60 percent of taxpayers, the IRS announced that it would not develop its own free federal e-filing system.

But the battle for state tax e-filing intensified. In August 2002, the *San Jose Mercury News* ran an editorial headlined "Software industry blocks easy e-filing." The editorial criticized the self-interested lobbying by the software tax industry in California and urged the California Franchise Tax Board to resist the industry's power. "Millions of Californians who don't use tax preparers and don't need complex software from Intuit or others deserve a free e-filing option. It's already available in seventeen other states," the editorial stated.[1]

As the gorilla in the industry, Intuit was at the center of a mini-controversy. In August 2002, the California state controller's office dropped the legislation and said it would offer free online e-filing only for Californians earning less than $50,000.[2] By summer 2003, two-thirds of California's taxpayers were eligible to complete their state income taxes on the Web in "real time" without even having to download forms.[3]

Intuit encountered a public relations mess at the height of tax season in winter 2003. In an effort to thwart TurboTax piracy by users who bought one copy of the software and shared it among ten, twenty, even thirty officemates or neighbors, Intuit required TurboTax to be connected briefly to an Intuit server for an activation code, so that users could only print out their tax forms from one PC. So customers who began their TurboTax preparation on one PC and then upgraded their computers could not use their new PCs to finish the job unless they telephoned the company for a new code.

This limitation on use infuriated many customers, who encouraged others to switch to longtime competitor TaxCut. Users mistook the security program in TurboTax, supplied by a vendor, as that vendor's more aggressive surveillance technology. Internet bulletin board users, spurred by those who had previously pirated TurboTax, seized on this mistaken claim and launched blistering attacks on the company. The *Wall Street Journal* ran an article with the headline: "Unpopular Security Feature Could Take a Toll on Intuit."[4]

To calm Wall Street, Bennett noted that the positive financial impact of eliminating many pirated copies outweighed lost sales due to the antipiracy feature. Still, tax head Tom Allanson admitted that the company had erred, and the antipiracy feature was dropped for the next tax year. Cook conceded that the new feature had had several problems. For one, the activation codes did not reliably work on all machines. Second, Intuit had failed to explain the new code, and its reason for including it, early enough in the tax season. Even when the complaints swelled, Intuit did not make its case to the press about the piracy problem they were trying to solve to head off some of the negative press. Users and press alike did not verify the untrue claims about the surveillance component of the code, and the complaints grew louder. Cook believed that 75 percent of the problem could have been prevented had the company addressed the issue more proactively, a stark contrast to the company's adept handling of previous tax crises.

And the brouhaha affected the bottom line. Even though the company's tax division in fiscal year 2002 drove the biggest portion of Intuit sales, generating more than $577 million of the company's $1.36 billion in revenues, by April 2003, Intuit warned that it would miss its fiscal 2003 earnings targets (which it had raised the previous month) by some $150 million. Prudential also lowered its recommendation on Intuit's stock, and investors punished the company by brutally driving down its share price nearly 24 percent in a single day.[5] Still buoyed by the 40 percent profit growth expected even after the warning, however, Intuit announced an ambitious stock buyback plan only a week later.[6]

TYRANNY OF THE TYPICAL

Under Bennett's leadership, Intuit also redoubled its focus on small businesses. In 2000, the business products group had developed and launched QuickBooks for the Web to attract multiple site firms and those focused on ease of use. It had also expanded the QuickBooks Web services gateway and introduced its first set of programming tools to entice third-party developers to link to its small business Web site services, called QuickBooks Site Solutions. And at the end of November 2000, Intuit had announced its intent to purchase Employee Matters, an online human resources company in Stamford, Connecticut, to increase its products and services for small business.

But this was the small stuff. By 2001 Bennett's arrival spurred a complete rethink around small business that forever changed the way Intuit would approach this important segment of its business. In late 2000, when Bennett took over as acting general manager for the business products group for several months while the group's VP slot was vacant, the team, led by Dan Levin, had realized that Intuit's typical "one size fits all" QuickBooks annual upgrade could not deliver the 30 to 40 percent growth the company needed. Ideas about how to capitalize on small businesses had been floating around Intuit since the 1997 restrategy effort, but the company had not fully addressed them.

"We were focused on the middle of the bell curve where we thought most small businesses were," noted Cook. "In fact, small business needs are more different from each other than we knew. It's the 'tyranny of the typical'—by just focusing on typical customers, you miss the differing needs of so many other customers. We needed to understand the needs of specific customer groups we'd never focused on before."[7] The top ideas for expanding QuickBooks including focusing on vertical industry segments, moving toward mid-sized businesses beyond twenty employees, and extending into business areas beyond accounting. Cook coined the moniker "Right For My Business" to describe the new approach.

Bennett and Cook thought the most interesting opportunity revolved around creating custom flavors for QuickBooks to appeal to different vertical markets. Given the significantly different needs of, for example, the retail store segment from the medical office segment, creating different versions of QuickBooks to appeal to these varying user groups made sense. Moreover, creating industry-specific versions of QuickBooks could make selling the new versions easier, as marketing could more effectively target specific groups or industries.

In mid-2001 Bennett had recruited Lorrie Norrington from GE to run Intuit's small business area, and the energetic Norrington immediately embraced the expanding QuickBooks strategy. "We dove into the market opportunity and came up with $18 billion in the areas fairly adjacent to accounting," the charismatic Harvard M.B.A. recalled. "This was such a compelling size that when we segmented it—vertical $4.6 billion, payroll and benefits, $11 billion, etc.—it became clear that a 'right for my business' approach would help us grow an enduringly big business that will create a legacy in the valley."[8]

Under Norrington's lead, Intuit identified potential customers interested in integrated software solutions beyond accounting. These "integration customers" were growing businesses with increasing revenues and staff. The team believed integration customers would upgrade more often and have a higher lifetime value for Intuit. Many QuickBooks users complained that they couldn't integrate the product with their other business software. Intuit began to envision QuickBooks as the center of a business's critical hub. From the hub, the team imagined, different spokes addressing important business needs would radiate.

A September 2001 Intuit press release publicly laid out the three elements of the company's new strategy for the first time: "The first element is delivering industry-specific solutions that meet the specialized requirements of vertical segments, such as construction and retail. The second element is developing accounting solutions for bigger businesses and more complex businesses. The third element is the continued expansion beyond accounting software to offer additional business management tools and services."[9] Simultaneously, the company announced the acquisition of its first vertically targeted company, OMware Software of Sebastopol, California, a company that provided business management software to the construction industry.

To aid in producing related services for small business customers in vertical markets, Intuit acquired several other companies in specific industries. With more than $1.5 billion in cash, Intuit could pursue the "Right For My Business" approach aggressively. Intuit's several purchases included companies focused on professional accountants, nonprofit organizations, outsourced payroll, property managers, and wholesale distributors. These companies added functionality that further extended QuickBooks' vertical approach to each market.

But Intuit could not purchase enough companies to offer complete, integrated solutions to customers in all vertical markets. Accordingly, in 2001, the company announced another Intuit first: an open architecture software effort to encourage other companies and programmers to create programs to link into and integrate with QuickBooks functionality. The Intuit Developer Network offered access to application programming interfaces and a channel containing millions of small businesses. The goal of the Network, according to a press release, was to "allow developers to profit from a direct channel and integration with the business management tools that small businesses use everyday."[10] Intuit was now strategically trying to transform QuickBooks from accounting software to a business management platform with accounting as its core.

Many Intuit engineers and marketers vehemently opposed the developer network idea. "Being a platform company is very different from being a product company," Cook noted. "There were many arguments against the idea. How do we know outside developers' programs won't screw up the customer's data? How will tech support be able to handle questions about outside products? Won't this dilute the QuickBooks brand name?"[11]

Even though no business case predicted sales results from creating a developer network, Cook's persistent arguments eventually persuaded the naysayers. "In old world thinking, QuickBooks customers could only get improvements from products that we made. Now customers can benefit from the labors of a lot of other engineers, not just our own."[12] Cook also realized that Microsoft could easily exploit Intuit's lack of outside developers if they wanted to, since the Redmond company had years of experience working with outside developers.

To convey more of the advantages of open architecture, Cook invited Carol Bartz, CEO of Autodesk, to Intuit's headquarters to answer developer network questions. Bartz told a room crowded with Intuit employees that without its developer network, Autodesk would lose half of its sales. "What makes you think you understand those customers' needs better than the other developers who serve them?" she asked.[13] Bartz's conviction converted the naysayers who had opposed opening QuickBooks as a platform.

As another element of "Right For My Business," Intuit launched a new version of QuickBooks to serve mid-sized businesses. Called QuickBooks Enterprise Solutions Business Management Software, this new version of QuickBooks, which debuted in April 2002, served businesses from 20 to 250 employees and could support up to 10 users simultaneously.

Intuit also introduced its QuickBooks Point of Sale solution for retail customers in 2002. This package included vertically targeted QuickBooks software along with several hardware components including a cash register, scanner, and credit card swipe. Intuit offered the QuickBooks POS system through office supply retailers, another first for such products. At a price of $1,500 for the entire software and hardware system, the QuickBooks POS business represented Intuit's serious interest in moving up-market. By providing a lower cost, easy to use, and reliable turnkey system for retail customers, Intuit once again aimed to redefine an entire category.

"Our definition of small business used to be QuickBooks," noted Carol Novello, VP of Construction Business Solutions. With its open architecture software, Intuit had expanded its definition to include payroll, employee administration benefits, support, supplies, and online gateway services. "We're recognizing that our customers spend something like ten hours per week in the QuickBooks product—it's really the hub of their business—so we had to extend the value of QuickBooks beyond just the accounting component," added Novello.[14]

CAN'T IMAGINE GOING BACK

At Intuit's first Developer Network Conference in 2002, Cook (figure 22-2) commented on the "Right For My Business" activ-

FIGURE 22-2

Scott Cook continues to devote himself to building Intuit as chairman of the executive committee, with a focus on fostering innovation.
Source: Courtesy of Intuit.

ity, "QuickBooks is no longer one-size fits all. One way to offer lots more to customers was to open up the QuickBooks code base and encourage software developers to develop products that work with QuickBooks. These offerings help provide many more solutions for customers than Intuit could ever do by itself and help establish QuickBooks as the hub of the small business desktop."[15]

By fiscal year 2002, small business had become a significant contributor of revenues, bringing in $544 million of Intuit's $1.36 billion in total revenues. The company's "Right For My Business" strategy, its string of acquisitions in support of its vertical approach, the creation of its enterprise version for larger businesses, and its newly opened architecture to encourage third-party development all pointed to a future with exploding small business revenues and profits—and increasing success.

But Cook and Bennett still struggled with organizational change. Gaining widespread support for the QuickBooks industry-specific approach had proved difficult. "In a well-run company, beliefs run deep," Cook noted. "Change is hard. Some middle managers here have a 'Version 11 syndrome' with very high standards for perfection. If you had those standards for Version 1, you'd never launch a new product. We need a split personality: Version 11 thinking for Version 11 products and Version 1 thinking for new products."[16] Despite this organizational bias toward impossibly high quality, Cook persevered.

To finally prove the vertical concept, a guerrilla team developed a "lite flavor" of QuickBooks for the nonprofit sector. To test concerns that the "lite" version would not satisfy customers, the group tested QuickBooks Non Profit in late 2002. To the relief of managers, customer satisfaction for this version came in just as high as satisfaction for regular QuickBooks. This success led Intuit's organization to finally commit to the vertical approach and initiate development of many new vertical industry flavors for release by late 2003. And Cook launched a new focus on fostering internal entrepreneurship to make such changes easier in the future.

Twenty years after dreaming up a product in his California kitchen, Scott Cook's company had grown into a fixture in millions of U.S. households. Signe Ostby's complaint had been answered in spades. The 2002 Intuit Annual Report showcased the record $1.36 billion revenues and $140 million in income, and the company expects fiscal 2003 to come in with a 40 percent increase in profit and 25 percent increase in revenue. The ever-driven son of Chester Cook was still not content to rest on his laurels, though. The report promised that Intuit was ready to "take it to the next level." The company planned, it said, to continue to create solutions so profound that its customers would never be able to imagine going back to their former ways.

EPILOGUE

I n 1983, Scott Cook founded a company on the idea of listening to customers and then delivering products that "wow" them. Two decades later, that remains Intuit's mission.

Although Quicken alone no longer drives its profits, Intuit's beloved software still dominates the personal finance category, with more than fifteen million devoted users. Twenty years ago pen and checkbook were the best way to manage finances. Today, individuals can analyze to the penny where their money goes and how it comes in. They can track investment performance, bank electronically, save virtually, and locate instantly reams of financial information on the Internet. All of this is possible because of Intuit.

"We don't know what's going to happen in the future," Cook said to a hushed crowd of seven hundred employees and developers at the San Francisco Hyatt Regency in 2002, at Intuit's first developer network conference. "But one thing we do know is that Intuit will continue to operate by the enduring values that we've always operated by: Integrity, do right by customers, and it's the people. Our values are the reason why Intuit has done so well. They shape and guide us and will carry us into the future."[1]

Strong leaders have also shaped Intuit. "There are few companies you could point to that have two active chairmen," notes thirteen-year board member John Doerr, when asked to reflect on how Cook and Bill Campbell will help CEO Steve Bennett steer Intuit toward continued success. "These are not ceremonial roles. Bennett has the last call, but Cook, Campbell, and Bennett all possess the properties to make a company great. They are modest, understated men who don't have gargantuan egos but do have keen ambition for the company."[2]

For his part, Bennett is focused on using his talents to make Intuit the best organization it can be.

> *At Intuit, we are making our customers' lives better. The only other time I felt like this in my whole career was in GE's medical unit, which improved mammography and other medical technologies. Here, too, we really make our customers' lives better. And our people sign up for that.*
>
> *At the same time, this isn't just a social organization. We're here for a reason. And matching that customer devotion up with organizational rigor is the whole reason I am here. We're here to be successful for employees and shareholders and to improve customers' lives. The future is great. That's the dream I share with people—Steve's dream for Intuit.*[3]

But who can predict that future? The world continues to change, and the next disruptive technology may render today's strategies obsolete.

If Intuit lives by its values, by its three guiding stars—integrity, customers, and its people—Cook is certain that it will continue to endure and contribute. Ten years from now, he predicts, Intuit's constant will remain its values, and these will help Intuit reach new heights.

What does Intuit show us? That a company built on the strong guiding values of its founders and employees—whose corporate body, through excellent management, is shaped to live and breathe its founding principles—can survive and endure. That a company starting with a fierce dedication to customers, then, surviving, thriving, competing, reinventing, leading, empowering, innovating, and growing in accordance with a set of core values, can make a meaningful, lasting contribution.

When asked to comment on the meaning of his company, Cook is partial to a quote by anthropologist Margaret Mead: "Never doubt that a small group of thoughtful, committed citizens can change the world. In fact, it's the only thing that ever has."[4] Through all the ups and downs, triumphs and disappointments, Cook and Intuit's employees remain energized and committed to the company's mission. And, Cook is sure to add, there is still so much left to do.

INTUIT VISION, MISSION, AND OPERATING VALUES

FOREWORD

Intuit was founded on strong principles and has always acted on them. As the company grew larger, employees felt it was important to capture the spirit of those principles in writing—to "institutionalize" them for the future. In 1993, the company shut down for a day. All the employees went to a convention center and spent the entire day brainstorming ideas of what the vision, mission, and operating values of Intuit were and should be.

All of the input from that day was gathered and honed down over the next few months by cross-functional teams of employees. The goal was not to create a statement of what existed at the time, but something that could guide us into the future. The sum of that work is what follows on these pages.

OUR VISION OF INTUIT IN THE YEAR 2010

Intuit is the preeminent provider of automated financial solutions for small businesses and individuals. We are renowned as the company whose leadership and revolutionary innovations in financial services and software have delivered breakthrough value to our customers in every facet of their financial lives: banking, borrowing, investing, and beyond.

We are a large, growing, multinational company. Both our competitors and our shareholders respect us for our continued ability to create and establish leadership in huge, new markets.

Intuit's customer focus is legendary. Our unwavering devotion to outstanding quality—in our customer care, as well as in our products and services—inspires our customers' confidence and enthusiasm.

Our products and services strike a careful balance between evolution—seeking out, understanding, and responding to our customers' needs and desires—and revolution—continually delighting our customers with valuable new ideas they haven't even thought of.

People around the world use our products and access our services both on the PC and other computing devices. We have become an integral part of their daily lives. Our customers rely on our solutions to help them simplify and organize their finances, make better financial decisions, save money, and do it all quickly, easily and with greater confidence thanks to our tools, information, and services.

Even though Intuit is known for the quality of its products and services, we know that the quality of our people is the foundation of our success.

OUR MISSION

Revolutionize how people manage their financial lives.[1]

OPERATING VALUES

WOW!

Many companies say their most important job is satisfying the customer. We don't. We believe that satisfying the customer is simply the minimum requirement for staying in business. Therefore, we don't seek merely to satisfy our customers; we seek to wow them.

What do we mean by wow? Wow means creating customer enthusiasm and delight. It means giving customers dramatically more value than they expect—whether measured by price, performance, quality, features, or service. We know we're succeeding when we inspire our customers to go out and tell others about our company.

But how do we continue to wow our customers year after year? We certainly can't do it by relying on a single product, person, or idea, no matter how brilliant. We must build an organization that enables us continually to do great things for our customers.

We do this by creating an environment in which the ability to make decisions rests with those closest to the issues. In this environment, we are surrounded with the trust and given the latitude to be creative. We can talk openly about what needs to change, and we can see and make improvements happen. We feel energized by our work. We feel our full potential is not only being tapped, but is growing.

Our fundamental belief is that people come to work seeking to do great things. So we've created an environment that does not bog us down with rules but frees us to achieve ever greater accomplishments.

We outline the guidelines for this organization in the following ten values. Living by these values creates the type of environment we all desire: an environment in which we exceed the expectations of our customers and those of each other, where we don't just satisfy people, we wow them.

1. *Integrity Without Compromise.*

   Intuit is built on integrity. In all we do, we maintain the highest standards, never approaching what could be considered questionable behavior. On this, we never compromise.

Having integrity means more to us than simply the absence of deception. It means we are completely forthright in all our dealings. We say what needs to be said, not simply what people want to hear.

Integrity builds trust. Only through trust do successful, long-term working relationships flourish.

2. *Do Right by All Our Customers.*

Doing right means acting with the best interests of the other party in mind. We commit ourselves not only to meeting expectations, but to exceeding them.

An important word in this phrase is *all*—it includes every relationship at Intuit. We treat each other, our business partners, and our shareholders with the same care and respect with which we treat our customers. In other words, there is a customer for everything we do. While some of us directly serve the customers who purchase our products, each of us serves customers within the company.

We know we've succeeded in doing right when all our customers feel that they have benefited from their association with us.

3. *It's the People.*

People are the foundation of Intuit's success. In fact, people are so important that the *primary* job of each manager here is to help people be more effective in their jobs and to help them grow and develop at Intuit.

We have great people who want to do well, are capable of doing great things, and come to work fired up to achieve them. Great people flourish in an environment that liberates and amplifies their energy. Managers create this environment through support, respect, and trust.

Support means giving people the tools, information, training, and coaching they need to succeed. It means continuous effort to develop people's skills. Great managers help people excel and grow.

Respect means understanding people's unique career goals and being sensitive to their life choices. It means helping people achieve these career goals consistent with the needs of the company.

Trust means freeing people to do their jobs and to make decisions. It means knowing people want to do well and believing that they will.

4. *Seek the Best.*

We seek the best in two ways: we cast wide nets to find the best people to hire and the best ideas to adopt, and we base decisions regarding them on facts. While all decisions involve some judgment, we use fact-based analysis as much as we can.

To ensure we find the best person for the job, we aggressively seek across diverse, qualified applicant pools. When we've done our job right, the best person for most jobs will be someone here at Intuit. Most importantly, we evaluate solely on the basis of performance and abilities. There are no other criteria for hiring and promoting at Intuit.

The same principle is true for ideas. We actively seek the best ideas whether they are developed here or are in practice at another company. We have no bias; we adopt the ideas that will most help our company.

5. *Continually Improve Processes.*

Quality is the result of a process of inputs, procedures, tools, training, support systems, and materials. Therefore, to improve the quality of results, we must improve the processes.

How do we know if a process needs improving? The answer is, it always does. We can always get better. We strive continually to improve our processes, to help people do their jobs better, and to produce higher quality at lower cost.

While managers have a special responsibility to focus on processes, everyone has a responsibility to improve them. We all have two jobs: doing the daily work and improving the processes we work with.

6. *Speak, Listen, and Respond.*

At Intuit, we all have the responsibility to speak up. When we do, we deserve an open ear and a thoughtful response. Without open communication and expression, ideas get lost, needed improvements aren't made, and people get frustrated.

Managers at Intuit have a responsibility to create an environment that encourages people to speak openly, knowing they will be listened to when they do. Listening, however, is only a first step. It's also key to respond—if not through direct action, then through acknowledgment or feedback.

Speaking up doesn't mean just talking openly with your manager. When you have an idea or a concern, the right thing to do is talk to the person who's best able to act on it, no matter what role that person has in the company or what department is involved.

7. *Teams Work.*

The reasons to work in teams are simple: by building on each other's ideas and skills, we make better decisions and produce better results than we could by working alone.

296

Teams are also important because so many decisions impact multiple areas of the company. We find it works best to assemble a team of people with the relevant skills and let them make the decisions.

Teamwork means focusing on the team's success, realizing that ultimately the team's success is your success. It also means you succeed by helping other members of the team to succeed. The result? Decisions that are not "mine," not "yours," but better.

Great teams elicit everyone's participation and actively seek out both dissenting and favorable opinions; however, once the team makes a decision, all members commit to it.

8. *Customers Define Quality.*

The customer is the most important judge of the quality of a product or process. Therefore, we gauge the success of a product, service, or internal process based upon how well it delights the customer.

Part of adapting to changing customer needs and desires is knowing what our customers want. Intuit has triumphed in part because we actively solicit input and invent new ways to solicit that input from our customers.

Quality is something we incorporate throughout all our processes. It's not something we simply look for at the end of a process. It means keeping all our customers in mind each step of the way.

9. *Think Fast, Move Fast [Changed in 2000 to "Think Smart, Move Fast"].*

Another aspect of quality is the ability to respond to customer needs quickly. In addition, the company's success often depends on our ability to act on market changes and new opportunities. To meet these challenges, we must think fast and move fast.

Customers want to benefit from our great ideas sooner, not later. So do we. Moving fast enables us to learn and make better decisions over time. That's because the best learning comes from trying out more things in the real world.

We operate in a fast moving market. Rapidly responding to competition and new opportunities is essential for our continued success.

Does this mean we endorse thoughtless action? Not at all. What enables us to move fast is rapid, but thoughtful, planning. And by improving our processes through focusing on what's essential, enabling people to take informed risks, and using mistakes as opportunities to learn, we permit ourselves to think faster and move faster.

10. *We Care and Give Back.*

At Intuit, one of our most enduring values is our genuine care for the people with whom we work. While our responsibility to Intuit people will always come first, we also believe that with our success comes the responsibility to give back to our community.

We seek to contribute to our community in ways that reflect broadly held values, have meaningful impact, draw upon our unique strengths as a corporation, and, whenever possible, reinforce our business objectives.

AFTERWORD

What about results—things like market share, growing our revenue, profits? We barely mention them in our values. Don't we care about results?

We do. Market share is a measure of how well we are serving customers. Long-term earnings growth creates shareholder value which also helps us attract and retain the best people, and further increases the confidence of our partners and customers in our company. And revenue growth and current profitability allow us to reinvest to deliver even more value to customers in the future.

Do we have to sacrifice our Operating Values to meet financial goals? By no means. Living up to our Operating Values has always required making thoughtful tradeoffs—for example, balancing the bias for action of "Think Smart, Move Fast" against the emphasis on careful analysis in "Seek the Best." Attention to the financial implications of our actions is simply an aspect of making these tradeoffs well.

What's more, if we do our jobs right, it's a chain reaction, not a series of tradeoffs. We get the best people and ideas, develop and energize our people, focus on the quality the customer wants, improve the process relentlessly, deliver higher quality at ever-lower costs, which wows the customer, and when we have done this consistently, higher revenues, higher profits, and greater shareholder value result.

Simply put, living and working by our operating values will create customer wow and shareholder value.

Chapter 1

1. IBM is headquartered in Armonk, NY.

2. Founded in 1954, Commodore Business Machines, Ltd., based in Toronto, Canada, produced the first consumer-friendly home computer (the PET 2001). From Zimmers.net, <http://www.zimmers.net/commie/index.html> (accessed 1 September 2002). Apple Computer is based in Cupertino, CA. The Apple II was released in 1977. Compaq is based in Houston, TX.

3. Otto Friedrich, "Man of the Year," *Time,* 3 January 1983.

4. Scott Cook, interview with authors, Mountain View, CA, 7 February 2003.

5. Scott Cook, interview with authors, Mountain View, CA, 18 October 2001.

Chapter 2

1. Scott Cook, interview with authors, Mountain View, CA, 2 October 2001.

2. Home Accountant was made by a company called PC Software Development in San Pedro, California.

Chapter 3

1. James Wallace and Jim Erickson, *Hard Drive: Bill Gates and the Making of the Microsoft Empire* (New York: Harper Business, 1993), 242.

2. Karen Southwick, *The Kingmakers: Venture Capital and the Money Behind the Net* (New York: John Wiley & Sons, 2001), 24.

3. John Cook, "Venture Capital Notebook: Karlgaard of *Forbes* sees tech rebound," *Seattle Post-Intelligencer* Web site, 1 June 2001, <http://seattlepi.nwsource.com/venture/25545_vco1.shtml> (accessed 23 September 2002).

4. Intuit business presentation developed for VCs, retailers, and the press included this quote, 1984.

5. Stephen Kindel and Robert Teitelman, "But What Do I Use It For?" *Forbes,* 24 October 1983, 76.

6. Scott Cook, interview with authors, Mountain View, CA, 2 October 2001.

Chapter 4

1. Scott Cook, interview with authors, Mountain View, CA, 15 January 2003.

2. Tom Proulx, e-mail to authors, 22 October 2002.

3. Virginia Boyd, interview with authors, Menlo Park, CA, 21 September 2001.

4. Eric Dunn, interview with authors, Palo Alto, CA, 10 July 2001.

5. Ken Landis, "The Quicken Breakthrough," *A+ Magazine* 4, no. 1 (1986): 22.

6. Geoffrey Moore, *Crossing the Chasm* (New York: HarperBusiness, 2002), 140.

7. Virginia Boyd, interview with authors, Menlo Park, CA, 21 September 2001.

8. Tom Proulx, interview with authors, Menlo Park, CA, 3 October 2001.

Chapter 5

1. Gordon Moore, <http://www.intel.com/update/archive/issue2/feature.htm> (accessed 15 July 2002).

2. Scott Cook, interview with authors, Mountain View, CA, 7 February 2003.

3. Eric Shenk, interview with author, Palo Alto, CA, 25 October 2001.

4. Tom Proulx, interview with authors, Menlo Park, CA, 3 October 2001.

5. Eric Dunn, interview with authors, Palo Alto, CA, 1 October 2001.

6. Peter Wendell, interview with author, Menlo Park, CA, 16 November 2001.

7. Eric Shenk, interview with author, Palo Alto, CA, 25 October 2001.

8. Jeffrey Kutler, "PC Banking for Midsize Firms—Intuit Software Speeds Check Reconciliation Process," *The American Banker,* 9 November 1988, 8.

9. Eric Shenk, interview with author, Palo Alto, CA 25 October 2001.

10. Virginia Boyd, interview with authors, Menlo Park, CA, 21 September 2001.

Chapter 6

1. Scott Cook, interview with authors, Mountain View, CA, 5 February 2002.

2. Scott Cook, interview with authors, Mountain View, CA, 15 January 2003.

3. Scott Cook, interview with authors, Mountain View, CA, 5 February 2002.

Chapter 7

1. Mari Baker, from interview with authors, Woodside, CA, 2 November 2001.

2. Lun Yuen, interview with author, Palo Alto, CA, 25 October 2001.

3. Scott Cook, interview with authors, Mountain View, CA, 17 May 2002.

4. Customer testimonials, Intuit advertisement, 1990.

5. Richard O'Reilly, "Intuit Upgrades Quicken, An Easy to Use Financial Program," *Washington Post,* 24 July 1989.

6. Mari Baker, interview with authors, Woodside, CA, 2 November 2001.

7. Eric Dunn, e-mail to authors, 26 February 2003.

8. Mari Baker, interview with authors, Woodside, CA, 2 November 2001.

9. Eric Dunn, from interview with authors, Palo Alto, CA, 1 October 2001.

10. Eric Dunn, e-mail to author, 13 January 2003.

11. Tom Proulx, interview with authors, Menlo Park, CA, 3 October 2001.

12. Tom Proulx, from e-mail to author, 10 December 2002.

13. John Doerr, interview with author, Menlo Park, CA, 14 November 2001.

Chapter 8

1. Michael A. Cusumano and Richard W. Selby, *Microsoft Secrets: How the World's Most Powerful Software Company Creates Technology, Shapes Markets, and Manages People* (New York: The Free Press, 1995), 3.

2. Heather Fleming Phillips, "Microsoft Gets Its Way," *San Jose Mercury News,* 2 November 2002.

3. Cusumano and Selby, *Microsoft Secrets,* 398.

4. Scott Cook, from interview with authors, Mountain View, CA, 5 December 2002.

5. Ibid.

6. Mari Baker, from e-mail to author, 26 January 2003.

7. Scott Cook, from interview with authors, Mountain View, CA, 18 October 2001.

8. Eric Dunn, interview with authors, Palo Alto, CA, 12 October 2001.

9. Eric Dunn, interview with authors, Palo Alto, CA, 22 January 2003.

10. Mari Baker, from interview with authors, Woodside, CA, 21 July 2001.

11. John Monson, e-mail to author, 27 January 2003.

12. Ibid.

13. John Monson, interview with authors, Palo Alto, CA, 28 June 2001.

14. Mike Hallman, telephone interview with author, 8 February 2002.

15. Scott Cook, interview with authors, Mountain View, CA, 7 January 2003.

16. Mari Baker, interview with authors, Woodside, CA, 21 July 2001.

17. Jacqueline Maartense, interview with author, Palo Alto, CA, 7 August 2001.

18. Steve Katz, interview with authors, Menlo Park, CA, 2 August 2001.

19. Jonathan Weber, "Slaying the Giant," *Los Angeles Times,* 8 August 1993.

20. Ibid.

21. Ibid.

22. Ibid.

23. Eric Dunn, interview with authors, Palo Alto, CA, 12 October 2001.

Chapter 9

1. Tom LeFevre, interview with author, Menlo Park, CA, 11 September 2001.

2. Ridge Evers, interview with authors, San Francisco, CA, 22 October 2001.

3. Ibid.

4. Dr. L. Murphy Smith's Official Web Site of Texas A&M University, <http://acct.tamu.edu/smith/ethics/pacioli.htm> (accessed 15 June 2002).

5. John Monson, interview with authors, Palo Alto, CA, 28 June 2001.

6. Ridge Evers, interview with authors, San Francisco, CA, 22 October 2001.

7. Ibid.

8. Ibid.

9. Jane Boutelle, telephone interview with author, 24 October 2001.

10. According to an Intuit press release of 10 May 1992, the leading low-end business accounting software included: Accpac Simply, version 3.4, Computer Associates, Islandia, NY, $199; DACEasy Instant Accounting, DACEasy, Dallas, $49.95; One Write Plus Accounting, version 3.0, Meca Software, Fairfield, CT, $129.95; Peachtree Basic Accounting, Peachtree Software, Norcross, GA, $99; Pacioli 2000, M-USA, Dallas, $49.95; QuickBooks, Intuit, Menlo Park, CA, $139.95; StageSoft, Accounting for SmallBusiness, StageSoft, Tampa, FL, StandardPak $249, bonus $349.

11. John Monson, interview with authors, Palo Alto, CA, 28 June 2001.

12. Jay O'Connor, interview with authors, Mountain View, CA, 17 September 2001.

13. Ibid.

14. Ibid.

15. Intuit Press Release, *Intuit rolls out Windows version of best-selling bookkeeping software; QuickBooks for DOS drove unprecedented growth in accounting category in 1992* (Menlo Park, CA, 27 August 1993). Software Publishing Association data.

16. Customer testimonials, QuickBooks advertising, 1992–1994.

Chapter 10

1. Steve Pelletier, interview with authors, Woodside, CA, 4 December 2001.

2. Ibid.

3. Mike Maples, telephone interview with author, 5 December 2002.

4. Microsoft Press Release, *Microsoft Ships Money 2.0, a Fast, Easy Tool for Managing Personal Finances; European Versions Simultaneously Announced* (Redmond, WA, 14 September 1992).

Chapter 11

1. Eric Dunn, from interview with authors, Palo Alto, CA, 22 January 2003.
2. Eric Dunn, from interview with authors, Palo Alto, CA, 6 January 2001.
3. Jamie Beckett, "Traders Embrace Intuit IPO—Stock Soars 60 Percent," *San Francisco Chronicle,* 13 March 1993.
4. Ibid.
5. Jim Heeger, interview with authors, Menlo Park, CA, 22 January 2002.
6. Ibid.
7. Scott Cook, internal company memo, March 1993.
8. Jim Collins (speech at Intuit company meeting, San Jose, CA, 25 March 1993).
9. Scott Cook, interview with authors, Mountain View, CA, 7 November 2001.
10. Scott Cook, from interview with authors, Mountain View, CA, 7 November 2001.
11. Scott Cook, interview with authors, Mountain View, CA, 7 November 2001.

Chapter 12

1. Bill Harris, interview with authors, Woodside, CA, 30 November 2001.
2. Ibid.
3. Tom Proulx, e-mail to author, 7 December 2002.
4. Ibid.
5. Bill Harris, interview with authors, Woodside, CA, 30 November 2001.
6. Scott Cook, interview with authors, Mountain View, CA, 15 January 2003.
7. Tom Proulx, e-mail to author, 7 December 2002.
8. Eric Dunn, from interview with authors, Palo Alto, CA, 6 November 2001.

Chapter 13

1. Scott Cook, interview with authors, Mountain View, CA, 7 February 2003.
2. Bill Campbell, interview with authors, Palo Alto, CA, 30 January 2002.
3. Ibid.
4. Scott Cook, interview with authors, Mountain View, CA, 10 January 2002.
5. Eric Dunn, interview with authors, Palo Alto, CA, 3 December 2001.
6. Bill Harris, interview with authors, Woodside, CA, 1 February 2002.
7. Bill Campbell, interview with authors, Palo Alto, CA, 20 July 2001.
8. Alan Gleicher, from interview with authors, Palo Alto, CA, 26 January 2002.
9. Dave Kinser, interview with author, Cupertino, CA, 17 January 2002.
10. Bill Harris, interview with authors, Woodside, CA, 1 February 2002.

Chapter 14

1. Bill Campbell, interview with authors, Palo Alto, CA, 17 December 2001.
2. Nancy F. Koehn, *Brand New* (Boston: Harvard Business School Press, 2001), 262.
3. Michael Oneal, "Scott Cook Wants to Control Your Checkbook," *BusinessWeek,* 26 September 1994.
4. Scott Cook, interview with authors, Mountain View, CA, 5 January 2003.

Chapter 15

1. Richard Brandt, "Sorry Bill, the Deal Is Off," *BusinessWeek,* 27 February 1995.
2. Mike Maples, telephone interview with author, 5 December 2002.

3. Scott Cook, interview with authors, Mountain View, CA, 5 January 2003.

4. Bill Campbell, interview with authors, Palo Alto, CA, 20 July 2001.

5. Bill Harris, interview with authors, Woodside, CA, 1 February 2002.

6. Ibid.

7. Intuit meeting videotape, 13 October 1994.

8. Ibid.

9. Ibid.

10. Ibid.

11. Intuit Company Research, Mercer Group, 1995.

12. Ibid.

13. Ibid.

14. Ibid.

15. Bill Gates, "Letters to *Fortune*," *Fortune,* 20 February 1995, 40.

16. Matt Cone, telephone interview with author, 20 December 2001.

17. Matt Cone, from telephone interview with author, 20 December 2001.

18. Karen Epper, "Software Deal Shakes Up Home Banking; Banks Fear Microsoft As Relationship Rival," *American Banker,* 17 October 1994.

19. Brandt, "Sorry Bill, the Deal Is Off."

Chapter 16

1. Martha Groves, "Microsoft Deal Facing Intense New Scrutiny," *Los Angeles Times,* 23 November 1994.

2. Scott Cook, interview with authors, Mountain View, CA, 12 December 2002.

3. Steve Lohr, "Gates, the Pragmatist, Walked Away," *New York Times,* 22 May 1995.

4. Jube Shiver Jr., "Justice Department Appeals Microsoft Ruling," *Los Angeles Times,* 17 February 1995.

5. Bill Harris, interview with authors, Woodside, CA, 1 February 2002.

6. Ibid.

7. Jube Shiver Jr., "Justice Department Appeals Microsoft Ruling," *Los Angeles Times,* 17 February 1995.

8. Bill Campbell, interview with authors, Palo Alto, CA, 25 September 2001.

9. Steve Pelletier, interview with authors, Woodside, CA, 4 December 2001.

10. Scott Cook, interview with authors, Mountain View, CA, 5 December 2002.

11. Bill Campbell, interview with authors, Palo Alto, CA, 25 September 2001.

12. Ibid.

13. Andy Cohen, telephone interview with author, 5 February 2003.

14. Scott Cook, interview with authors, Mountain View, CA, 9 January 2002.

15. Ibid.

16. Bill Harris, interview with authors, Woodside, CA, 1 February 2002.

Chapter 17

1. Hobbes Internet Timeline, <http://www.zakon.org/robert/internet/timeline/> (accessed 15 November 2002).

2. Bill Harris, interview with authors, Woodside, CA, 1 February 2002.

3. Intuit Press Release, *Intuit to Provide Internet Access Directly From Quicken* (Menlo Park, CA, 19 October 1995).

4. John Monson, interview with authors, Palo Alto, CA, 12 July 2001.

5. John Monson, e-mail to author, 4 February 2003.

6. Andy Cohen, telephone interview with author, 5 February 2003.

7. Steven Aldrich, interview with author, Mountain View, CA, 8 April 2002.

8. Intuit Press Release, *America Online and Intuit Announce Strategic Alliance to Provide Electronic Banking to AOL Subscribers* (Menlo Park, CA, 13 November 1995).

9. Steve Grey, e-mail to author, 31 October 2002.

10. Ibid.

11. Steve Pelletier, interview with authors, Woodside, CA, 4 December 2001.

Chapter 18

1. AP, "Intuit Warns of Flaws in Tax Software, Again," *New York Times,* 15 February 1996.

2. Andy Cohen, telephone interview with author, 5 February 2003.

3. Roger Bass, telephone interview with author, 17 December 2001.

4. Andy Cohen, interview with authors, Palo Alto, CA, 16 January 2001.

5. Scott Cook, interview with authors, Mountain View, CA, 6 February 2002.

6. Bill Harris, interview with authors, Woodside, CA, 1 February 2002.

7. Eric Dunn, interview with authors, Palo Alto, CA, 22 January 2003.

8. Scott Cook, interview with authors, Mountain View, CA, 9 January 2002.

9. Kathy Rebello, "Gut Feel at Intuit," *BusinessWeek,* 30 September 1996.

10. Carl Reese, telephone interview with author, 15 July 2002.

11. John Swartz, "Intuit Buys a Piece of Excite; Quicken-Maker OKs Deal a Day After It Cuts Staff," *San Francisco Chronicle,* 12 June 1997.

12. W. Royal, "Intuit's Equity Stake in Excite Creates Banking's Version of 'Seinfeld': The Deal Means That Banks Must Pay to Play—and Keep Their Customers' Attention," *American Banker,* 1 December 1997.

13. Elizabeth Corcoran, "What Intuit Didn't Bank On: Counting Its Click Fees Before They Hatched, the Online Financial Service Leader Laid an Egg," *Washington Post,* 22 June 1997.

14. Eryn Brown, "Is Intuit Headed for a Meltdown?" *Fortune,* 18 August 1997.

Chapter 19

1. Tapan Bhat, interview with author, Mountain View, CA, 29 January 2002.

2. Intuit Press Release, *Intuit and Excite Now Offer Complete Online Tax Preparation and Filing; TurboTax Online Now Available on Excite Business & Investing Channel by Quicken.com* (Mountain View, CA, 23 February 1998).

3. Bill Campbell, interview with authors, Palo Alto, CA, 13 March 2002.

4. Alison Wagonfeld, interview with authors, Menlo Park, CA, 12 February 2002.

5. John Monson, e-mail to author, 4 February 2003.

6. Bill Harris, interview with authors, Woodside, CA, 18 March 2002.

7. Intuit video, "A Tribute to the Coach," August 1998.

8. Mari Baker, e-mail to author, 11 November 2002.

9. Lisa Wirthman, "Intuit Installs 'Deal Maker' At the Helm," *Investor's Business Daily,* 21 May 1998.

10. Scott Cook, telephone interview with author, Mountain View, CA, 5 December 2002.

11. Scott Cook, interview with authors, Mountain View, CA, 6 February 2002.

12. Bill Harris, interview with authors, Woodside, CA, 18 March 2002.

13. Dave Kinser, interview with author, Cupertino, CA, 17 January 2002.

14. Bill Campbell, e-mail to authors, Palo Alto, CA, 12 August 2002.

15. Ibid.

16. Scott Cook, from interview with authors, Mountain View, CA, 9 January 2002.

17. Megan Barnett, "Intuit's Identity Crisis," *IDG,* 20 August 1999.

18. Scott Cook, interview with authors, Mountain View, CA, 9 January 2002.

19. Scott Cook, e-mail to author, 10 December 2002.

Chapter 20

1. WebEx (Web-based meetings) is headquartered in San Jose, CA; Signio (online payment processing, now owned by VeriSign) is in Mountain View, CA; Autoweb (car-based site) is based in Irvine, CA; First Sierra (online lending) is located in Houston, TX; UpShot (online sales lead management) is in Mountain View, CA; and E–Stamp (online postage company, now Stamps.com) is in Santa Monica, CA.

2. Fidelity is based in Boston, MA, and Vanguard in Valley Forge, PA.

3. Steve Bennett, interview with authors, Mountain View, CA, 15 March 2002.

4. Ibid.

5. Ibid.

6. Bill Campbell, interview with authors, Palo Alto, CA, 13 March 2002.

7. Eric Dunn, interview with authors, Palo Alto, CA, 22 January 2003.

8. Steve Bennett, interview with authors, Mountain View, CA, 15 March 2002.

9. Mary Meeker, "Intuit Appoints GE Capital EVP as President, CEO," Morgan Stanley Dean Witter, 25 January 2000.

10. Craig Peckham, "INTU: The Search Is Over—We Like the Result," *Bear Stearns,* 25 January 2000.

11. Steve Bennett, interview with authors, Mountain View, CA, 15 March 2002.

12. Scott Cook, interview with authors, Mountain View, CA, 7 February 2003.

13. Steve Bennett, interview with authors, Mountain View, CA, 15 March 2002.

14. Constance Gustke, "Sharing Secrets," *The Industry Standard,* 15 May 2000.

15. Sam Jaffe, "How Intuit Dispatched Mighty Microsoft," *BusinessWeek Online,* 30 March 2000.

Chapter 21

1. Steve Bennett, interview with authors, Mountain View, CA, 15 March 2002.

2. Jack Welch, *Jack: Straight from the Gut* (New York: Warner Books, 2001), 383–385.

3. Steve Bennett, interview with authors, Mountain View, CA, 15 March 2002.

4. Ibid.

5. Ibid.

6. Ibid.

7. Ibid.

8. Ibid.

9. Steve Grey, interview with authors, Mountain View, CA, 8 January 2002.

10. Dennis Adsit, telephone interview with author, 1 April 2002.

11. Alan Gleicher, interview with authors, Palo Alto, CA, 26 January 2002.

12. Scott Cook, interview with authors, Mountain View, CA, 22 March 2002.

13. Scott Cook, from interview with authors, Mountain View, CA, 7 February 2003.

14. Dennis Adsit, from telephone interview with author, 1 April 2002.

15. Tom Allanson, telephone interview with author, 2 May 2002.

16. Pankaj Shukla, interview with author, Mountain View, CA, 15 May 2002.

17. Dennis Adsit, telephone interview with author, 1 April 2002.

18. Steve Bennett, interview with authors, Mountain View, CA, 15 March 2002.

19. Scott Cook, interview with authors, Mountain View, CA, 7 February 2003.

20. Intuit Press Release, *Intuit Signs Agreement to Sell its QuickenLoans Business* (Mountain View, CA, 20 June 2002).

21. Steve Aldrich, interview with author, Mountain View, CA, 8 April 2002.

22. Scott Cook, interview with authors, Mountain View, CA, 17 May 2002.

23. Alan Gleicher, from interview with authors, Palo Alto, CA, 26 January 2002.

Chapter 22

1. Editorial staff, "Software Industry Blocks Easy E-Filing," *San Jose Mercury News,* 2 August 2002.

2. Ann E. Marimow, "Online State Tax Filing Has Easier Road Ahead," *San Jose Mercury News,* 8 August 2002.

3. Marimow, "Tax e-Filing Gets Boost," *San Jose Mercury News,* 27 November 2002.

4. Marcelo Prince, "Unpopular Security Feature Could Take Toll on Intuit," *Wall Street Journal,* 7 February 2003.

5. Yahoo News, "Intuit Shares Drop 24 Percent After Target Cuts," <http://biz. yahoo.com/rc/030321/tech_intuit_stocks_3.html> (accessed 12 April 2003).

6. Yahoo News, "Intuit Says To Buy Back $500 Million Of Stock,"<http://biz. yahoo.com/rf/030324/tech_intuit_7.html> (accessed 12 April 2003).

7. Scott Cook, interview with authors, Mountain View, CA, 7 February 2003.

8. Lorrie Norrington, interview with authors, Mountain View, CA, 6 May 2002.

9. Intuit Press Release, *Intuit Announces Strategy to Tackle $17 Billion Small Business Management Opportunity* (Mountain View, CA, 24 September 2001).

10. Intuit Press Release, *New Initiative to Help Developers Profit From Small Business Channel* (Mountain View, CA, 12 February 2001).

11. Scott Cook, interview with authors, Mountain View, CA, 7 February 2003.

12. Ibid.

13. Scott Cook, from interview with authors, Mountain View, CA, 7 February 2003.

14. Carol Novello, interview with author, Mountain View, CA, 1 April 2002.

15. Scott Cook, keynote speech at Intuit Developer Network Conference, San Francisco, CA, 13 November 2002.

16. Scott Cook, interview with authors, Mountain View, CA, 7 February 2003.

Appendix

1. Changed in 2000 to "Revolutionize how people manage their financial lives and small businesses manage their businesses."

Epilogue

1. Scott Cook, keynote speech at Intuit Developer Network Conference, San Francisco, CA, 13 November 2002.

2. John Doerr, telephone interview with author, 12 November 2002.

3. Steve Bennett, interview with authors, Mountain View, CA, 15 March 2002.

4. The Institute for Intercultural Studies, "Margaret Mead," <http://www. mead2001.org> (accessed 11 August 2002).

SUZANNE TAYLOR is a marketing consultant, and has practiced independently since 1998. Her area of expertise is in optimizing the customer experience, with a focus on customer insight and metrics. Taylor's client list includes WebTV, Palm Computing, and several high-tech start-ups. Prior to 1998, Taylor worked for Intuit, Inc., for eight years in a variety of marketing positions, including Quicken Product Manager and Customer Insight Group Manager. She also worked in brand management at the Clorox Company, leading marketing efforts for Fresh Step cat litter and Formula 409 spray cleaner brands.

Taylor has led product teams through the full product development life cycle and has managed all elements of the marketing mix, both online and offline. She taught an Internet marketing class at Stanford University and holds Stanford B.A. and M.B.A. degrees.

KATHY SCHROEDER is a full-time author. She spent seven years in marketing for Ford Motor Company. While in the Stanford M.B.A. program, Kathy was the Features Editor of the Stanford Business School newspaper and Staff Writer for the *Stanford Daily News*. She also served as Copy Editor for a health textbook publisher. After her M.B.A., Schroeder spent four years in Project Management and Corporate Marketing for Risk Management Solutions, leading consulting teams utilizing the company's complex software. She then led the Business Development effort at

NetEarnings.com, making the first small business finance distribution deals with Yahoo!, Microsoft, and Quicken.com.

Schroeder has written three unpublished novels and a play, contributed to various newsletters and publications, and taught an Internet marketing class at Stanford in 2001. She holds a B.S. in Business with highest distinction from Indiana University and an M.B.A. from Stanford.

www.InsideIntuit.com